ELIANA.

ELIANA:

BEING

THE HITHERTO UNCOLLECTED WRITINGS

OF

CHARLES LAMB.

"The king's chaff is as good as other people's corn."—OLD PROVERB.

NEW YORK:
HURD AND HOUGHTON.
BOSTON: WILLIAM VEAZIE.
1865.

BOSTON:

STEREOTYPED AND PRINTED BY JOHN WILSON AND SON,

No. 5, Water Street.

PREFACE.

Sir Thomas More, in the dedicatory epistle of the "Utopia," addressed to his friend Peter Giles, says, speaking of the readers of books in his day, "There be some so unkind and ungenteel, that though they take great pleasure and delectation in the work, yet, for all that, they cannot find in their hearts to love the author thereof, nor to afford him a good word; being much like uncourteous, unthankful, and churlish guests, which, when they have with good and dainty meat well filled their bellies, depart home, giving no thanks to the feast-maker." *

This, and indeed all that the wise, witty, and learned Lord High Chancellor says of the reading public in the times of Henry VIII., — a literary San Marino, — is true of the reading public of the present day.

If, however, it is the misfortune of most authors to be perused by such unkind and unthankful readers as those Sir Thomas speaks of, there are a few favorite and fortunate penmen that not only obtain their readers' admiration, but also win their reader's love.

Such a one is Charles Lamb. Other writers may have more readers; but none have so many true, hearty, enthusiastic admirers as he. If to the public at large — the miscellaneous rabble of whom Milton speaks so scornfully in "Paradise Regained" — he is but little known, by the truest

* I quote from the old translation of Raphe Robinson.

and most intelligent lovers of literature he is read with unusual pleasure and delight. If ordinary readers — those who —

> "Distinguish not rare peacock from vile swan,
> Nor Mareotic juice from Cœcuban" —

find but little in him to praise or to admire, with all lovers and appreciators of true wit, genuine humor, fine fancy, beautiful imagination, and exquisite pathos, he is a prodigious favorite. Indeed, there is something — a nameless, indescribable charm — about this author's productions, which captivates and enravishes his readers. By those whose mental palate is fine enough to taste and appreciate the exquisite flavor of his style, and to relish and enjoy his rich, peculiar, delicious humor, the "Essays of Elia" are read with extraordinary satisfaction, and prized as highly as the curate in "Don Quixote" prized the "Diana" of Gil Polo.

And though Lamb found many admiring readers in his lifetime, since his death his fame and popularity have increased greatly. Then he was generally looked upon as a mere eccentric, — a person of more quaintness than humor, of more oddity than genius. Now he is acknowledged to be a most beautiful and original genius, — one of the "fixed stars of the literary system," whose light will never pale or grow dim, and whose peculiar brightness and beauty will long be the wonder and delight of a choice and select number of men and women.

Yet, despite all their love and admiration of Charles Lamb, — nay, rather in consequence of it, — his admirers must blame him for what Mr. Barron Field was pleased to eulogize him for, — writing so little. Undoubtedly, in most authors, suppression in writing would be a virtue. In Lamb it was a fault. Instead of writing only two volumes of essays,

Elia should have written a dozen. He had read, heard, thought, and seen enough to furnish matter for twice that number. He himself confesseth, in a letter written a year or two before his death, that he felt as if he had a thousand essays swelling within him. Oh that Elia, like Mr. Spectator, had printed himself out before he died!

But notwithstanding Lamb's fame and popularity, notwithstanding all readers of his inimitable Essays lament that one who wrote so delightfully as Elia did should have written so little, there has not yet been published a complete collection of his writings. The standard edition of his works, edited by Talfourd, is far from being complete. Surely the author of "Ion" was unwise in not publishing all of Lamb's productions. Carlyle said he wanted to know all about Margaret Fuller, even to the color of her stockings; and the admirers of Elia want to possess every scrap and fragment of his inditing. They cannot let oblivion have the least "notelet" or "essaykin" of his. For, however inferior to his best productions these uncollected articles may be, they must contain more or less of Lamb's humor, sense, and observation. Somewhat of his delightful individuality must be stamped upon them. In brief, they cannot but contain much that would amuse and entertain all admirers of their author. For myself, I would rather read the poorest of these uncollected Essays of Elia than the best productions of some of the most popular of modern authors. "The king's chaff is as good as other people's corn," saith the old proverb. "There is a pleasure arising from the very bagatelles of men renowned for their knowledge and genius," says Goldsmith; "and we receive with veneration those pieces, after they are dead, which would lessen them in our estimation while living: sensible that we shall enjoy them no more, we treasure up, as precious relics, every saying and word that has escaped them; but their writings of every kind we deem inestimable."

For years I have been hopefully and patiently waiting for somebody to collect and publish these scattered and all but forgotten articles of Lamb's; but at last, seeing no likelihood of its being done at present, if ever in my day, and fearing that I might else never have an opportunity of perusing these strangely neglected writings of my favorite author, I commenced the task of searching out and discovering them myself for mine own delectation. And after a deal of fruitless and aimless labor (for, unlike Johannes Scotus Erigena, in his quest of a treatise of Aristotle, I had no oracle to consult), after spending nearly as many weeks in turning over the leaves of I know not how many volumes of old, dusty, musty, fusty periodicals, as Mr. Vernon ran miles after a butterfly, I was amply rewarded for all my pains; for I not only found all, or nearly all, of Lamb's uncollected writings that are spoken of in his "Life and Letters," but a goodly number of articles from his pen which neither he nor his biographer has even alluded to. As I read these (to me) new essays, poems, and letters of Elia, I could not but feel somewhat indignant that such excellent productions of such an excellent writer should have been "underkept and down suppress" so long. I was as much ravished with these new-found Essays of Lamb's as good old Nicholas Gerbelius (see Burton's "Anatomy of Melancholy," partition ii., section 2, member 4) was with a few Greek authors restored to light. If I had had one or two loving, enthusiastic admirers of Charles Lamb to enjoy with me the delight of perusing these uncollected Elias, I should have been "all felicity up to the brim." For with me, as with Michael de Montaigne and Hans Andersen, there is no pleasure without communication; and therefore, partly to please myself, and partly to please the admirers of Elia, I have collected and published all of Charles Lamb's writings that I found "sleeping" in out-of-fashion books and out-of-date periodicals.

To ninety-nine hundredths of their author's readers, the contents of this volume will be as good as manuscript; and not only will the contents of "Eliana" be new to most readers, but they will be found to be not wholly unworthy of him who wrote the immortal dissertation on "Roast Pig." Albeit not to be compared with Elia's best and most finished productions, many of the articles in this collection contain some of the finest qualities and peculiarities of his genius; and most of them — especially the essays and sketches — are, as good old Bishop Hall would say, flowered with the blossoms of learning and observation.

Though the generality of readers may not find much to amuse or entertain them in this volume, without doubt all genuine admirers, all true lovers, of the gentle, genial, delightful Elia, to whom almost every word of their favorite author's inditing is —

"Farsed with pleasaunce,"

will be mightily pleased with these productions of his inimitable pen, now first collected together.

J. E. B.

CHELSEA, May, 1864.

CONTENTS.

ESSAYS AND SKETCHES.

ESSAYS AND SKETCHES (*continued*).

TALES.

POEMS.

LETTERS.

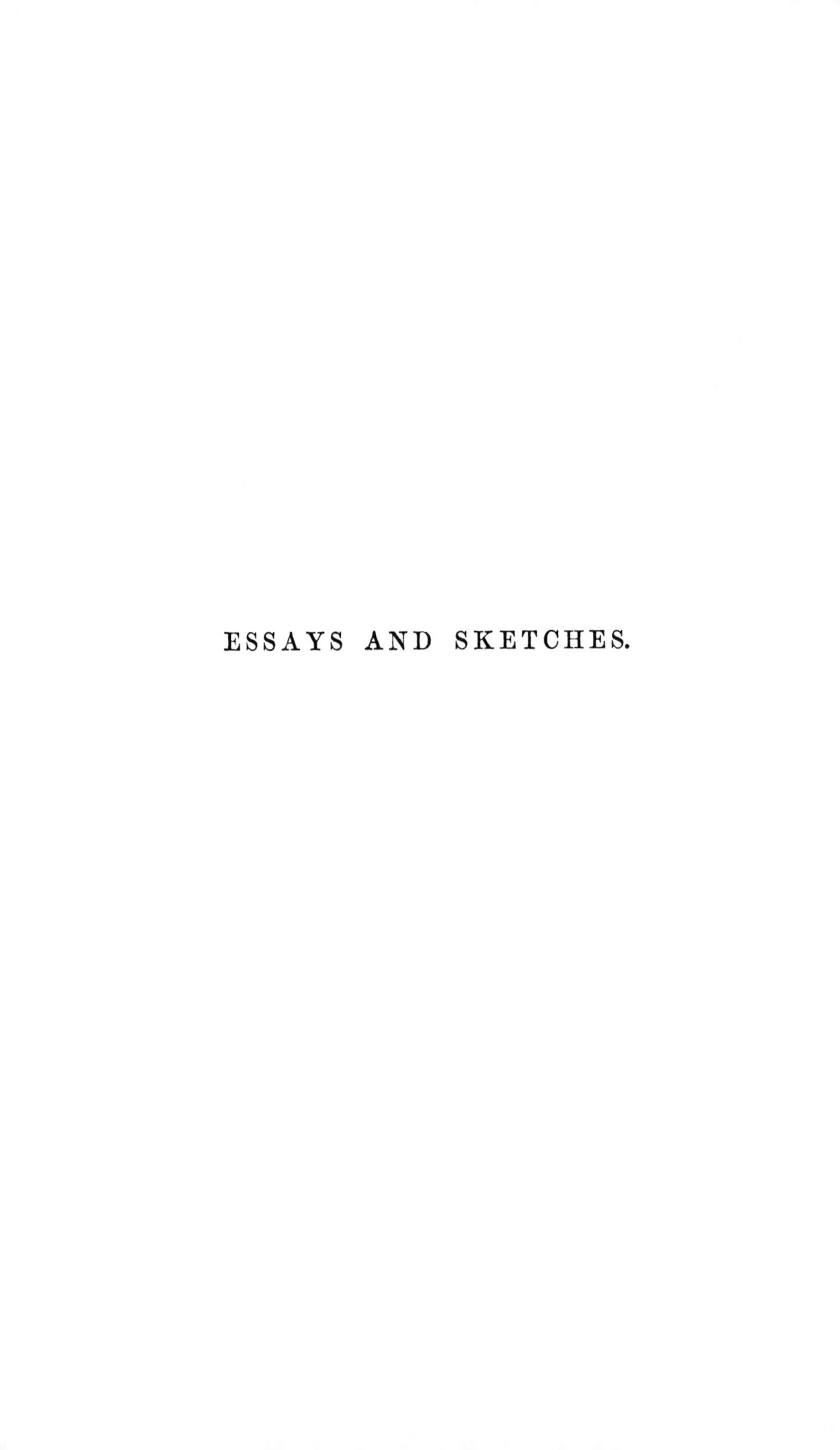

ESSAYS AND SKETCHES.

ESSAYS AND SKETCHES.

TABLE-TALK.*

It is a desideratum in works that treat *de re culinariâ*, that we have no *rationale* of sauces, or theory of mixed flavors: as to show why cabbage is reprehensible with roast beef, laudable with bacon; why the haunch of mutton seeks the alliance of currant-jelly, the shoulder civilly declineth it; why loin of veal (a pretty problem), being itself unctuous, seeketh the adventitious lubricity of melted butter, — and why the same part in pork, not more oleaginous, abhorreth from it; why the French bean sympathizes with the flesh of deer; why salt fish points to parsnip, brawn makes a dead-set at mustard; why cats prefer valerian to heart's-ease, old ladies *vice versâ*, — though this is rather travelling out of the road of the dietetics, and may be thought a question more curious than relevant; why salmon (a strong sapor *per se*) fortifieth its condition with the mighty lobster-sauce, whose embraces are fatal to the delicater relish of the turbot; why oysters in death rise up against the contamination of brown sugar, while

* From the "London Athenæum," 1834.

they are posthumously amorous of vinegar; why the sour mango and the sweet jam by turns court and are accepted by the compliable mutton-hash, — she not yet decidedly declaring for either. We are as yet but in the empirical stage of cookery. We feed ignorantly, and want to be able to give a reason of the relish that is in us; so that, if Nature should furnish us with a new meat, or be prodigally pleased to restore the phœnix, upon a *given* flavor, we might be able to pronounce instantly, on philosophical principles, what the sauce to it should be, — what the curious adjuncts.

The greatest pleasure I know is to do a good action by stealth, and to have it found out by accident.

'Tis unpleasant to meet a beggar. It is painful to deny him; and, if you relieve him, it is so much out of your pocket.

Men marry for fortune, and sometimes to please their fancy; but, much oftener than is suspected, they consider what the world will say of it, — how such a woman in their friends' eyes will look at the head of a table. Hence we see so many insipid beauties made wives of, that could not have struck the particular fancy of any man that had any fancy at all. These I call *furniture wives;* as men buy *furniture pictures*, because they suit this or that niche in their dining-parlors.

Your universally cried-up beauties are the very last choice which a man of taste would make. What pleases all cannot have that individual charm which makes this or that countenance engaging to you, and to you only perhaps, you know not why. What gained the fair Gunnings titled husbands, who, after all, turned out very sorry wives? Popular repute.

It is a sore trial when a daughter shall marry against her father's approbation. A little hard-heartedness, and aversion to a reconcilement, is almost pardonable. After all, Will Dockwray's way is, perhaps, the wisest. His best-loved daughter made a most imprudent match; in fact, eloped with the last man in the world that her father would have wished her to marry. All the world said that he would never speak to her again. For months she durst not write to him, much less come near him. But, in a casual rencounter, he met her in the streets of Ware, — Ware, that will long remember the mild virtues of William Dockwray, Esq. What said the parent to his disobedient child, whose knees faltered under her at the sight of him? "Ha, Sukey! is it you?" with that benevolent aspect with which he paced the streets of Ware, venerated as an angel: "come and dine with us on Sunday." Then turning away, and again turning back, as if he had forgotten something, he added, "And, Sukey, do you hear? — bring your husband with you." This was all the reproof she ever heard from him. Need it be added, that the match turned out better for Susan than the world expected?

The vices of some men are magnificent. Compare the amours of Henry the Eighth and Charles the Second. The Stuart had mistresses: the Tudor *kept* wives.

"We read the 'Paradise Lost' as a task," says Dr. Johnson. Nay, rather as a celestial recreation, of which the dullard mind is not at all hours alike recipient. "Nobody ever wished it longer;" nor the moon rounder, he might have added. Why, 'tis the perfectness and completeness of it which makes us imagine that not a line could be added to it, or diminished from it, with advantage. Would we have a cubit added to the stature of the Medicean Venus? Do we wish her taller?

Amidst the complaints of the wide spread of infidelity among us, it is consolatory that a sect has sprung up in the heart of the metropolis, and is daily on the increase, of teachers of that healing doctrine which Pope upheld, and against which Voltaire directed his envenomed wit: we mean those practical preachers of optimism, or the belief that *whatever is is best;* the cads of omnibuses, who from their little back pulpits, not once in three or four hours, as those proclaimers of "God and his prophet" in Mussulman countries, but every minute, at the entry or exit of a brief passenger, are heard, in an almost prophetic tone, to exclaim (Wisdom crying out, as it were, in the streets), "ALL'S RIGHT!"

Advice is not so commonly thrown away as is imagined. We seek it in difficulties. But, in common speech, we are apt to confound with it *admonition;* as when a friend reminds one that drink is prejudicial to the health, &c. We do not care to be told of that which we know better than the good man that admonishes. M—— sent to his friend L——, who is no water-drinker, a twopenny tract "Against the Use of Fermented Liquors." L—— acknowledged the obligation, as far as to *twopence*. Penotier's advice was the safest, after all: —

"I advised him" —

But I must tell you. The dear, good-meaning, no-thinking creature had been dumfounding a company of us with a detail of inextricable difficulties, in which the circumstances of an acquaintance of his were involved. No clew of light offered itself. He grew more and more misty as he proceeded. We pitied his friend, and thought, —

> "God help the man so rapt in Error's endless maze!"

when, suddenly brightening up his placid countenance, like one that had found out a riddle, and looked to have the solution admired, —

"At last," said he, "I advised him" —

Here he paused, and here we were again interminably thrown back. By no possible guess could any of us aim at the drift of the meaning he was about to be delivered of.

"I advised him," he repeated, "to have some *advice* upon the subject."

A general approbation followed; and it was unanimously agreed, that, under all the circumstances of the case, no sounder or more judicious counsel could have been given.

A laxity pervades the popular use of words.

Parson W—— is not quite so continent as Diana, yet prettily dissembleth his frailty. Is Parson W——, therefore, a *hypocrite?* I think, not. Where the concealment of a vice is less pernicious than the barefaced publication of it would be, no additional delinquency is incurred in the secrecy. Parson W—— is simply an immoral clergyman. But if Parson W—— were to be for ever haranguing on the opposite virtue; choosing for his perpetual text, in preference to all other pulpit-topics, the remarkable resistance recorded in the 39th of Exodus [Genesis?]; dwelling, moreover, and dilating upon it, — then Parson W—— might be reasonably suspected of hypocrisy. But Parson W—— rarely diverteth into such line of argument, or toucheth it briefly. His ordinary topics are fetched from "obedience to the powers that are," "submission to the civil magistrate in all commands that are not absolutely unlawful;" on which he can delight to expatiate with equal fervor and sincerity.

Again: to *despise* a person is properly to *look down* upon him with none or the least possible emotion; but when Clementina, who has lately lost her lover, with bosom heaving, eyes flashing, and her whole frame in agitation, pronounces with a peculiar emphasis that she "*despises* the fellow," depend upon it that he is not quite so despicable in her eyes as she would have us imagine.

One more instance. If we must naturalize that portentous phrase, *a truism*, it were well that we limited the use of it. Every commonplace or trite observation is not a truism. For example: A good name helps a man on in the world. This is nothing but a simple truth, however hackneyed. It has a distinct subject and predicate. But when the thing predicated is involved in the term of the subject, and so necessarily involved that by no possible conception they can be separated, then it becomes a truism; as to say, "A good name is a proof of a man's estimation in the world." We seem to be saying something, when we say nothing. I was describing to F—— some knavish tricks of a mutual friend of ours. "If he did so and so," was the reply, "he cannot be an honest man." Here was a genuine truism, truth upon truth, inference and proposition identical, or rather a dictionary definition usurping the place of an inference.

We are ashamed at sight of a monkey, — somehow as we are shy of poor relations.

C—— imagined a Caledonian compartment in Hades, where there should be fire without sulphur.

Absurd images are sometimes irresistible. I will mention two, — an elephant in a coach-office gravely coming to have his trunk booked; a mermaid over a fish-kettle cooking her own tail.

It is the praise of Shakspeare, with reference to the playwriters his contemporaries, that he has so few revolting characters. Yet he has one that is singularly mean and disagreeable, — the King in "Hamlet." Neither has he characters of insignificance, unless the phantom that stalks over the stage as Julius Cæsar, in the play of that name, may be accounted one. Neither has he envious characters, excepting the short part of Don John, in "Much Ado about Nothing." Neither has he unentertaining characters, if we except Parolles, and the little that there is of the Clown, in "All's Well that Ends Well."

Is it possible that Shakspeare should never have read Homer, in Chapman's version at least? If he had read it, could he mean to *travesty* it in the parts of those big boobies, Ajax and Achilles? Ulysses, Nestor, and Agamemnon are true to their parts in the "Iliad:" they are gentlemen at least. Thersites, though unamusing, is fairly deducible from it. Troïlus and Cressida are a fine graft upon it. But those two big bulks —

It would settle the dispute as to whether Shakspeare intended Othello for a jealous character, to consider how differently we are affected towards him and for Leontes in the "Winter's Tale." Leontes *is* that character. Othello's fault was simply credulity.

"*Lear.* Who are you?
Mine eyes are none o' the best. I'll tell you straight.
Are you not Kent?
Kent. The same; your servant Kent.
Where is your servant Caius?
Lear. 'Twas a good fellow, I can tell you that;
He'd strike, and quickly too: he is dead and rotten.
Kent. No, my good lord: I am the very man —
Lear. I'll see that straight —
Kent. That from your first of difference and decay
Have followed your sad steps.
Lear. You are welcome hither.
Albany. He knows not what he says; and vain is it
That we present us to him.
Edgar. Look up, my lord.
Kent. Vex not his ghost. Oh! let him pass. He hates him
That would upon the rack of this rough world
Stretch him out longer."

So ends "King Lear," the most stupendous of the

Shakspearian dramas; and Kent, the noblest feature of the conceptions of his divine mind. This is the magnanimity of authorship, when a writer, having a topic presented to him, fruitful of beauties for common minds, waives his privilege, and trusts to the judicious few for understanding the reason of his abstinence. What a pudder would a common dramatist have raised here of a reconciliation-scene, a perfect recognition, between the assumed Caius and his master! — to the suffusing of many fair eyes, and the moistening of cambric handkerchiefs. The old dying king partially catching at the truth, and immediately lapsing into obliviousness, with the high-minded carelessness of the other to have his services appreciated, — as one that —

> "Served not for gain,
> Or followed out of form," —

are among the most judicious, not to say heart-touching, strokes in Shakspeare.

Allied to this magnanimity it is, where the pith and point of an argument, the amplification of which might compromise the modesty of the speaker, is delivered briefly, and, as it were, *parenthetically;* as in those few but pregnant words, in which the man in the old "Nut-brown Maid" rather intimates than reveals his unsuspected high birth to the woman: —

> "Now understand, to Westmoreland,
> *Which is my heritage,*
> I will you bring, and with a ring,
> By way of marriage,
> I will you take, and lady make."

Turn we to the version of it, ten times diluted, of dear Mat. Prior, — in his own way unequalled, and a poet now-a-days too much neglected. "In me," quoth Henry, addressing the astounded Emma, — with a flourish and an attitude, as we may conceive, —

"In me behold the potent Edgar's heir,
Illustrious earl! him terrible in war,
Let Loire confess."

And with a deal of skimble-skamble stuff, as Hotspur would term it, more, presents the lady with a full and true enumeration of his papa's rent-roll in the fat soil by Deva.

But, of all parentheses (not to quit the topic too suddenly), commend me to that most significant one, at the commencement of the old popular ballad of "Fair Rosamond:" —

"When good King Henry ruled this land
The second of that name,"

Now mark, —

"(Besides the queen) he dearly loved
A fair and comely dame."

There is great virtue in this *besides*.

THE GENTLE GIANTESS.*

THE Widow Blacket, of Oxford, is the largest female I ever had the pleasure of beholding. There may be her parallel upon the earth; but surely I never saw it. I take her to be lineally descended from the maid's aunt of Brainford, who caused Master Ford such uneasiness. She hath Atlantean shoulders; and, as she stoopeth in

* From the "London Magazine," 1822.

her gait, — with as few offences to answer for in her own particular as any of Eve's daughters, — her back seems broad enough to bear the blame of all the peccadilloes that have been committed since Adam. She girdeth her waist — or what she is pleased to esteem as such — nearly up to her shoulders; from beneath which, that huge dorsal expanse, in mountainous declivity, emergeth. Respect for her alone preventeth the idle boys, who follow her about in shoals, whenever she cometh abroad, from getting up, and riding. But her presence infallibly commands a reverence. She is indeed, as the Americans would express it, something awful. Her person is a burthen to herself no less than to the ground which bears her. To her mighty bone, she hath a pinguitude withal, which makes the depth of winter to her the most desirable season. Her distress in the warmer solstice is pitiable. During the months of July and August, she usually renteth a cool cellar, where ices are kept, whereinto she descendeth when Sirius rageth. She dates from a hot Thursday, — some twenty-five years ago. Her apartment in summer is pervious to the four winds. Two doors, in north and south direction, and two windows, fronting the rising and the setting sun, never closed, from every cardinal point, catch the contributory breezes. She loves to enjoy what she calls a quadruple draught. That must be a shrewd zephyr that can escape her. I owe a painful face-ache, which oppresses me at this moment, to a cold caught, sitting by her, one day in last July, at this receipt of coolness. Her fan, in ordinary, resembleth a banner spread, which she keepeth continually on the alert to detect the least breeze. She possesseth an active and gadding mind, totally incommensurate with her person. No one delighteth more than herself in country exercises and pastimes. I have passed many an agreeable holy-day with her in her favorite park at Woodstock. She performs her part in these delightful ambulatory excursions by the aid of a portable garden chair. She setteth out with you at a fair foot-gallop, which she keepeth up till you are both well breathed, and then she reposeth for a few seconds. Then she is up again for a hundred paces or so, and again resteth; her movement, on these sprightly occasions, being something between walking and flying. Her great weight seemeth to propel her forward, ostrich-fashion. In this kind of relieved marching, I have traversed with her many scores of acres on those well-wooded and well-watered domains. Her delight at Oxford is in the public walks and gardens, where, when the weather is not too oppressive, she passeth much of her valuable time. There is a bench at Maudlin, or rather situated between the frontiers of that and ——'s College (some litigation, latterly, about repairs, has vested the property of it finally in ——'s), where, at the hour of noon, she is ordinarily to be found sitting, — so she calls it by courtesy, — but, in fact, pressing and breaking of it down with her enormous settlement; as both those foundations, who, however, are good-natured enough to wink at it, have found, I believe, to their cost. Here she taketh the fresh air, principally at vacation-times, when the walks are freest from interruption of the younger fry of students. Here she passeth her idle hours, not idly, but generally accompanied with a book, — blessed if she can but intercept some resident Fellow (as usually there are some of that brood left behind at these periods) or stray Master of Arts (to most of whom she is better known than their dinner-bell), with whom she may confer upon any curious topic of literature. I have seen these shy gownsmen, who truly set but a very slight value upon female conversation, cast a hawk's eye upon her from the length of Maudlin Grove, and warily glide off into into another walk, — true monks as they are, and ungently neglecting the delicacies of her polished converse for their own perverse and uncommunicating solitariness! Within-doors, her principal diversion is music, vocal and instrumental; in both which she is no mean professor. Her voice is wonderfully fine; but, till I got used to it, I confess it staggered me. It is, for all the world, like that of a piping bulfinch; while, from her size and stature, you would expect notes to drown the deep organ. The shake, which most fine singers reserve for the close or cadence, by some unaccountable flexibility, or tremulousness of pipe, she carrieth quite through the composition; so that her time, to a common air or ballad, keeps double motion, like the earth, — running the primary circuit of the tune, and still revolving upon its own axis. The effect, as I said before, when you are used to it, is as agreeable as it is altogether new and surprising. The spacious apartment of her outward frame lodgeth a soul in all respects disproportionate. Of more than mortal make, she evinceth withal a trembling sensibility, a yielding infirmity of purpose, a quick susceptibility to reproach, and all the train of diffident and blushing virtues, which for their habitation usually seek out a feeble frame, an attenuated and meagre constitution. With more than man's bulk, her humors and occupations are eminently feminine. She sighs, — being six foot high. She languisheth, — being two feet wide. She worketh slender sprigs upon the delicate muslin, — her fingers being capable of moulding a Colossus. She sippeth her wine out of her glass daintily, — her capacity being that of a tun of Heidelberg. She goeth mincingly with those feet of hers, whose solidity need not fear the black ox's pressure. Softest and largest of thy sex, adieu! By what parting attribute may I salute thee, last and best of the Titanesses, — Ogress, fed with milk instead of blood; not least, or least handsome, among Oxford's stately structures, — Oxford, who, in its deadest time of vacation, can never properly be said to be empty, having thee to fill it.*

* Lamb, in the following extract from a letter to Miss Wordsworth, gives the original sketch of "The Gentle Giantess:" "Ask anybody you meet who is the biggest woman in Cambridge, and I'll hold you a wager they'll say Mrs. ——. She broke down two benches in Trinity Gardens; one on the confines of St. John's, which occasioned a litigation between the societies as to repairing it. In warm weather, she retires into an ice-cellar (literally), and dates from a hot Thursday some twenty years back. She sits in a room with opposite doors and windows, to let in a thorough draught, which gives her slenderer friends toothaches. She is to be seen in the market every morning at ten, cheapening fowls; which I observe the Cambridge poulterers are not sufficiently careful to stump." The reader will observe, that, in the essay, Elia has changed the locality of the stout woman, and places her in Oxford, instead of Cambridge. — EDITOR.

THE REYNOLDS GALLERY.*

THE Reynolds Gallery has, upon the whole, disappointed me. Some of the portraits are interesting. They are faces of characters whom we (middle-aged gentlemen) were born a little too late to remember, but about whom we have heard our fathers tell stories till we almost fancy to have seen them. There is a charm in the portrait of a Rodney or a Keppel, which even a picture of Nelson must want for me. I should turn away after a slight inspection from the best likeness that could be made of Mrs. Anne Clarke; but Kitty Fisher is a considerable personage. Then the dresses of some of the women so exactly remind us of modes which we can just recall; of the forms under which the venerable relationship of aunt or mother first presented themselves to our young eyes; the aprons, the coifs, the lappets, the hoods. Mercy on us! what a load of head-ornaments seem to have conspired to bury a pretty face in the picture of Mrs. Long, *yet could not!* Beauty must have some "charmed life" to have been able to surmount the conspiracy of fashion in those days to destroy it.

The portraits which least pleased me were those of boys, as infant Bacchuses, Jupiters, &c. But the artist is not to be blamed for the disguise. No doubt, the parents wished to see their children deified in their lifetime. It was but putting a thunderbolt (instead of a squib) into young master's hands; and a

* From the "London Examiner," 1813.

whey-faced chit was transformed into the infant ruler of Olympus, — him who was afterward to shake heaven and earth with his black brow. Another good boy pleased his grandmamma with saying his prayers so well, and the blameless dotage of the good old woman imagined in him an adequate representative of the infancy of the awful Prophet Samuel. *But the great historical compositions, where the artist was at liberty* to paint from *his own idea, — the Beaufort and the Ugolino:* why, then, I must confess, pleading the liberty of table-talk for my presumption, that they have not left any very elevating impressions on my mind. Pardon a ludicrous comparison. I know, madam, you admire them both; but placed opposite to each other as they are at the gallery, as if to set the one work in competition with the other, they did remind me of the famous contention for the prize of deformity, mentioned in the 173d number of the "Spectator." The one stares, and the other grins; but is there common dignity in their countenances? Does any thing of the history of their life gone by peep through the ruins of the mind in the face, like the unconquerable grandeur that surmounts the distortions of the Laocoön? The figures which stand by the bed of Beaufort are indeed happy representations of the plain unmannered old nobility of the English historical plays of Shakspeare; but, for any thing else, give me leave to recommend those macaroons.

After leaving the Reynolds Gallery (where, upon the whole, I received a good deal of pleasure), and feeling that I had quite had my fill of paintings, I stumbled upon a picture in Piccadilly (No. 22, I think), which purports to be a portrait of Francis the First by Leonardo da Vinci. Heavens, what a difference! It is but a portrait, as most of those I had been seeing; but, placed by them, it would kill them, swallow them up as Moses' rod the other rods. Where did these old painters get their models? I see no such figures, not in my dreams, as this Francis, in the character, or rather with the attributes, of John the Baptist. A more than martial majesty in the brow and upon the eyelid; an arm muscular, beautifully formed; the long, graceful, massy fingers compressing, yet so as not to hurt, a lamb more lovely, more sweetly shrinking, than we can conceive that milk-white one which followed Una; the picture altogether looking as if it were eternal, — combining the truth of flesh with a promise of permanence like marble.

Leonardo, from the one or two specimens we have of him in England, must have been a stupendous genius. I scarce can think he has had his full fame, — he who could paint that wonderful personification of the Logos, or third person of the Trinity, grasping a globe, late in the possession of Mr. Troward of Pall Mall, where the hand was, by the boldest license, twice as big as the truth of drawing warranted; yet the effect, to every one that saw it, by some magic of genius was confessed to be not *monstrous*, but *miraculous* and *silencing*. It could not be gainsaid.

GUY FAUX.*

A VERY ingenious and subtle writer,† whom there is good reason for suspecting to be an ex-Jesuit, not unknown at Douay some five and twenty years since (he will not obtrude himself at M——th again in a hurry), about a twelvemonth back set himself to prove the character of the Powder-Plot conspirators to have been that of heroic self-devotedness and true Christian martyrdom. Under the mask of Protestant candor, he actually gained admission for his treatise into a London weekly paper‡ not particularly distinguished for its zeal towards either religion. But, admitting Catholic principles, his arguments are shrewd and incontrovertible. He says, —

"Guy Faux was a fanatic; but he was no hypocrite. He ranks among *good haters*. He was cruel, bloody-minded, reckless of all considerations but those of an infuriated and bigoted faith; but he was a true son of the Catholic Church, a martyr, and a confessor, for all that. He who can prevail upon himself to devote his life for a cause, however we may condemn his opinions or abhor his actions, vouches at least for the honesty of his principles and the disinterestedness of his motives. He may be guilty of the worst practices; but he is capable of the greatest. He is no longer a slave, but free.

* From the "London Magazine," 1823.

† William Hazlitt.

‡ The "London Examiner," then edited by Leigh Hunt.

The contempt of death is the beginning of virtue. The hero of the Gunpowder Plot was, if you will, a fool, a madman, an assassin; call him what names you please: still he was neither knave nor coward. He did not propose to blow up the parliament, and come off, scot-free, himself: he showed that he valued his own life no more than theirs in such a cause, where the integrity of the Catholic faith and the salvation of perhaps millions of souls was at stake. He did not call it a murder, but a sacrifice, which he was about to achieve: he was armed with the Holy Spirit and with fire; he was the Church's chosen servant and her blessed martyr. He comforted himself as 'the best of cut-throats.' How many wretches are there that would have undertaken to do what he intended, for a sum of money, if they could have got off with impunity! How few are there who would have put themselves in Guy Faux's situation to save the universe! Yet, in the latter case, we affect to be thrown into greater consternation than at the most unredeemed acts of villany; as if the absolute disinterestedness of the motive doubled the horror of the deed! The cowardice and selfishness of mankind are in fact shocked at the consequences to themselves (if such examples are held up for imitation); and they make a fearful outcry against the violation of every principle of morality, lest they, too, should be called on for any such tremendous sacrifices; lest they, in their turn, should have to go on the forlorn hope of extra-official duty. *Charity begins at home* is a maxim that prevails as well in the courts of conscience as in those of prudence. We would be thought to shudder at the consequences of crime to others, while we tremble for them to ourselves. We talk of the dark and cowardly assassin; and this is well, when an individual shrinks from the face of an enemy, and purchases his own safety by striking a blow in the dark: but how the charge of cowardly can be applied to the public assassin, who, in the very act of destroying another, lays down his life as the pledge and forfeit of his sincerity and boldness, I am at a loss to devise. There may be barbarous prejudice, rooted hatred, unprincipled treachery, in such an act; but he who resolves to take all the danger and odium upon himself can no more be branded with cowardice, than Regulus devoting himself for his country, or Codrus leaping into the fiery gulf. A wily Father Inquisitor, coolly and with plenary authority condemning hundreds of helpless, unoffending victims to the flames, or to the horrors of a living tomb, while he himself would not suffer a hair of his head to be hurt, is, to me, a character without any qualifying trait in it. Again: the Spanish conqueror and hero, the favorite of his monarch, who enticed thirty thousand poor Mexicans into a large open building under promise of strict faith and cordial good-will, and then set fire to it, making sport of the cries and agonies of these deluded creatures, is an instance of uniting the most hardened cruelty with the most heartless selfishness. His plea was, keeping no faith with heretics; this was Guy Faux's too: but I am sure at least that the latter kept faith with himself; he was in earnest in his professions. *His* was not gay, wanton, unfeeling depravity; he did not murder in sport: it was serious work that he had taken in hand. To see this arch-bigot, this heart-whole traitor, this pale miner in the infernal regions, skulking in his retreat with his cloak and dark lantern, moving cautiously about among his barrels of gunpowder loaded with death, but not yet ripe for destruction, regardless of the lives of others, and more than indifferent to his own, presents a picture of the strange infatuation of the human understanding, but not of the depravity of the human will, without an equal. There were thousands of pious Papists privy to and ready to applaud the deed when done: there was no one but our old fifth-of-November friend, who still flutters in rags and straw on the occasion, that had the courage to attempt it. In him stern duty and unshaken faith prevailed over natural frailty."*

It is impossible, upon Catholic principles, not to admit the force of this reasoning: we can only not help smiling (with the writer) at the simplicity of the gulled editor, swallowing the dregs of Loyola for the very quintessence of sublimated reason in England at the commencement of the nineteenth century. We will just, as a contrast, show what we Protestants (who are a party concerned) thought upon the same subject at a period rather nearer to the heroic project in question.

The Gunpowder Treason was the subject which called

* In Hazlitt's delightful report of the conversation at one of Charles Lamb's Wednesday-evening parties (it is to be regretted that he did not report the conversation at all of these assemblages of wits, humorists, and good fellows), Elia thus speaks in defence of the hero of the Gunpowder Plot: "I cannot but think that Guy Faux, that poor fluttering annual scarecrow of straw and rags, is an ill-used gentleman. I would give something to see him sitting pale and emaciated, surrounded by his matches and his barrels of gunpowder, and expecting the moment that was to transport him to Paradise for his heroic self-devotion. But, if I say any more, there is that fellow Godwin will make something out of it." —EDITOR.

forth the earliest specimen which is left us of the pulpit eloquence of Jeremy Taylor. When he preached the sermon on that anniversary, which is printed at the end of the folio edition of his Sermons, he was a young man, just commencing his ministry under the auspices of Archbishop Laud. From the learning and maturest oratory which it manifests, one should rather have conjectured it to have proceeded from the same person after he was ripened by time into a Bishop and Father of the Church. "And, really, these *Romano-barbari* could never pretend to any precedent for an act so barbarous as theirs. Adramelech, indeed, killed a king; but he spared the people. Haman would have killed the people, but spared the king; but that both king and people, princes and judges, branch and rush and root, should die at once (as if Caligula's wish were actuated, and all England upon one head), was never known till now, that all the malice of the world met in this as in a centre. The Sicilian even-song, the matins of St. Bartholomew, known for the pitiless and damned massacres, were but κάπνου σκίας ὄναρ, the dream of the shadow of smoke, if compared with this great fire. *In tam occupato sæculo fabulas vulgares nequitia non invenit.* This was a busy age. Herostratus must have invented a more sublimed malice than the burning of one temple, or not have been so much as spoke of since the discovery of the powder treason. But I must make more haste; I shall not else climb the sublimity of this impiety. Nero was sometimes the *populare odium*, was popularly hated, and deserved it too: for he slew his master, and his wife, and all his family, once or twice over; opened his mother's womb; fired the city, laughed at it, slandered the Christians for it: but yet all these were but *principia malorum*, the very first rudiments of evil. Add, then, to these, Herod's masterpiece at Ramah, as it was deciphered by the tears and sad threnes of the matrons in a universal mourning for the loss of their pretty infants; yet this of Herod will prove but an infant wickedness, and that of Nero the evil but of one city. I would willingly have found out an example, but see I cannot. Should I put into the scale the extract of all the old tyrants famous in antique stories, —

> 'Bistonii stabulum regis, Busiridis aras,
> Antiphatæ mensas, et Taurica regna Thoantis;' —

should I take for true story the highest cruelty as it was fancied by the most hieroglyphical Egyptian, — this alone would weigh them down, as if the Alps were put in scale against the dust of a balance. For, had this accursed treason prospered, we should have had the whole kingdom mourn for the inestimable loss of its chiefest glory, its life, its present joy, and all its very hopes for the future. For such was their destined malice, that they would not only have inflicted so cruel a blow, but have made it incurable, by cutting off our supplies of joy, the whole succession of the Line Royal. Not only the vine itself, but all the *gemmulæ*, and the tender olive branches, should either have been bent to their intentions, and made to grow crooked, or else been broken.

"And now, after such a sublimity of malice, I will not instance in the sacrilegious ruin of the neighboring temples, which needs must have perished in the flame; nor in the disturbing the ashes of our entombed kings, devouring their dead ruins like sepulchral dogs: these are but minutes in respect of the ruin prepared for the living temples:—

> 'Stragem sed istam non tulit
> Christus cadentum Principum
> Impune, ne forsan sui
> Patris periret fabrica.
> Ergo quæ poterit lingua retexere
> Laudes, Christe, tuas, qui domitum struis
> Infidum populum cum Duce perfido!'"

In such strains of eloquent indignation did Jeremy Taylor's young oratory inveigh against that stupendous attempt which he truly says had no parallel in ancient or modern times. A century and a half of European crimes has elapsed since he made the assertion, and his position remains in its strength. He wrote near the time in which the nefarious project had like to have been completed. Men's minds still were shuddering from the recentness of the escape. It must have been within his memory, or have been sounded in his ears so young by his parents, that he would seem, in his maturer years, to have remembered it. No wonder, then, that he describes it in words that burn. But to us, to whom the tradition has come slowly down, and has had time to cool, the story of Guido Vaux sounds rather like a tale, a fable, and an invention, than true history. It supposes such gigantic audacity of daring, combined with such more than infantile stupidity in the motive,—such a combination of the fiend and the monkey,—that credulity is almost swallowed up in contemplating the singularity of the attempt. It has accordingly, in some degree, shared the fate of fiction. It is familiarized to us in a kind of serio-ludicrous way, like the story of

Guy of Warwick, or *Valentine and Orson*. The way which we take to perpetuate the memory of this deliverance is well adapted to keep up this fabular notion. Boys go about the streets annually with a beggarly scare-crow dressed up, which is to be burnt indeed, at night, with holy zeal; but, meantime, they beg a penny for *poor Guy:* this periodical petition, which we have heard from our infancy, combined with the dress and appearance of the effigy, so well calculated to move compassion, has the effect of quite removing from our fancy the horrid circumstances of the story which is thus commemorated; and in *poor Guy* vainly should we try to recognize any of the features of that tremendous madman in iniquity, Guido Vaux, with his horrid crew of accomplices, that sought to emulate earthquakes and bursting volcanoes in their more than mortal mischief.

Indeed, the whole ceremony of burning Guy Faux, or *the Pope*, as he is indifferently called, is a sort of *Treason Travestie*, and admirably adapted to lower our feelings upon this memorable subject. The printers of the little duodecimo *Prayer Book*, printed by T. Baskett,* in 1749, which has the effigy of his sacred majesty George II. piously prefixed, have illustrated the service (a very fine one in itself), which is appointed for the anniversary of this day, with a print, which it is not very easy to describe; but the contents appear to

* The same, I presume, upon whom the clergyman in the song of the "Vicar and Moses," not without judgment, passes this memorable censure: —

> " Here, Moses the king:
> 'Tis a scandalous thing
> That this Baskett should print for the Crown."

be these: The scene is a room, I conjecture, in the king's palace. Two persons — one of whom I take to be James himself, from his wearing his hat, while the other stands bare-headed — are intently surveying a sort of speculum, or magic mirror, which stands upon a pedestal in the midst of the room, in which a little figure of Guy Faux with his dark lantern, approaching the door of the Parliament House, is made discernible by the light proceeding from a *great eye* which shines in from the topmost corner of the apartment, by which eye the pious artist no doubt meant to designate Providence. On the other side of the mirror is a figure doing something, which puzzled me when a child, and continues to puzzle me now. The best I can make of it is, that it is a conspirator busy laying the train; but, then, why is he represented in the king's chamber? Conjecture upon so fantastical a design is vain; and I only notice the print as being one of the earliest graphic representations which woke my childhood into wonder, and doubtless combined, with the mummery before mentioned, to take off the edge of that horror which the naked historical mention of Guido's conspiracy could not have failed of exciting.

Now that so many years are past since that abominable machination was happily frustrated, it will not, I hope, be considered a profane sporting with the subject, if we take no very serious survey of the consequences that would have flowed from this plot if it had had a successful issue. The first thing that strikes us, in a selfish point of view, is the material change which it must have produced in the course of the nobility. All the ancient peerage being extinguished, as it was intended, at one blow, the *Red-Book* must have been closed for ever, or a new race of peers must have been created to supply the deficiency. As the first part of this dilemma is a deal too shocking to think of, what a fund of mouth-watering reflections does this give rise to in the breast of us plebeians of A.D. 1823! Why, you or I, reader, might have been Duke of ——, or Earl of ——. I particularize no titles, to avoid the least suspicion of intention to usurp the dignities of the two noblemen whom I have in my eye; but a feeling more dignified than envy sometimes excites a sigh, when I think how the posterity of Guido's Legend of Honor (among whom you or I might have been) might have rolled down, "dulcified," as Burke expresses it, "by an exposure to the influence of heaven in a long flow of generations, from the hard, acidulous, metallic tincture of the spring." * What new orders of merit think you this English Napoleon would have chosen? Knights of the Barrel, or Lords of the Tub, Grand Almoners of the Cellar, or Ministers of Explosion. We should have given the train *couchant*, and the fire *rampant*, in our arms; we should have quartered the dozen white matches in our coats: the Shallows would have been nothing to us.

Turning away from these mortifying reflections, let us contemplate its effects upon the *other house;* for they were all to have gone together, — king, lords, commons.

To assist our imagination, let us take leave to suppose (and we do it in the harmless wantonness of fancy) — to suppose that the tremendous explosion had taken

* Letter to a Noble Lord.

place in our days. We better know what a House of Commons is in our days, and can better estimate our loss. Let us imagine, then, to ourselves, the united members sitting in full conclave above; Faux just ready with his train and matches below,—in his hand a "reed tipt with fire." He applies the fatal engine.

To assist our notions still further, let us suppose some lucky dog of a reporter, who had escaped by miracle upon some plank of St. Stephen's benches, and came plump upon the roof of the adjacent Abbey; from whence descending, at some neighboring coffee-house, first wiping his clothes and calling for a glass of lemonade, he sits down and reports what he had heard and seen (*quorum pars magna fuit*), for the "Morning Post" or the "Courier." We can scarcely imagine him describing the event in any other words but some such as these:—

"A *motion* was put and carried, that this house do *adjourn;* that the speaker do *quit the chair*. The house ROSE amid clamors for order."

In some such way the event might most technically have been conveyed to the public. But a poetical mind, not content with this dry method of narration, cannot help pursuing the effects of this tremendous blowing up, this adjournment in the air, *sine die*. It seems the benches mount,—the chair first, and then the benches; and first the treasury bench, hurried up in this nitrous explosion,—the members, as it were, pairing off; Whigs and Tories taking their friendly apotheosis together (as they did their sandwiches below in Bellamy's room). Fancy, in her flight, keeps pace with the aspiring legislators: she sees the awful seat of order mounting, till it becomes finally fixed, a constellation, next to Cassiopeia's chair, — the wig of him that sat in it taking its place near Berenice's curls. St. Peter, at heaven's wicket, — no, not St. Peter, — St. Stephen, with open arms, receives his own.

While Fancy beholds these celestial appropriations, Reason, no less pleased, discerns the mighty benefit which so complete a renovation must produce below. Let the most determined foe to corruption, the most thorough-paced redresser of abuses, try to conceive a more absolute purification of the house than this was calculated to produce. Why, pride's purge was nothing to it. The whole borough-mongering system would have been got rid of, fairly *exploded;* with it the senseless distinctions of party must have disappeared, faction must have vanished, corruption have expired in air. From Hundred, Tything, and Wapentake, some new Alfred would have convened, in all its purity, the primitive Witenagemote, — fixed upon a basis of property or population permanent as the poles.

From this dream of universal restitution, Reason and Fancy with difficulty awake to view the real state of things. But, blessed be Heaven! St. Stephen's walls are yet standing, all her seats firmly secured; nay, some have doubted (since the Septennial Act) whether gunpowder itself, or any thing short of a *committee above stairs*, would be able to shake any one member from his seat. That great and final improvement to the Abbey, which is all that seems wanting, — the removing Westminster Hall and its appendages, and letting in the view of the Thames, — must not be expected in our days. Dismissing, therefore, all such speculations as mere tales of a tub, it is the duty of every honest Englishman to endeavor, by means less wholesale than Guido's, to ameliorate, without extinguishing, parliaments; to hold the *lantern* to the dark places of corruption; to apply the *match* to the rotten parts of the system only; and to wrap himself up, not in the muffling mantle of conspiracy, but in the warm, honest *cloak* of integrity and patriotic intention.

A VISION OF HORNS.*

My thoughts had been engaged last evening in solving the problem, why in all times and places the *horn* has been agreed upon as the symbol, or honorable badge, of married men. Moses' horn, the horn of Ammon, of Amalthea, and a cornucopia of legends besides, came to my recollection, but afforded no satis-

* From the "London Magazine," 1825.

In a letter to Miss Hutchinson, Lamb thus speaks of this article: "The 'Horns' is in a poor taste, resembling the most labored papers in the 'Spectator.' I had signed it 'Jack Horner:' but Taylor and Hessey said it would be thought an offensive article, unless I put my known signature to it; and wrung from me my slow consent." It seems that the "Vision" ("the foolish Vision," Lamb calls it) displeased Bernard Barton's daughter; but Elia hoped she would receive, in atonement for the "Horns" (as no doubt the "quiet Quakeress" gladly did), his beautiful story, "Barbara S." But despite the disparaging words of its writer, and the wounded sensibility of Miss Lucy Barton, I venture to say that "The Vision of Horns" is a pleasant and entertaining paper. — Editor.

factory solution, or rather involved the question in deeper obscurity. Tired with the fruitless chase of inexplicant analogies, I fell asleep, and dreamed in this fashion: —

Methought certain scales or films fell from my eyes, which had hitherto hindered these little tokens from being visible. I was somewhere in the Cornhill (as it might be termed) of some Utopia. Busy citizens jostled each other, as they may do in our streets, with care (the care of making a penny) written upon their foreheads; and *something else*, which is rather imagined than distinctly imaged, upon the brows of my own friends and fellow-townsmen.

In my first surprise, I supposed myself gotten into some forest, — Arden, to be sure, or Sherwood; but the dresses and deportment, all civic, forbade me to continue in that delusion. Then a scriptural thought crossed me (especially as there were nearly as many Jews as Christians among them), whether it might not be the children of Israel going up to besiege Jericho. I was undeceived of both errors by the sight of many faces which were familiar to me. I found myself strangely (as it will happen in dreams) at one and the same time in an unknown country with known companions. I met old friends, not with new faces, but with their old faces oddly adorned in front, with each man a certain corneous excresence. Dick Mitis, the little cheesemonger in St. ——'s Passage, was the first that saluted me, with his hat off (you know Dick's way to a customer); and, I not being aware of him, he thrust a strange beam into my left eye, which pained and grieved me exceedingly; but, instead of apology, he only grinned and fleered in my face, as much as to say, "It is the custom of the country," and passed on.

I had scarce time to send a civil message to his lady, whom I have always admired as a pattern of a wife, and do indeed take Dick and her to be a model of conjugal agreement and harmony, when I felt an ugly smart in my neck, as if something had gored it behind; and, turning round, it was my old friend and neighbor, Dulcet, the confectioner, who, meaning to be pleasant, had thrust his protuberance right into my nape, and seemed proud of his power of offending.

Now I was assailed right and left, till in my own defence I was obliged to walk sideling and wary, and look about me, as you guard your eyes in London streets; for the horns thickened, and came at me like the ends of umbrellas poking in one's face.

I soon found that these towns-folk were the civilest, best-mannered people in the world; and that, if they had offended at all, it was entirely owing to their blindness. They do not know what dangerous weapons they protrude in front, and will stick their best friends in the eye with provoking complacency. Yet the best of it is, they can see the beams on their neighbors' foreheads, if they are as small as motes; but their own beams they can in no wise discern.

There was little Mitis, that I told you I just encountered. He has simply (I speak of him at home in his own shop) the smoothest forehead in his own conceit. He will stand you a quarter of an hour together, contemplating the serenity of it in the glass, before he begins to shave himself in a morning; yet you saw what a desperate gash he gave me.

Desiring to be better informed of the ways of this extraordinary people, I applied myself to a fellow of some assurance, who (it appeared) acted as a sort of interpreter to strangers: he was dressed in a military uniform, and strongly resembled Col. ——, of the Guards. And "Pray, sir," said I, "have all the inhabitants of your city these troublesome excrescences? I beg pardon: I see you have none. You perhaps are single." — "Truly, sir," he replied with a smile, "for the most part we have, but not all alike. There are some, like Dick, that sport but one tumescence. Their ladies have been tolerably faithful, have confined themselves to a single aberration or so: these we call Unicorns. Dick, you must know, is my Unicorn. [He spoke this with an air of invincible assurance.] Then we have Bicorns, Tricorns, and so on up to Millecorns. [Here methought I crossed and blessed myself in my dream.] Some again we have, — there goes one: you see how happy the rogue looks, — how he walks smiling, and perking up his face, as if he thought himself the only man. He is not married yet; but on Monday next he leads to the altar the accomplished widow Dacres, relict of our late sheriff."

"I see, sir," said I, "and observe that he is happily free from the national *goitre* (let me call it) which distinguishes most of your countrymen."

"Look a little more narrowly," said my conductor.

I put on my spectacles; and, observing the man a little more diligently, above his forehead I could mark a thousand little twinkling shadows dancing the hornpipe; little hornlets, and rudiments of horn, of a soft and pappy consistence (for I handled some of them), but which, like coral out of water, my guide informed me, would infallibly stiffen and grow rigid within a week or two from the expiration of his bachelorhood.

Then I saw some horns strangely growing out behind; and my interpreter explained these to be married men, whose wives had conducted themselves with infinite propriety since the period of their marriage, but were thought to have antedated their good men's titles, by certain liberties they had indulged themselves in, prior to the ceremony. This kind of gentry wore their horns backwards, as has been said, in the fashion of the old pig-tails; and, as there was nothing obtrusive or ostentatious in them, nobody took any notice of it.

Some had pretty little budding antlers, like the first essays of a young fawn. These, he told me, had wives, whose affairs were in a hopeful way, but not quite brought to a conclusion.

Others had nothing to show: only by certain red angry marks and swellings in their foreheads, which itched the more they kept rubbing and chafing them, it was to be hoped that something was brewing.

I took notice that every one jeered at the rest, only none took notice of the sea-captains; yet these were as well provided with their tokens as the best among them. This kind of people, it seems, taking their wives upon so contingent tenures, their lot was considered as nothing but natural: so they wore their marks without impeachment, as they might carry their cockades; and nobody respected them a whit the less for it.

I observed, that the more sprouts grew out of a man's head, the less weight they seemed to carry with them; whereas a single token would now and then appear to give the wearer some uneasiness. This shows that use is a great thing.

Some had their adornings gilt, which needs no explanation; while others, like musicians, went sounding theirs before them, — a sort of music which I thought might very well have been spared.

It was pleasant to see some of the citizens encounter between themselves; how they smiled in their sleeves at the shock they received from their neighbor, and none seemed conscious of the shock which their neighbor experienced in return.

Some had great corneous stumps, seemingly torn off and bleeding. These, the interpreter warned me, were husbands who had retaliated upon their wives, and the badge was in equity divided between them.

While I stood discerning these things, a slight tweak on my cheek unawares, which brought tears into my eyes, introduced to me my friend Placid, between whose lady and a certain male cousin some idle flirtations I remember to have heard talked of; but that was all. He saw he had somehow hurt me, and asked my pardon with that round, unconscious face of his; and looked so tristful and contrite for his no-offence, that I was ashamed for the man's penitence. Yet I protest it was but a scratch. It was the least little hornet of a horn that could be framed. "Shame on the man," I secretly exclaimed, "who could thrust so much as the value of a hair into a brow so unsuspecting and inoffensive! What, then, must they have to answer for, who plant great, monstrous, timber-like, projecting antlers upon the heads of those whom they call their friends, when a puncture of this atomical tenuity made my eyes to water at this rate! All the pincers at Surgeons' Hall cannot pull out for Placid that little hair."

I was curious to know what became of these frontal excrescences when the husbands died; and my guide informed me that the chemists in their country made a considerable profit by them, extracting from them certain subtile essences: and then I remembered that nothing was so efficacious in my own, for restoring swooning matrons, and wives troubled with the vapors, as a strong sniff or two at the composition appropriately called hartshorn, — far beyond *sal volatile*.

Then also I began to understand why a man, who is the jest of the company, is said to be the butt, — as much as to say, such a one butteth with the horn.

I inquired if by no operation these wens were ever extracted; and was told that there was indeed an order of dentists, whom they call canonists in their language, who undertook to restore the forehead to its pristine smoothness; but that ordinarily it was not done without much cost and trouble; and, when they succeeded in plucking out the offending part, it left a painful void, which could not be filled up; and that many patients who had submitted to the excision were eager to marry again, to supply with a good second antler the baldness and deformed gap left by the extraction of the former, as men losing their natural hair substitute for it a less becoming periwig.

Some horns I observed beautifully taper, smooth, and (as it were) flowering. These I understand were the portions brought by handsome women to their spouses; and I pitied the rough, homely, unsightly deformities on the brows of others, who had been deceived by plain and ordinary partners. Yet the latter I observed to be by far the most common; the solution of which I leave to the natural philosopher.

One tribe of married men I particularly admired at, who, instead of horns, wore ingrafted on their forehead a sort of horn-book. "This," quoth my guide, "is the greatest mystery in our country, and well worth an explanation. You must know that all infidelity is not of the senses. We have as well intellectual as material wittols. These, whom you see decorated with the order of the book, are triflers, who encourage about their wives' presence the society of your men of genius, (their good friends, as they call them), — literary disputants, who ten to one out-talk the poor husband, and commit upon the understanding of the woman a violence and estrangement in the end, little less painful than the coarser sort of alienation. Whip me these knaves, — [my conductor here expressed himself with a becoming warmth], — whip me them, I say, who, with no excuse from the passions, in cold blood seduce the minds, rather than the persons, of their friends' wives; who, for the tickling pleasure of hearing themselves prate, dehonestate the intellects of married women, dishonoring the husband in what should be his most sensible part. If I must be — [here he used a plain word] let it be by some honest sinner like myself, and not by one of these gad-flies, these debauchers of the understanding, these flattery-buzzers." He was going on in this manner, and I was getting insensibly pleased with my friend's manner (I had been a little shy of him at first), when the dream suddenly left me, vanishing, as Virgil speaks, through the gate of Horn.

JOHN KEMBLE, AND GODWIN'S TRAGEDY OF "ANTONIO."*

THE story of his swallowing opium-pills to keep him lively upon the first night of a certain tragedy, we may presume to be a piece of retaliatory pleasantry on the part of the suffering author. But, indeed, John had the art of diffusing a complacent equable dulness (which you knew not where to quarrel with) over a piece which he did not like, beyond any of his contemporaries. John Kemble had made up his mind early, that all the good tragedies which could be written had been written; and he resented any new attempt. His shelves were full. The old standards were scope enough for his ambition. He ranged in them absolute; and "fair in Otway, full in Shakspeare shone." He succeeded to the old lawful thrones, and did not care to adventure bottomry with a Sir Edward Mortimer, or any casual speculator that offered.

I remember, too acutely for my peace, the deadly extinguisher which he put upon my friend G.'s "Antonio." G., satiate with visions of political justice (possibly not to be realized in our time), or willing to let the sceptical worldlings see that his anticipations of

* From the "London Magazine," 1822.

To Elia's essay on "The Artificial Comedy of the Last Century," as originally published in the "London Magazine," this circumstantial account of the cold and stately manner in which John Kemble performed the part of Antonio, in Godwin's unfortunate play of that name, was the conclusion. In reprinting the article, Lamb omitted this part of it. — EDITOR.

the future did not preclude a warm sympathy for men as they are and have been, wrote a tragedy. He chose a story, affecting, romantic, Spanish; the plot simple, without being naked; the incidents uncommon, without being overstrained. Antonio, who gives the name to the piece, is a sensitive young Castilian, who, in a fit of his country honor, immolates his sister —

But I must not anticipate the catastrophe. The play, reader, is extant in choice English; and you will employ a spare half-crown not injudiciously in the quest of it.

The conception was bold; and the *dénouement*, the time and place in which the hero of it existed, considered, not much out of keeping: yet it must be confessed that it required a delicacy of handling, both from the author and the performer, so as not much to shock the prejudices of a modern English audience. G., in my opinion, had done his part. John, who was in familiar habits with the philosopher, had undertaken to play Antonio. Great expectations were formed. A philosopher's first play was a new era. The night arrived. I was favored with a seat in an advantageous box, between the author and his friend M. G. sat cheerful and confident. In his friend M.'s looks, who had perused the manuscript, I read some terror. Antonio, in the person of John Philip Kemble, at length appeared, starched out in a ruff which no one could dispute, and in most irreproachable mustachios. John always dressed most provokingly correct on these occasions. The first act swept by, solemn and silent. It went off, as G. assured M., exactly as the opening act of a piece — the *protasis* — should do. The cue of the spectators was to be mute. The characters were but in their introduction. The passions and the incidents would be developed hereafter. Applause hitherto would be impertinent. Silent attention was the effect all-desirable. Poor M. acquiesced; but in his honest, friendly face I could discern a working which told how much more acceptable the plaudit of a single hand (however misplaced) would have been than all this reasoning. The second act (as in duty bound) rose a little in interest; but still John kept his forces under,—in policy, as G. would have it,—and the audience were most complacently attentive. The *protasis*, in fact, was scarcely unfolded. The interest would warm in the next act, against which a special incident was provided. M. wiped his cheek, flushed with a friendly perspiration,—'tis M.'s way of showing his zeal,—"from every pore of him a perfume falls." I honor it above Alexander's. He had once or twice during this act joined his palms in a feeble endeavor to elicit a sound; they emitted a solitary noise without an echo: there was no deep to answer to his deep. G. repeatedly begged him to be quiet. The third act at length brought on the scene which was to warm the piece progressively to the final flaming-forth of the catastophe. A philosophic calm settled upon the clear brow of G. as it approached. The lips of M. quivered. A challenge was held forth upon the stage, and there was promise of a fight. The pit roused themselves on this extraordinary occasion, and, as their manner is, seemed disposed to make a ring; when suddenly Antonio, who was the challenged, turning the tables upon the hot challenger, Don Gusman (who, by the way, should have had his sister), balks his humor, and the pit's reasonable expectation at the same time, with some speeches out of the new philosophy against duelling. The audience were here fairly caught; their courage was up, and on the alert; a few blows, *ding dong*, as R——s, the dramatist, afterwards expressed it to me, might have done the business, — when their most exquisite moral sense was suddenly called in to assist in the mortifying negation of their own pleasure. They could not applaud, for disappointment; they would not condemn, for morality's sake. The interest stood stone-still; and John's manner was not at all calculated to unpetrify it. It was Christmas-time, and the atmosphere furnished some pretext for asthmatic affections. One began to cough: his neighbor sympathized with him, till a cough became epidemical. But when, from being half artificial in the pit, the cough got frightfully naturalized among the fictitious persons of the drama, and Antonio himself (albeit it was not set down in the stage directions) seemed more intent upon relieving his own lungs than the distresses of the author and his friends, then G. "first knew fear," and, mildly turning to M., intimated that he had not been aware that Mr. Kemble labored under a cold, and that the performance might possibly have been postponed with advantage for some nights further, — still keeping the same serene countenance, while M. sweat like a bull.

It would be invidious to pursue the fates of this ill-starred evening. In vain did the plot thicken in the scenes that followed, in vain the dialogue wax more passionate and stirring, and the progress of the sentiment point more and more clearly to the arduous development which impended. In vain the action was accelerated, while the acting stood still. From the beginning, John had taken his stand, — had wound himself up to an even tenor of stately declamation, from which no exigence of dialogue or person could make him swerve for an instant. To dream of his rising with the scene (the common trick of tragedians) was preposterous; for from the onset he had planted himself, as upon a terrace, on an eminence vastly above the audience, and he kept that sublime level to the end. He looked from his throne of elevated sentiment upon the under-world of spectators with a most sovereign and becoming contempt. There was excellent pathos delivered out to them: an they would receive it, so; an they would not receive it, so. There was no offence against decorum in all this; nothing to condemn, to damn: not an irreverent symptom of a sound was to be heard. The procession of verbiage stalked on through four and five acts, no one venturing to predict what would come of it; when, towards the winding-up of the latter, Antonio, with an irrelevancy that seemed to stagger Elvira herself, — for she had been coolly arguing the point of honor with him, — suddenly whips out a poniard, and stabs his sister to the heart. The effect was as if a murder had been committed in cold blood. The whole house rose up in clamorous indignation, demanding justice. The feeling rose far above hisses. I believe at that instant, if they could have got him, they would have torn the unfortunate author to pieces. Not that the act itself was so exorbitant, or of a complexion different from what they themselves would have applauded upon another occasion in a Brutus or an Appius; but, for want of attending to Antonio's *words*, which palpably led to the expectation of no less dire an event, instead of being seduced by his *manner*, which seemed to promise a sleep of a less alarming nature than it was his cue to inflict upon Elvira, they found themselves betrayed into an accompliceship of murder, a perfect misprision of parricide, while they dreamed of nothing less.

M., I believe, was the only person who suffered acutely from the failure; for G. thenceforward, with a serenity unattainable but by the true philosophy, abandoning a precarious popularity, retired into his fast hold of speculation, — the drama in which the world was to be his tiring-room, and remote posterity his applauding spectators at once and actors.

THE GOOD CLERK, A CHARACTER;

WITH SOME ACCOUNT OF "THE COMPLETE ENGLISH TRADESMAN." *

THE GOOD CLERK. — He writeth a fair and swift hand, and is competently versed in the four first rules of arithmetic, in the Rule of Three (which is sometimes called the Golden Rule), and in Practice. We mention these things that we may leave no room for cavillers to say that any thing essential hath been omitted in our definition; else, to speak the truth, these are but ordinary

* From the "Reflector," No. 4.

accomplishments, and such as every understrapper at a desk is commonly furnished with. The character we treat of soareth higher.

He is clean and neat in his person, not from a vain-glorious desire of setting himself forth to advantage in the eyes of the other sex, with which vanity too many of our young sparks now-a-days are infected; but to do credit, as we say, to the office. For this reason, he evermore taketh care that his desk or his books receive no soil; the which things he is commonly as solicitous to have fair and unblemished, as the owner of a fine horse is to have him appear in good keep.

He riseth early in the morning; not because early rising conduceth to health (though he doth not altogether despise that consideration), but chiefly to the intent that he may be first at the desk. There is his post, there he delighteth to be, unless when his meals or necessity calleth him away; which time he alway esteemeth as lost, and maketh as short as possible.

He is temperate in eating and drinking, that he may preserve a clear head and steady hand for his master's service. He is also partly induced to this observation of the rules of temperance by his respect for religion and the laws of his country; which things, it may once for all be noted, do add special assistances to his actions, but do not and cannot furnish the main spring or motive thereto. His first ambition, as appeareth all along, is to be a good clerk; his next, a good Christian, a good patriot, &c.

Correspondent to this, he keepeth himself honest, not for fear of the laws, but because he hath observed how unseemly an article it maketh in the day-book or ledger when a sum is set down lost or missing; it being his pride to make these books to agree and to tally, the one side with the other, with a sort of architectural symmetry and correspondence.

He marrieth, or marrieth not, as best suiteth with his employer's views. Some merchants do the rather desire to have married men in their counting-houses, because they think the married state a pledge for their servants' integrity, and an incitement to them to be industrious; and it was an observation of a late Lord-Mayor of London, that the sons of clerks do generally prove clerks themselves, and that merchants encouraging persons in their employ to marry, and to have families, was the best method of securing a breed of sober, industrious young men attached to the mercantile interest. Be this as it may, such a character as we have been describing will wait till the pleasure of his employer is known on this point; and regulateth his desires by the custom of the house or firm to which he belongeth.

He avoideth profane oaths and jesting, as so much time lost from his employ. What spare time he hath for conversation, which, in a counting-house such as we have been supposing, can be but small, he spendeth in putting seasonable questions to such of his fellows (and sometimes *respectfully* to the master himself) who can give him information respecting the price and quality of goods, the state of exchange, or the latest improvements in book-keeping; thus making the motion of his lips, as well as of his fingers, subservient to his master's interest. Not that he refuseth a brisk saying, or a cheerful sally of wit, when it comes unforced, is free of offence, and hath a convenient brevity. For this reason, he hath commonly some such phrase as this in his mouth: —

"It's a slovenly look
To blot your book."

Or,

"Red ink for ornament, black for use:
The best of things are open to abuse."

So upon the eve of any great holy-day, of which he keepeth one or two at least every year, he will merrily say, in the hearing of a confidential friend, but to none other, —

"All work and no play
Makes Jack a dull boy."

Or,

"A bow always bent must crack at last."

But then this must always be understood to be spoken confidentially, and, as we say, *under the rose.*

Lastly, his dress is plain, without singularity; with no other ornament than the quill, which is the badge of his function, stuck behind the dexter ear, and this rather for convenience of having it at hand, when he hath been called away from his desk, and expecteth to resume his seat there again shortly, than from any delight which he taketh in foppery or ostentation. The color of his clothes is generally noted to be black rather than brown, brown rather than blue or green. His whole deportment is staid, modest, and civil. His motto is "Regularity."

This character was sketched in an interval of business, to divert some of the melancholy hours of a counting-house. It is so little a creature of fancy, that it is scarce any thing more than a recollection of some of those frugal and economical maxims, which, about the beginning of the last century (England's meanest period), were endeavored to be inculcated and instilled into the breasts of the London Apprentices* by a class of instructors who might not inaptly be termed "The Masters of Mean Morals." The astonishing narrowness and illiberality of the lessons contained in some of those books is inconceivable by those whose studies have not led them that way, and would almost induce one to subscribe to the hard censure which Drayton has passed upon the mercantile spirit: —

> "The gripple merchant, born to be the curse
> Of this brave isle."

I have now lying before me that curious book by Daniel Defoe, "The Complete English Tradesman." The pompous detail, the studied analysis of every little mean art, every sneaking address, every trick and subterfuge, short of larceny, that is necessary to the tradesman's occupation, with the hundreds of anecdotes, dialogues (in Defoe's liveliest manner) interspersed, all tending to the same amiable purpose, — namely, the sacrificing of every honest emotion of the soul to what he calls the main chance, — if you read it in an *ironical sense*, and as a piece of *covered satire*, make it one of the most amusing books which Defoe ever writ, as much so as any of his best novels. It is difficult to say what his intention was in writing it. It is almost impossible to suppose him in earnest. Yet such is the bent of the book to narrow and to degrade the heart, that if such maxims were as catching and infectious as those of a licentious cast, which happily is not the case, had I been living at

* This term designated a larger class of young men than that to which it is now confined. It took in the articled clerks of merchants and bankers, the George Barnwells of the day.

that time, I certainly should have recommended to the Grand Jury of Middlesex, who presented "The Fable of the Bees," to have presented this book of Defoe's in preference, as of a far more vile and debasing tendency. I will give one specimen of his advice to the young tradesman on the *government of his temper:* "The retail tradesman in especial, and even every tradesman in his station, must furnish himself with a competent stock of patience. I mean that sort of patience which is needful to bear with all sorts of impertinence, and the most provoking curiosity that it is impossible to imagine the buyers, even the worst of them, are, or can be, guilty of. *A tradesman behind his counter must have no flesh and blood about him, no passions, no resentment;* he must never be angry, no, not so much as seem to be so, if a customer tumbles him five hundred pounds' worth of goods, and scarce bids money for any thing; nay, though they really come to his shop with no intent to buy, as many do, only to see what is to be sold, and though he knows they cannot be better pleased than they are at some other shop where they intend to buy, 'tis all one; the tradesman must take it; he must place it to the account of his calling, that *'tis his business to be ill used, and resent nothing;* and so must answer as obligingly to those that give him an hour or two's trouble, and buy nothing, as he does to those, who, in half the time, lay out ten or twenty pounds. The case is plain; and if some do give him trouble, and do not buy, others make amends, and do buy; and as for the trouble, 'tis the business of the shop."

Here follows a most admirable story of a mercer, who by his indefatigable meanness, and more than Socratic patience under affronts, overcame and reconciled a lady, who, upon the report of another lady that he had behaved saucily to some third lady, had determined to shun his shop, but, by the over-persuasions of a fourth lady, was induced to go to it; which she does, declaring beforehand that she will buy nothing, but give him all the trouble she can. Her attack and his defence, her insolence and his persevering patience, are described in colors worthy of a Mandeville; but it is too long to recite. "The short inference from this long discourse," says he, "is this, — that here you see, and I could give you many examples like this, how and in what manner a shop-keeper is to behave himself in the way of his business; what impertinences, what taunts, flouts, and ridiculous things, he must bear in his trade; and must not show the least return, or the least signal of disgust: he must have no passions, no fire in his temper; he must be all soft and smooth; nay, if his real temper be naturally fiery and hot, he must show none of it in his shop; he must be a perfect *complete hypocrite* if he will be a *complete tradesman*.* It is true, natural tempers are not to be always counterfeited: the man cannot easily be a lamb in his shop, and a lion in himself; but, let it be easy or hard, it must be done, and is done. There are men who have by custom and usage brought themselves to it, that nothing could be meeker and milder than they when behind the counter, and yet nothing be more furious and raging in every other part of life: nay, the provocations they have met with in their shops have so irritated their rage, that they would go up stairs from their shop, and fall into frenzies, and a kind of mad-

* As no qualification accompanies this maxim, it must be understood as the genuine sentiment of the author!

ness, and beat their heads against the wall, and perhaps mischief themselves, if not prevented, till the violence of it had gotten vent, and the passions abate and cool. I heard once of a shop-keeper that behaved himself thus to such an extreme, that, when he was provoked by the impertinence of the customers beyond what his temper could bear, he would go up stairs and beat his wife, kick his children about like dogs, and be as furious for two or three minutes as a man chained down in Bedlam; and again, when that heat was over, would sit down, and cry faster than the children he had abused; and, after the fit, he would go down into the shop again, and be as humble, courteous, and as calm, as any man whatever; so absolute a government of his passions had he in the shop, and so little out of it: in the shop, a soulless animal that would resent nothing; and in the family, a madman: in the shop, meek like a lamb; but in the family outrageous, like a Lybian lion. The sum of the matter is, it is necessary for a tradesman to subject himself, by all the ways possible, to his business; *his customers are to be his idols: so far as he may worship idols by allowance, he is to bow down to them, and worship them;* at least, he is not in any way to displease them, or show any disgust or distaste, whatsoever they may say or do. The bottom of all is, that he is intending to get money by them; and it is not for him that gets money to offer the least inconvenience to them by whom he gets it: he is to consider, that, as Solomon says, "the borrower is servant to the lender;" so the seller is servant to the buyer. What he says on the head of "Pleasures and Recreations" is not less amusing: "The tradesman's pleasure should be in his business;

his companions should be his books (he means his ledger, waste-book, &c.); and, if he has a family, he makes *his excursions up stairs, and no further.* None of my cautions aim at restraining a tradesman from diverting himself, as we call it, with his fireside, or keeping company with his wife and children." Liberal allowance! nay, almost licentious and criminal indulgence! But it is time to dismiss this Philosopher of Meanness. More of this stuff would illiberalize the pages of the "Reflector." Was the man in earnest, when he could bring such powers of description, and all the charms of natural eloquence, in commendation of the meanest, vilest, wretchedest degradations of the human character? or did he not rather laugh in his sleeve at the doctrines which he inculcated; and, retorting upon the grave citizens of London their own arts, palm upon them a sample of disguised satire under the name of wholesome instruction?

REMINISCENCE OF SIR JEFFERY DUNSTAN.

To the Editor of the "Every-day Book."

To your account of Sir Jeffery Dunstan, in columns 829–30 (where, by an unfortunate erratum, the effigies of *two Sir Jefferys* appear, when the uppermost figure is clearly meant for Sir Harry Dimsdale), you may add that the writer of this has frequently met him in his latter days, about 1790 or 1791, returning in an evening, after his long day's itineracy, to his domicile, — a wretched shed in the most beggarly purlieu of Bethnal

Green, a little on this side the Mile-end Turnpike. The lower figure in that leaf most correctly describes his then appearance, except that no graphic art can convey an idea of the general squalor of it, and of his bag (his constant concomitant) in particular. Whether it contained "old wigs" at that time, I know not; but it seemed a fitter repository for bones snatched out of kennels than for any part of a gentleman's dress, even at second-hand.

The ex-member for Garrat was a melancholy instance of a great man whose popularity is worn out. He still carried his sack; but it seemed a part of his identity rather than an implement of his profession; a badge of past grandeur: could any thing have divested him of *that*, he would have shown a "poor forked animal" indeed. My life upon it, it contained no curls at the time I speak of. The most decayed and spiritless remnants of what was once a peruke would have scorned the filthy case; would absolutely have "burst its cerements." No: it was empty, or brought home bones, or a few cinders possibly. A strong odor of burnt bones, I remember, blended with the scent of horse-flesh seething into dog's meat, and, only relieved a little by the breathings of a few brick-kilns, made up the atmosphere of the delicate suburban spot which this great man had chosen for the last scene of his earthly vanities. The cry of "old wigs" had ceased with the possession of any such fripperies: his sack might have contained not unaptly a little mould to scatter upon that grave to which he was now advancing; but it told of vacancy and desolation. His quips were silent too, and his brain was empty as his sack: he slank along, and seemed to decline popular observation. If a few boys followed him, it seemed rather from habit than any expectation of fun.

> "Alas! how changed from *him*,
> The life of humor, and the soul of whim,
> Gallant and gay on Garrat's hustings proud!"

But it is thus that the world rewards its favorites in decay. What faults he had, I know not. I have heard something of a peccadillo or so. But some little deviation from the precise line of rectitude might have been winked at in so tortuous and stigmatic a frame. Poor Sir Jeffery! it were well if some M.P.'s in earnest have passed their parliamentary existence with no more offences against integrity than could be laid to thy charge! A fair dismissal was thy due, not so unkind a degradation; some little snug retreat, with a bit of green before thine eyes, and not a burial alive in the fetid beggaries of Bethnal. Thou wouldst have ended thy days in a manner more appropriate to thy pristine dignity, installed in munificent mockery (as in mock honors you had lived), — a poor knight of Windsor!

Every distinct place of public speaking demands an oratory peculiar to itself. The forensic fails within the walls of St. Stephen. Sir Jeffery was a living instance of this; for, in the flower of his popularity, an attempt was made to bring him out upon the stage (at which of the winter theatres I forget, but I well remember the anecdote) in the part of *Doctor Last.** The announcement drew a crowded house; but, notwithstanding infinite tutoring, — by Foote or Garrick, I forget which, — when the curtain drew up, the heart of Sir Jeffery

* It was at the Haymarket Theatre. — *Editor of "Every-day Book."*

failed, and he faltered on, and made nothing of his part, till the hisses of the house at last, in very kindness, dismissed him from the boards. Great as his parliamentary eloquence had shown itself, brilliantly as his off-hand sallies had sparkled on a hustings, they here totally failed him. Perhaps he had an aversion to borrowed wit, and, like my Lord Foppington, disdained to entertain himself (or others) with the forced products of another man's brain. Your man of quality is more diverted with the natural sprouts of his own.

ON A PASSAGE IN "THE TEMPEST."*

As long as I can remember the play of "The Tempest," one passage in it has always set me upon wondering. It has puzzled me beyond measure. In vain I strove to find the meaning of it. I seemed doomed to cherish infinite, hopeless curiosity.

It is where Prospero, relating the banishment of Sycorax from Argier, adds,—

> "For one thing that she did,
> They would not take her life."

How have I pondered over this when a boy! How have I longed for some authentic memoir of the witch to clear up the obscurity! Was the story extant in the chronicles of Algiers? Could I get at it by some fortunate introduction to the Algerine ambassador? Was a voyage thither practicable? The Spectator, I knew,

* From the "London Magazine" for 1823

went to Grand Cairo only to measure the pyramid. Was not the object of my quest of at least as much importance? The blue-eyed hag! could *she* have done any thing good or meritorious? might that succubus relent? then might there be hope for the Devil. I have often admired since, that none of the commentators have boggled at this passage; how they could swallow this camel, — such a tantalizing piece of obscurity, such an abortion of an anecdote.

At length, I think I have lighted upon a clew which may lead to show what was passing in the mind of Shakspeare when he dropped this imperfect rumor. In the "Accurate Description of Africa, by John Ogilby (folio), 1670," page 230, I find written as follows. The marginal title to the narrative is, "Charles the Fifth besieges Algier."

"In the last place, we will briefly give an account of the emperour, Charles the Fifth, when he besieg'd this city; and of the great loss he suffer'd therein.

"This prince, in the year one thousand five hundred forty-one, having embarqued upon the sea an army of twenty-two thousand men aboard eighteen gallies, and an hundred tall ships, not counting the barques and shallops, and other small boats, in which he had engaged the principal of the Spanish and Italian nobility, with a good number of the Knights of Malta; he was to land on the coast of Barbary, at a cape call'd Matifou. From this place unto the city of Algier, a flat shore or strand extends itself for about four leagues, the which is exceeding favorable to gallies. There he put ashore with his army, and in a few days caused a fortress to be built, which unto this day is call'd the castle of the Emperour.

"In the meantime the city of Algier took the alarm, having in it at that time but eight hundred Turks, and six thousand Moors, poor-spirited men, and unexercised in martial affairs; besides it was at that time fortifi'd only with walls, and had no out-works: insomuch that by reason of its weakness, and the great forces of the Emperour, it could not in appearance escape taking. In fine, it was attempted with such order, that the army came up to the very gates, where the Chevalier de Sauignac, a Frenchman by nation, made himself remarkable above all the rest, by the miracles of his valor. For having repulsed the Turks, who, having made a sally at the gate call'd Babason, and there desiring to enter along with them, when he saw that they shut the gate upon him, he ran his ponyard into the same, and left it sticking deep therein. They next fell to battering the city by the force of cannon; which the assailants so weakened, that in that great extremity the defendants lost their courage, and resolved to surrender.

"But as they were thus intending, there was a witch of the town, whom the history doth not name, which went to seek out Assam Aga, that commanded within, and pray'd him to make it good yet nine days longer, with assurance, that within that time he should infallibly see Algier delivered from that siege, and the whole army of the enemy dispersed, so that Christians should be as cheap as birds. In a word, the thing did happen in the manner as foretold; for upon the twenty-first day of October, in the same year, there fell a continual rain upon the land, and so furious a storm at sea, that one might have seen ships hoisted into the clouds, and in one instant again precipitated into the bottom of the water: insomuch that that same dreadful tempest was followed with the loss of fifteen gallies, and above an hundred other vessels; which was the cause why the Emperour, seeing his army wasted by the bad weather, pursued by a famine, occasioned by wrack of his ships, in which was the greatest part of his victuals and amunition, he was constrain'd to raise the siege, and set sail for Sicily, whither he retreated with the miserable reliques of his fleet.

"In the meantime that witch being acknowledged the deliverer of Algier, was richly remunerated, and the credit of her charms authorized. So that ever since, witchcraft hath been very freely tolerated; of which the chief of the town, and even those who are esteem'd to be of greatest sanctity among them, such as are the Marabous, a religious order of their sect, do for the most part make profession of it, under a goodly pretext of certain revelations which they say they have had from their prophet, Mahomet.

"And hereupon those of Algier, to palliate the shame and the reproaches that are thrown upon them for making use of a witch in the danger of this siege, do say that the loss of the forces of Charles V. was caused by a prayer of one of their Marabous, named Cidy Utica, which was at that time in great credit, not under the notion of a magitian, but for a person of a holy life. Afterwards in remembrance of their success, they have erected unto him a small mosque without the Babason gate, where he is buried, and in which they keep sundry lamps burning in honor of him: nay they sometimes repair thither to make their *sala*, for a testimony of greater veneration."

Can it be doubted, for a moment, that the dramatist had come fresh from reading some *older narrative* of this deliverance of Algier by a witch, and transferred the merit of the deed to his Sycorax, exchanging only the "rich remuneration," which did not suit his purpose, to the simple pardon of her life? Ogilby wrote in 1670; but the authorities to which he refers for his account of Barbary are Johannes de Leo or Africanus, Louis Marmol, Diego de Haedo, Johannes Gramaye, Braeves, Cel. Curio, and Diego de Torres, names totally unknown to me, and to which I beg leave to refer the curious reader for his fuller satisfaction.

THE MONTHS.*

RUMMAGING over the contents of an old stall at a half *book*, half *old-iron shop*, in an alley leading from Wardour Street to Soho Square, yesterday, I lit upon a ragged duodecimo which had been the strange delight of my infancy, and which I had lost sight of for more than forty years, — the "Queen-like Closet, or Rich Cabinet;" written by Hannah Woolly, and printed for R. C. and T. S., 1681; being an abstract of receipts in cookery, confectionery, cosmetics, needle-work, morality, and all such branches of what were then considered as female accomplishments. The price demanded was sixpence, which the owner (a little squab

* From Hone's "Every-day Book."

duodecimo of a character himself) enforced with the assurance that his "own mother should not have it for a farthing less." On my demurring at this extraordinary assertion, the dirty little vender re-enforced his assertion with a sort of oath, which seemed more than the occasion demanded: "And now," said he, "I have put my soul to it." Pressed by so solemn an asseveration, I could no longer resist a demand which seemed to set me, however unworthy, upon a level with his dearest relations; and, depositing a tester, I bore away the tattered prize in triumph. I remembered a gorgeous description of the twelve months of the year, which I thought would be a fine substitute for those poetical descriptions of them which your "Every-day Book" had nearly exhausted out of Spenser. "This will be a treat," thought I, "for friend Hone." To memory they seemed no less fantastic and splendid than the other. But what are the mistakes of childhood! On reviewing them, they turned out to be only a set of commonplace receipts for working the seasons, months, heathen gods and goddesses, &c., in *samplers!* Yet, as an instance of the homely occupations of our great-grandmothers, they may be amusing to some readers. "I have seen," says the notable Hannah Woolly, "such ridiculous things done in work, as it is an abomination to any artist to behold. As for example: You may find, in some pieces, *Abraham* and *Sarah*, and many other persons of old time, clothed as they go now-a-days, and truly sometimes worse; for they most resemble the pictures on ballads. Let all ingenious women have regard, that when they work any image, to represent it aright. First, let it be drawn well, and then observe the directions which are given by knowing men. I do assure you, I never durst work any Scripture-story without informing myself from the ground of it; nor any other story, or single person, without informing myself both of the visage and habit; as followeth: —

"If you work *Jupiter*, *the imperial feigned God*, he must have long, black, curled hair, a purple garment trimmed with gold, and sitting upon a golden throne, with bright yellow clouds about him."

THE TWELVE MONTHS OF THE YEAR.

March. Is drawn in tawny, with a fierce aspect; a helmet upon his head, and leaning on a spade; and a basket of garden seeds in his left hand, and in his right hand the sign of *Aries;* and winged.

April. A young man in green, with a garland of myrtle and hawthorn-buds; winged; in one hand primroses and violets, in the other the sign *Taurus*.

May. With a sweet and lovely countenance; clad in a robe of white and green, embroidered with several flowers; upon his head a garland of all manner of roses; on the one hand a nightingale, in the other a lute. His sign must be *Gemini*.

June. In a mantle of dark grass-green; upon his head a garland of bents, kings-cups, and maiden-hair; in his left hand an angle, with a box of cantharides; in his right, the sign *Cancer;* and upon his arms a basket of seasonable fruits.

July. In a jacket of light yellow, eating cherries; with his face and bosom sun-burnt; on his head a wreath of centaury and wild thyme; a scythe on his shoulder, and a bottle at his girdle; carrying the sign *Leo*.

August. A young man of fierce and choleric aspect, in a flame-colored garment; upon his head a garland of wheat and rye; upon his arm a basket of all manner of ripe fruits; at his belt a sickle: his sign *Virgo*.

September. A merry and cheerful countenance, in a purple robe; upon his head a wreath of red and white grapes; in his left hand a handful of oats; withal carrying a horn of plenty, full of all manner of ripe fruits; in his right hand the sign *Libra*.

October. In a garment of yellow and carnation; upon his head a garland of oak-leaves with acorns; in his right hand the sign *Scorpio;* in his left hand a basket of medlars, services, and chestnuts, and any other fruits then in season.

November. In a garment of changeable green and black; upon his head a garland of olives, with the fruit in his left hand; bunches of parsnips and turnips in his right: his sign *Sagittarius*.

December. A horrid and fearful aspect, clad in Irish rags, or coarse frieze girt unto him; upon his head three or four night-caps, and over them a Turkish turban; his nose red, his mouth and beard clogged with icicles; at his back a bundle of holly, ivy, or mistletoe; holding in furred mittens the sign of *Capricornus*.

January. Clad all in white, as the earth looks with the snow, blowing his nails; in his left arm a billet; the sign *Aquarius* standing by his side.

February. Clothed in a dark sky-color, carrying in his right hand the sign *Pisces*.

The following receipt, "To dress up a chimney very

fine for the summer time, as I have done many, and they have been liked very well," may not be unprofitable to the housewives of this century: —

"First, take a pack-thread, and fasten it even to the inner part of the chimney, so high as that you can see no higher as you walk up and down the house. You must drive in several nails to hold up all your work. Then get good store of old green moss from trees, and melt an equal proportion of beeswax and rosin together; and, while it is hot, dip the wrong ends of the moss in it, and presently clap it upon your pack-thread, and press it down hard with your hand. You must make haste, else it will cool before you can fasten it, and then it will fall down. Do so all around where the pack-thread goes; and the next row you must join to that, so that it may seem all in one: thus do till you have finished it down to the bottom. Then take some other kind of moss, of a whitish color and stiff, and of several sorts or kinds, and place that upon the other, here and there carelessly, and in some places put a good deal, and some a little; then any kind of fine snail-shells, in which the snails are dead, and little toad-stools, which are very old, and look like velvet, or *any other thing that was old and pretty:* place it here and there as your fancy serves, and fasten all with wax and rosin. Then, for the hearth of your chimney, you may lay some orpan-sprigs in order all over, and it will grow as it lies; and, according to the season, get what flowers you can, and stick in as if they grew, and a few sprigs of sweet-brier: the flowers you must renew every week; but the moss will last all the summer, till it will be time to make a fire; and the orpan will last near two months. A chimney thus done doth grace a room exceedingly." *

One phrase in the above should particularly recommend it to such of your female readers as, in the nice language of the day, have done growing some time, — "little toad-stools, &c., and any thing that is *old and pretty*." Was ever antiquity so smoothed over? The culinary recipes have nothing remarkable in them, except the costliness of them. Every thing (to the meanest meats) is sopped in claret, steeped in claret, basted with claret, as if claret were as cheap as ditch-water. I remember Bacon recommends opening a turf or two in your garden-walks, and pouring into each a bottle of claret, to recreate the sense of smelling, being no less grateful than beneficial. We hope the chancellor of the exchequer will attend to this in his next reduction of French wines, that we may once more water our gardens with right Bourdeaux. The medical recipes are as whimsical as they are cruel. Our ancestors were not at all effeminate on this head. Modern sentimentalists would shrink at a cock plucked and bruised in a mortar alive to make a cullis, or a live mole baked in an oven (*be sure it be alive*) to make a powder for consumption. But the whimsicalist of all are the directions to servants (for this little book is a compendium of all duties): the footman is seriously admonished not to stand lolling against his master's chair while he waits at table; for "to lean on a chair when they wait is a particular favor shown to any

* Alas! in these days of stoves and furnaces, we have no "chimneys" or fireplaces to "dress up" in the beautiful manner Mistress Woolly describes. — EDITOR.

superior servant, as the chief gentleman, or the waiting-woman when she rises from the table." Also he must not "hold the plates before his mouth to be defiled with his breath, nor touch them on the right [inner] side." Surely Swift must have seen this little treatise.

Hannah concludes with the following address, by which the self-estimate which she formed of her usefulness may be calculated: —

"*Ladies*, I hope you're pleas'd and so shall I
If what I've writ, you may be gainers by:
If not; it is your fault, it is not mine,
Your benefit in this I do design.
Much labor and much time it hath me cost,
Therefore I beg, let none of it be lost.
The money you shall pay for this my book,
You'll not repent of, when in it you look.
No more at present to you I shall say,
But wish you all the happiness I may."

BIOGRAPHICAL MEMOIR OF MR. LISTON.*

THE subject of our Memoir is lineally descended from Johan de L'Estonne (see "Domesday Book," where he is so written), who came in with the Conqueror, and had lands awarded him at Lupton Magna, in Kent. His particular merits or services, Fabian, whose authority I chiefly follow, has forgotten, or perhaps thought it immaterial, to specify. Fuller thinks that he was standard-bearer to Hugo de Agmondesham, a powerful Norman baron, who was slain by the hand

* From the "London Magazine," 1825.

of Harold himself at the fatal battle of Hastings. Be this as it may, we find a family of that name flourishing some centuries later in that county. John Delliston, knight, was high sheriff for Kent, according to Fabian, *quinto Henrici Sexti;* and we trace the lineal branch flourishing downwards, — the orthography varying, according to the unsettled usage of the times, from Delleston to Leston or Liston, between which it seems to have alternated, till, in the latter end of the reign of James I., it finally settled into the determinate and pleasing dissyllabic arrangement which it still retains. Aminadab Liston, the eldest male representative of the family of that day, was of the strictest order of Puritans. Mr. Foss, of Pall Mall, has obligingly communicated to me an undoubted tract of his, which bears the initials only, A. L., and is entitled, "The Grinning Glass, or Actor's Mirrour; where in the vituperative Visnomy of Vicious Players for the Scene is as virtuously reflected back upon their mimetic Monstrosities as it has viciously (hitherto) vitiated with its vile Vanities her Votarists." A strange title, but bearing the impress of those absurdities with which the title-pages of that pamphlet-spawning age abounded. The work bears date 1617. It preceded the "Histriomastix" by fifteen years; and, as it went before it in time, so it comes not far short of it in virulence. It is amusing to find an ancestor of Liston's thus bespattering the players at the commencement of the seventeenth century: —

"Thinketh He" (the actor), "with his costive countenances, to wry a sorrowing soul out of her anguish, or by defacing the divine denotement of destinate dignity (daignely described in the face humane and no other) to reinstamp the Paradice-plotted similitude with a novel and naughty approximation (not in the first intention) to those abhorred and ugly God-forbidden correspondences, with flouting Apes' jeering gibberings, and Babion babbling-like, to hoot out of countenance all modest measure, as if our sins were not sufficing to stoop our backs without He wresting and crooking his members to mistimed mirth (rather malice) in deformed fashion, leering when he should learn, prating for praying, goggling his eyes (better upturned for grace), whereas in Paradice (if we can go thus high for His profession) that devilish Serpent appeareth his undoubted Predecessor, first induing a mask like some roguish roistering Roscius (I spit at them all) to beguile with Stage shows the gaping Woman, whose Sex hath still chiefly upheld these Mysteries, and are voiced to be the chief Stage-haunters, where, as I am told, the custom is commonly to mumble (between acts) apples, not ambiguously derived from that pernicious Pippin (worse in effect than the Apples of Discord), whereas sometimes the hissings sounds of displeasure, as I hear, do lively reintonate that snake-taking-leave, and diabolical goings off, in Paradice."

The Puritanic effervescence of the early Presbyterians appears to have abated with time, and the opinions of the more immediate ancestors of our subject to have subsided at length into a strain of moderate Calvinism. Still a tincture of the old leaven was to be expected among the posterity of A. L.

Our hero was an only son of Habakkuk Liston, settled as an Anabaptist minister upon the patrimonial soil of his ancestors. A regular certificate appears, thus entered in the Church-book at Lupton Magna: "*Johannes, filius Habakkuk et Rebeccæ Liston, Dissentientium, natus quinto Decembri*, 1780, *baptizatus sexto Februarii sequentis; Sponsoribus J. et W. Woollaston, unâ cum Maria Merryweather.*" The singularity of an Anabaptist minister conforming to the child-rites of the Church would have tempted me to doubt the authenticity of this entry, had I not been obliged with the actual sight of it by the favor of Mr. Minns, the intelligent and worthy parish clerk of Lupton. Possibly some expectation in point of worldly advantages from some of the sponsors might have induced this unseemly deviation, as it must have appeared, from the practice and principles of that generally rigid sect. The term *Dissentientium* was possibly intended by the orthodox clergyman as a slur upon the supposed inconsistency. What, or of what nature, the expectations we have hinted at may have been, we have now no means of ascertaining. Of the Woollastons no trace is now discoverable in the village. The name of Merryweather occurs over the front of a grocer's shop at the western extremity of Lupton.

Of the infant Liston we find no events recorded before his fourth year, in which a severe attack of the measles bid fair to have robbed the rising generation of a fund of innocent entertainment. He had it of the confluent kind, as it is called; and the child's life was for a week or two despaired of. His recovery he always attributes (under Heaven) to the humane inter-

sudden giddiness (probably a mixture of both), suddenly lost his footing, and, to use Mr. Liston's phrase, disappeared, and was doubtless broken into a thousand pieces. The sound of his head, &c., dashing successively upon the projecting masses of the chasm, had such an effect upon the child, that a serious sickness ensued; and, even for many years after his recovery, he was not once seen so much as to smile.

The joint death of both his parents, which happened not many months after this disastrous accident, and were probably (one or both of them) accelerated by it, threw our youth upon the protection of his maternal great-aunt, Mrs. Sittingbourn. Of this aunt we have never heard him speak but with expressions amounting almost to reverence. To the influence of her early counsels and manners he has always attributed the firmness with which, in maturer years, thrown upon a way of life commonly not the best adapted to gravity and self-retirement, he has been able to maintain a serious character, untinctured with the levities incident to his profession. Ann Sittingbourn (we have seen her portrait by Hudson) was stately, stiff, tall, with a cast of features strikingly resembling the subject of this memoir. Her estate in Kent was spacious and well wooded; the house one of those venerable old mansions which are so impressive in childhood, and so hardly forgotten in succeeding years. In the venerable solitudes of Charnwood, among thick shades of the oak and beach (this last his favorite tree), the young Liston cultivated those contemplative habits which have never entirely deserted him in after-years. Here he was commonly in the summer months to be met with, with a book in his hand, — not a play-book, — meditating. Boyle's "Reflections" was at one time the darling volume; which, in its turn, was superseded by Young's "Night Thoughts," which has continued its hold upon him through life. He carries it always about him; and it is no uncommon thing for him to be seen, in the refreshing intervals of his occupation, leaning against a side-scene, in a sort of Herbert-of-Cherbury posture, turning over a pocket-edition of his favorite author.

But the solitudes of Charnwood were not destined always to obscure the path of our young hero. The premature death of Mrs. Sittingbourn, at the age of seventy, occasioned by incautious burning of a pot of charcoal in her sleeping-chamber, left him in his nineteenth year nearly without resources. That the stage at all should have presented itself as an eligible scope for his talents, and, in particular, that he should have chosen a line so foreign to what appears to have been his turn of mind, may require some explanation.

At Charnwood, then, we behold him thoughtful, grave, ascetic. From his cradle averse to flesh-meats and strong drink; abstemious even beyond the genius of the place, and almost in spite of the remonstrances of his great-aunt, who, though strict, was not rigid, — water was his habitual drink, and his food little beyond the mast and beech-nuts of his favorite groves. It is a medical fact, that this kind of diet, however favorable to the contemplative powers of the primitive hermits, &c., is but ill adapted to the less robust minds and bodies of a later generation. Hypochondria almost constantly ensues. It was so in the case of the young

Liston. He was subject to sights, and had visions. Those arid beech-nuts, distilled by a complexion naturally adust, mounted into an occiput already prepared to kindle by long seclusion and the fervor of strict Calvinistic notions. In the glooms of Charnwood, he was assailed by illusions similar in kind to those which are related of the famous Anthony of Padua. Wild antic faces would ever and anon protrude themselves upon his sensorium. Whether he shut his eyes, or kept them open, the same illusions operated. The darker and more profound were his cogitations, the droller and more whimsical became the apparitions. They buzzed about him thick as flies, flapping at him, flouting him, hooting in his ear, yet with such comic appendages, that what at first was his bane became at length his solace; and he desired no better society than that of his merry phantasmata. We shall presently find in what way this remarkable phenomenon influenced his future destiny.

On the death of Mrs. Sittingbourn, we find him received into the family of Mr. Willoughby, an eminent Turkey merchant, resident in Birchin Lane, London. We lose a little while here the chain of his history,—by what inducements this gentlemen was determined to make him an inmate of his house. Probably he had had some personal kindness for Mrs. Sittingbourn formerly; but, however it was, the young man was here treated more like a son than a clerk, though he was nominally but the latter. Different avocations, the change of scene, with that alternation of business and recreation which in its greatest perfection is to be had only in London, appear to have weaned him in a short time from the hypochondriacal affections which had beset him at Charnwood.

In the three years which followed his removal to Birchin Lane, we find him making more than one voyage to the Levant, as chief factor for Mr. Willoughby at the Porte. We could easily fill our biography with the pleasant passages which we have heard him relate as having happened to him at Constantinople; such as his having been taken up on suspicion of a design of penetrating the seraglio, &c.: but, with the deepest convincement of this gentleman's own veracity, we think that some of the stories are of that whimsical, and others of that romantic nature, which, however diverting, would be out of place in a narrative of this kind, which aims not only at strict truth, but at avoiding the very appearance of the contrary.

We will now bring him over the seas again, and suppose him in the counting-house in Birchin Lane, his protector satisfied with the returns of his factorage, and all going on so smoothly, that we may expect to find Mr. Liston at last an opulent merchant upon 'Change, as it is called. But see the turns of destiny! Upon a summer's excursion into Norfolk in the year 1801, the accidental sight of pretty Sally Parker, as she was called (then in the Norwich company), diverted his inclinations at once from commerce; and he became, in the language of commonplace biography, stage-struck. Happy for the lovers of mirth was it that our hero took this turn; he might else have been to this hour that unentertaining character, a plodding London merchant.

We accordingly find him shortly after making his *début*, as it is called, upon the Norwich boards, in the season of that year, being then in the twenty-second year of his age. Having a natural bent to tragedy, he chose the part of Pyrrhus, in the "Distressed Mother," to Sally Parker's Hermione. We find him afterwards as Barnwell, Altamont, Chamont, &c.; but, as if Nature had destined him to the sock, an unavoidable infirmity absolutely discapacitated him for tragedy. His person, at this latter period of which I have been speaking, was graceful, and even commanding; his countenance set to gravity: he had the power of arresting the attention of an audience at first sight almost beyond any other tragic actor. But he could not hold it. To understand this obstacle, we must go back a few years to those appalling reveries at Charnwood. Those illusions, which had vanished before the dissipation of a less recluse life and more free society, now in his solitary tragic studies, and amid the intense calls upon feeling incident to tragic acting, came back upon him with tenfold vividness. In the midst of some most pathetic passage (the parting of Jaffier with his dying friend, for instance), he would suddenly be surprised with a fit of violent horse-laughter. While the spectators were all sobbing before him with emotion, suddenly one of those grotesque faces would peep out upon him, and he could not resist the impulse. A timely excuse once or twice served his purpose; but no audiences could be expected to bear repeatedly this violation of the continuity of feeling. He describes them (the illusions) as so many demons haunting him, and paralyzing every effect. Even now, I am told, he cannot recite the famous soliloquy in "Hamlet," even in private, without immoderate bursts of laughter. However, what he had not force of reason sufficient to overcome he had good sense enough to turn into emolument, and determined to make a commodity of his distemper. He prudently exchanged the buskin for the sock, and the illusions instantly ceased; or, if they occurred for a short season, by their very co-operation added a zest to his comic vein, — some of his most catching faces being (as he expresses it) little more than transcripts and copies of those extraordinary phantasmata.

We have now drawn out our hero's existence to the period when he was about to meet, for the first time, the sympathies of a London audience. The particulars of his success since have been too much before our eyes to render a circumstantial detail of them expedient. I shall only mention, that Mr. Willoughby, his resentments having had time to subside, is at present one of the fastest friends of his old renegado factor; and that Mr. Liston's hopes of Miss Parker vanishing along with his unsuccessful suit to Melpomene, in the autumn of 1811 he married his present lady, by whom he has been blessed with one son, Philip, and two daughters, Ann and Angustina.*

* Lamb once said, of all the lies he ever put off, — and he put off a good many, — indeed, he valued himself on being "a matter-of-lie man," believing truth to be too precious to be wasted upon everybody, — of all the lies he ever put off, he valued his "Memoir of Liston" the most. "It is," he confessed to Miss Hutchinson, "from top to toe, every paragraph, pure invention, and has passed for gospel, — has been republished in the newspapers, and in the penny play-bills of the night, as an authentic account." And yet, notwithstanding its incidents are all imaginary, its facts all fictions, is not Lamb's "Memoir of Liston" a truer and more trustworthy work than any of the productions of those contemptible biographers, unfortunately not yet extinct, so admirably ridiculed in the thirty-fifth number of the "Freeholder"? In fact, is not this "lying Life of Liston" a very clever satire on those biographers, who, like the monkish historians mentioned by

AUTOBIOGRAPHY OF MR. MUNDEN,*

IN A LETTER TO THE EDITOR OF THE "LONDON MAGAZINE." †

HARK'EE, Mr. Editor. A word in your ear. They tell me you are going to put me in print, — in print, sir; to publish my life. What is my life to you, sir? What is it to you whether I ever lived at all? My life is a very good life, sir. I am insured at the Pelican, sir. I am threescore years and six, — six; mark me, sir: but I can play Polonius, which, I believe, few of your corre — correspondents can do, sir. I suspect tricks, sir: I smell a rat; I do, I do. You would cog the die upon us; you would, you would, sir. But I will forestall you, sir. You would be deriving me from William the Conqueror, with a murrain to you. It is

Fuller in his "Church History of Britain," swell the bowels of their books with empty wind, in default of sufficient solid food to fill them; who, according to Addison, ascribe to the unfortunate persons, whose lives they pretend to write, works which they never wrote, and actions which they never performed; celebrate virtues which they were never famous for, and excuse faults they were never guilty of? And does not Lamb, in this work, very happily ridicule the pedantry and conceit of certain grave and dignified biographers whose works are to be found in most gentlemen's libraries?— EDITOR.

* From the "London Magazine," 1825.

† This is another of Lamb's "lie-children." Leigh Hunt, in his Autobiography, speaking of some of Elia's contributions to the "London Magazine," thus mentions the mock Memoirs of Liston and Munden: "He [Lamb] wrote in the same magazine two Lives of Liston and Munden, which the public took for serious, and which exhibit an extraordinary jumble of imaginary facts and truth of by-painting. Munden he made born at Stoke Pogis; the very sound of which was like the actor speaking and digging his words." — EDITOR.

no such thing, sir. The town shall know better, sir. They begin to smoke your flams, sir. Mr. Liston may be born where he pleases, sir; but I will not be born at Lup—Lupton Magna for anybody's pleasure, sir. My son and I have looked over the great map of Kent together, and we can find no such place as you would palm upon us, sir; palm upon us, I say. Neither Magna nor Parva, as my son says, and he knows Latin, sir; Latin. If you write my life true, sir, you must set down, that I, Joseph Munden, comedian, came into the world upon Allhallows Day, Anno Domini 1759—1759; no sooner nor later, sir: and I saw the first light—the first light, remember, sir, at Stoke Pogis—Stoke Pogis, *comitatu* Bucks, and not at Lup—Lup Magna, which I believe to be no better than moonshine—moonshine; do you mark me, sir? I wonder you can put such flim-flams upon us, sir; I do, I do. It does not become you, sir; I say it,—I say it. And my father was an honest tradesman, sir: he dealt in malt and hops, sir; and was a corporation-man, sir; and of the Church of England, sir, and no Presbyterian; nor Ana—Anabaptist, sir; however you may be disposed to make honest people believe to the contrary, sir. Your bams are found out, sir. The town will be your stale puts no longer, sir; and you must not send us jolly fellows, sir,—we that are comedians, sir,—you must not send us into groves and char—charnwoods a moping, sir. Neither charns, nor charnel-houses, sir. It is not our constitution, sir: I tell it you—I tell it you. I was a droll dog from my cradle. I came into the world tittering, and the midwife tittered, and the gossips spilt their caudle with tittering;

and, when I was brought to the font, the parson could not christen me for tittering. So I was never more than half baptized. And, when I was little Joey, I made 'em all titter; there was not a melancholy face to be seen in Pogis. Pure nature, sir. I was born a comedian. Old Screwup, the undertaker, could tell you, sir, if he were living. Why, I was obliged to be locked up every time there was to be a funeral at Pogis. I was — I was, sir. I used to *grimace* at the mutes, as he called it, and put 'em out with my mops and my mows, till they couldn't stand at a door for me. And when I was locked up, with nothing but a cat in my company, I followed my bent with trying to make her laugh; and sometimes she would, and sometimes she would not. And my schoolmaster could make nothing of me: I had only to thrust my tongue in my cheek — in my cheek, sir, and the rod dropped from his fingers; and so my education was limited, sir. And I grew up a young fellow, and it was thought convenient to enter me upon some course of life that should make me serious; but it wouldn't do, sir. And I was articled to a dry-salter. My father gave forty pounds premium with me, sir. I can show the indent — dent — dentures, sir. But I was born to be a comedian, sir: so I ran away, and listed with the players, sir; and I topt my parts at Amersham and Gerrard's Cross, and played my own father to his face, in his own town of Pogis, in the part of Gripe, when I was not full seventeen years of age; and he did not know me again, but he knew me afterwards; and then he laughed, and I laughed, and, what is better, the dry-salter laughed, and gave me up my articles for the joke's sake: so that I came into court afterwards with clean hands — with clean hands — do you see, sir?

[Here the manuscript becomes illegible for two or three sheets onwards, which we presume to be occasioned by the absence of Mr. Munden, jun., who clearly transcribed it for the press thus far. The rest (with the exception of the concluding paragraph, which is seemingly resumed in the first handwriting) appears to contain a confused account of some lawsuit, in which the elder Munden was engaged; with a circumstantial history of the proceedings or a case of breach of promise of marriage, made to or by (we cannot pick out which) Jemima Munden, spinster; probably the comedian's cousin, for it does not appear he had any sister; with a few dates, rather better preserved, of this great actor's engagements, — as "Cheltenham (spelt Cheltnam), 1776;" "Bath, 1779;" "London, 1789;" together with stage anecdotes of Messrs. Edwin, Wilson, Lee, Lewis, &c.; over which we have strained our eyes to no purpose, in the hope of presenting something amusing to the public. Towards the end, the manuscript brightens up a little, as we said, and concludes in the following manner.]

—— stood before them for six and thirty years, [we suspect that Mr. Munden is here speaking of his final leave-taking of the stage], and to be dismissed at last. But I was heart-whole to the last, sir. What though a few drops did course themselves down the old veteran's cheeks: who could help it, sir? I was a giant that night, sir; and could have played fifty parts, each as arduous as Dozy. My faculties were never better, sir. But I was to be laid upon the shelf. It did not suit the public to laugh with their old servant any longer, sir. [Here some moisture has blotted a sentence or two.] But I can play Polonius still, sir; I can, I can.

Your servant, sir,

JOSEPH MUNDEN.

THE ILLUSTRIOUS DEFUNCT.*

"Nought but a blank remains, a dead void space,
A step of life that promised such a race." — DRYDEN.

NAPOLEON has now sent us back from the grave sufficient echoes of his living renown: the twilight of posthumous fame has lingered long enough over the spot where the sun of his glory set; and his name must at length repose in the silence, if not in the darkness, of night. In this busy and evanescent scene, other spirits of the age are rapidly snatched away, claiming our undivided sympathies and regrets, until in turn they yield to some newer and more absorbing grief. Another name is now added to the list of the mighty departed, — a name whose influence upon the hopes and

* From the "New Monthly Magazine," 1825.

Since writing this article, we have been informed that the object of our funeral oration is not definitively dead, but only moribund. So much the better: we shall have an opportunity of granting the request made to Walter by one of the children in the wood, and "kill him two times." The Abbé de Vertot having a siege to write, and not receiving the materials in time, composed the whole from his invention. Shortly after its completion, the expected documents arrived, when he threw them aside, exclaiming, "You are of no use to me now: I have carried the town."

fears, the fates and fortunes, of our countrymen, has rivalled, and perhaps eclipsed, that of the defunct "child and champion of Jacobinism," while it is associated with all the sanctions of legitimate government, all the sacred authorities of social order and our most holy religion. We speak of one, indeed, under whose warrant heavy and incessant contributions were imposed upon our fellow-citizens, but who exacted nothing without the signet and the sign-manual of most devout Chancellors of the Exchequer. Not to dally longer with the sympathies of our readers, we think it right to premonish them that we are composing an epicedium upon no less distinguished a personage than the Lottery, whose last breath, after many penultimate puffs, has been sobbed forth by sorrowing contractors, as if the world itself were about to be converted into a blank. There is a fashion of eulogy, as well as of vituperation; and, though the Lottery stood for some time in the latter predicament, we hesitate not to assert that *multis ille bonis flebilis occidit.* Never have we joined in the senseless clamor which condemned the only tax whereto we became voluntary contributors, — the only resource which gave the stimulus without the danger or infatuation of gambling; the only alembic which in these plodding days sublimized our imaginations, and filled them with more delicious dreams than ever flitted athwart the sensorium of Alnaschar.

Never can the writer forget, when, as a child, he was hoisted upon a servant's shoulder in Guildhall, and looked down upon the installed and solemn pomp of the then drawing Lottery. The two awful cabinets of iron, upon whose massy and mysterious portals the royal initials were gorgeously emblazoned, as if, after having deposited the unfulfilled prophecies within, the king himself had turned the lock, and still retained the key in his pocket; the blue-coat boy, with his naked arm, first converting the invisible wheel, and then diving into the dark recess for a ticket; the grave and reverend faces of the commissioners eying the announced number; the scribes below calmly committing it to their huge books; the anxious countenances of the surrounding populace; while the giant figures of Gog and Magog, like presiding deities, looked down with a grim silence upon the whole proceeding, — constituted altogether a scene, which, combined with the sudden wealth supposed to be lavished from those inscrutable wheels, was well calculated to impress the imagination of a boy with reverence and amazement. Jupiter, seated between the two fatal urns of good and evil, the blind goddess with her cornucopia, the Parcæ wielding the distaff, the thread of life, and the abhorred shears, seemed but dim and shadowy abstractions of mythology, when I had gazed upon an assemblage exercising, as I dreamt, a not less eventful power, and all presented to me in palpable and living operation. Reason and experience, ever at their old spiteful work of catching and destroying the bubbles which youth delighted to follow, have indeed dissipated much of this illusion: but my mind so far retained the influence of that early impression, that I have ever since continued to deposit my humble offerings at its shrine, whenever the ministers of the Lottery went forth with type and trumpet to announce its periodical dispensations; and though nothing has been doled out to me from its undiscerning coffers but blanks, or those more vexatious tantalizers of the spirit, denominated small prizes, yet do I hold myself largely indebted to this most generous diffuser of universal happiness. Ingrates that we are! are we to be thankful for no benefits that are not palpable to sense, to recognize no favors that are not of marketable value, to acknowledge no wealth unless it can be counted with the five fingers? If we admit the mind to be the sole depository of genuine joy, where is the bosom that has not been elevated into a temporary Elysium by the magic of the Lottery? Which of us has not converted his ticket, or even his sixteenth share of one, into a nest-egg of Hope, upon which he has sate brooding in the secret roosting-places of his heart, and hatched it into a thousand fantastical apparitions?

What a startling revelation of the passions if all the aspirations engendered by the Lottery could be made manifest! Many an impecuniary epicure has gloated over his locked-up warrant for future wealth, as a means of realizing the dream of his namesake in the "Alchemist:" —

> " My meat shall all come in in Indian shells, —
> Dishes of agate set in gold, and studded
> With emeralds, sapphires, hyacinths, and rubies;
> The tongues of carps, dormice, and camels' heels,
> Boiled i' the spirit of Sol, and dissolved in pearl,
> (Apicius' diet 'gainst the epilepsy.)
> And I will eat these broths with spoons of amber,
> Headed with diamant and carbuncle.
> My footboy shall eat pheasants, calvered salmons,
> Knots, godwits, lampreys: I myself will have
> The beards of barbels served, instead of salads;
> Oiled mushrooms, and the swelling unctuous paps
> Of a fat pregnant sow, newly cut off,
> Dressed with an exquisite and poignant sauce,
> For which I'll say unto my cook, 'There's gold:
> Go forth, and be a knight.' "

Many a doting lover has kissed the scrap of paper whose promissory shower of gold was to give up to him his otherwise unattainable Danaë; Nimrods have transformed the same narrow symbol into a saddle, by which they have been enabled to bestride the backs of peerless hunters; while nymphs have metamorphosed its Protean form into —

> "Rings, gauds, conceits,
> Knacks, trifles, nosegays, sweetmeats,"

and all the braveries of dress, to say nothing of the obsequious husband, the two-footmaned carriage, and the opera-box. By the simple charm of this numbered and printed rag, gamesters have, for a time at least, recovered their losses; spendthrifts have cleared off mortgages from their estates; the imprisoned debtor has leapt over his lofty boundary of circumscription and restraint, and revelled in all the joys of liberty and fortune; the cottage-walls have swelled out into more goodly proportion than those of Baucis and Philemon; poverty has tasted the luxuries of competence; labor has lolled at ease in a perpetual arm-chair of idleness; sickness has been bribed into banishment; life has been invested with new charms; and death deprived of its former terrors. Nor have the affections been less gratified than the wants, appetites, and ambitions of mankind. By the conjurations of the same potent spell, kindred have lavished anticipated benefits upon one another, and charity upon all. Let it be termed a delusion, — a fool's paradise is better than the wise man's Tartarus; be it branded as an ignis-fatuus, — it was at least a benevolent one, which, instead of beguiling its followers into swamps, caverns, and pitfalls, allured them on with all the blandishments of enchantment to a garden of Eden, — an ever-blooming Elysium of delight. True, the pleasures it bestowed were evanescent: but which of our joys are permanent? and who so inexperienced as not to know that anticipation is always of higher relish than reality, which strikes a balance both in our sufferings and enjoyments? "The fear of ill exceeds the ill we fear;" and fruition, in the same proportion, invariably falls short of hope. "Men are but children of a larger growth," who may amuse themselves for a long time in gazing at the reflection of the moon in the water; but, if they jump in to grasp it, they may grope for ever, and only get the farther from their object. He is the wisest who keeps feeding upon the future, and refrains as long as possible from undeceiving himself by converting his pleasant speculations into disagreeable certainties.

The true mental epicure always purchased his ticket early, and postponed inquiry into its fate to the last possible moment, during the whole of which intervening period he had an imaginary twenty thousand locked up in his desk; and was not this well worth all the money? Who would scruple to give twenty pounds interest for even the ideal enjoyment of as many thousands during two or three months? *Crede quod habes, et habes;* and the usufruct of such a capital is surely not dear at such a price. Some years ago, a gentleman in passing along Cheapside saw the figures 1,069, of which number he was the sole proprietor, flaming on the window of a lottery-office as a capital prize. Somewhat flurried by this discovery, not less welcome than unexpected, he resolved to walk round St. Paul's that he might consider in what way to communicate the happy tidings to his wife and family; but, upon repassing the shop, he observed that the number was altered to 10,069, and, upon inquiry, had the mortification to learn that his ticket was a blank, and had only been stuck up in the window by a mistake of the clerk. This effectually calmed his agitation; but he always speaks of himself as having once possessed twenty thousand pounds, and maintains that his ten-minutes' walk round St. Paul's was worth ten times the purchase-money of the ticket. A prize thus obtained, has, moreover, this special advantage, — it is beyond the reach of fate; it cannot be squandered; bankruptcy cannot lay siege to it; friends cannot pull it down, nor enemies blow it up; it bears a charmed life, and none of woman born can break its integrity, even by the dissipation of a single fraction. Show me the property in these perilous times that is equally compact and impregnable. We can no longer become enriched for a quarter of an hour; we can no longer succeed in such splendid failures: all our chances of making such a miss have vanished with the last of the Lotteries.

Life will now become a flat, prosaic routine of matter-of-fact; and sleep itself, erst so prolific of numerical configurations and mysterious stimulants to lottery adventure, will be disfurnished of its figures and figments. People will cease to harp upon the one lucky number suggested in a dream, and which forms the exception, while they are scrupulously silent upon the ten thousand falsified dreams which constitute the rule. Morpheus will stifle Cocker with a handful of poppies, and our pillows will be no longer haunted by the book of numbers.

And who, too, shall maintain the art and mystery of puffing, in all its pristine glory, when the lottery professors shall have abandoned its cultivation? They were the first, as they will assuredly be the last, who fully developed the resources of that ingenious art; who cajoled and decoyed the most suspicious and wary reader into a perusal of their advertisements by devices of endless variety and cunning; who baited their lurking schemes with midnight murders, ghost-stories, crim-cons, bon-mots, balloons, dreadful catastrophes, and every diversity of joy and sorrow, to catch newspaper-gudgeons.* Ought not such talents to be encouraged? Verily the abolitionists have much to answer for!

And now, having established the felicity of all those who gained imaginary prizes, let us proceed to show that the equally numerous class who were presented with real blanks have not less reason to consider themselves happy. Most of us have cause to be thankful for that which is bestowed; but we have all, probably, reason to be still more grateful for that which is withheld, and more especially for our being denied the sudden possession of riches. In the Litany, indeed, we call upon the Lord to deliver us "in all time of our wealth;" but how few of us are sincere in deprecating such a cala-

* "Of all the puffs," says Hazlitt, "lottery-puffs are the most ingenious." He thinks a collection of them would be an amusing *vade-mecum*. Byron, you know, was accused of writing lottery-puffs: and Lamb, in his younger days, to eke out "a something contracted income," essayed to write them; but he did not succeed very well in the task. His samples were returned on his hands, as "done in too severe and terse a style." Some Grub-street hack — a nineteenth-century Tom Brown or Mr. Dash — succeeded in composing these popular and ingenious productions; but the man who wrote the Essays of Elia could not write a successful lottery-puff! At this, exult, O mediocrity! and take courage, man of genius! — EDITOR.

mity! Massinger's Luke, and Ben Jonson's Sir Epicure Mammon, and Pope's Sir Balaam, and our own daily observation, might convince us that the Devil "now tempts by making rich, not making poor." We may read in the "Guardian" a circumstantial account of a man who was utterly ruined by gaining a capital prize; we may recollect what Dr. Johnson said to Garrick, when the latter was making a display of his wealth at Hampton Court, — "Ah, David, David! these are the things that make a death-bed terrible;" we may recall the Scripture declaration, as to the difficulty a rich man finds in entering into the kingdom of Heaven; and, combining all these denunciations against opulence, let us heartily congratulate one another upon our lucky escape from the calamity of a twenty or thirty thousand pound prize! The fox in the fable, who accused the unattainable grapes of sourness, was more of a philosopher than we are generally willing to allow. He was an adept in that species of moral alchemy which turns every thing to gold, and converts disappointment itself into a ground of resignation and content. Such we have shown to be the great lesson inculcated by the Lottery, when rightly contemplated; and, if we might parody M. de Chateaubriand's jingling expression, — "*le Roi est mort: vive le Roi!*" — we should be tempted to exclaim, "The Lottery is no more: long live the Lottery!"

THE RELIGION OF ACTORS.*

THE world has hitherto so little troubled its head with the points of doctrine held by a community which contributes in other ways so largely to its amusement, that, before the late mischance of a celebrated tragic actor, it scarce condescended to look into the practice of any individual player, much less to inquire into the hidden and abscondite springs of his actions. Indeed, it is with some violence to the imagination that we conceive of an actor as belonging to the relations of private life, so closely do we identify these persons in our mind with the characters which they assume upon the stage. How oddly does it sound, when we are told that the late Miss Pope, for instance, — that is to say, in our notion of her, Mrs. Candor, — was a good daughter, an affectionate sister, and exemplary in all the parts of domestic life! With still greater difficulty can we carry our notions to church, and conceive of Liston kneeling upon a hassock, or Munden uttering a pious ejaculation,— "making mouths at the invisible event." But the times are fast improving; and, if the process of sanctity begun under the happy auspices of the present licenser go on

* From the "New Monthly Magazine," 1826.

Writing to Bernard Barton in the spring of 1826, Lamb says, speaking of his literary projects, "A little thing without name will also be printed on the 'Religion of the Actors:' but it is out of your way; so I recommend you, with true author's hypocrisy, to skip it." I wonder if "good B. B." read the article; and, if he did, how he liked it. Quaker though he was, he could not but have been pleased with it. — EDITOR.

to its completion, it will be as necessary for a comedian to give an account of his faith as of his conduct. Fawcett must study the five points; and Dicky Suett, if he were alive, would have had to rub up his catechism. Already the effects of it begin to appear. A celebrated performer has thought fit to oblige the world with a confession of his faith, — or Br——'s "Religio Dramatici." This gentleman, in his laudable attempt to shift from his person the obloquy of Judaism, with the forwardness of a new convert, in trying to prove too much, has, in the opinion of many, proved too little. A simple declaration of his Christianity was sufficient; but, strange to say, his apology has not a word about it. We are left to gather it from some expressions which imply that he is a Protestant; but we did not wish to inquire into the niceties of his orthodoxy. To his friends of the *old persuasion*, the distinction was impertinent; for what cares Rabbi Ben Kimchi for the differences which have split our novelty? To the great body of Christians that hold the pope's supremacy — that is to say, to the major part of the Christian world — his religion will appear as much to seek as ever. But perhaps he conceived that all Christians are Protestants, as children and the common people call all, that are not animals, Christians. The mistake was not very considerable in so young a proselyte, or he might think the general (as logicians speak) involved in the particular. All Protestants are Christians; but I am a Protestant; *ergo*, &c.: as if a marmoset, contending to be a man, overleaping that term as too generic and vulgar, should at once roundly proclaim himself to be a gentleman. The argument would be, as we say, *ex abundanti*. From whichever cause this *excessus in terminis* proceeded, we can do no less than congratulate the general state of Christendom upon the accession of so extraordinary a convert. Who was the happy instrument of the conversion, we are yet to learn: it comes nearest to the attempt of the late pious Dr. Watts to Christianize the Psalms of the Old Testament. Something of the old Hebrew raciness is lost in the transfusion; but much of its asperity is softened and pared down in the adaptation.

The appearance of so singular a treatise at this conjuncture has set us upon an inquiry into the present state of religion upon the stage generally. By the favor of the church-wardens of St. Martin's in the Fields, and St. Paul's, Covent Garden, who have very readily, and with great kindness, assisted our pursuit, we are enabled to lay before the public the following particulars. Strictly speaking, neither of the two great bodies is collectively a religious institution. We had expected to have found a chaplain among them, as at St. Stephen's and other court establishments; and were the more surprised at the omission, as the last Mr. Bengough at the one house, and Mr. Powell at the other, from a gravity of speech and demeanor, and the habit of wearing black at their first appearances in the beginning of *fifth* or the conclusion of *fourth acts*, so eminently pointed out their qualifications for such office. These corporations, then, being not properly congregational, we must seek the solution of our question in the tastes, attainments, accidental breeding, and education of the individual members of them. As we were prepared to expect, a majority at both houses adhere to the religion of the Church Established,—only that at one of them a pretty strong leaven of Catholicism is suspected; which, considering the notorious education of the manager at a foreign seminary, is not so much to be wondered at. Some have gone so far as to report that Mr. T——y, in particular, belongs to an order lately restored on the Continent. We can contradict this: that gentleman is a member of the Kirk of Scotland; and his name is to be found, much to his honor, in the list of seceders from the congregation of Mr. Fletcher. While the generality, as we have said, are content to jog on in the safe trammels of national orthodoxy, symptoms of a sectarian spirit have broken out in quarters where we should least have looked for it. Some of the ladies at both houses are deep in controverted points. Miss F——e, we are credibly informed, is a *Sub-* and Madame V—— a *Supra-* Lapsarian. Mr. Pope is the last of the exploded sect of the Ranters. Mr. Sinclair has joined the Shakers. Mr. Grimaldi, sen., after being long a Jumper, has lately fallen into some whimsical theories respecting the fall of man; which he understands, not of an allegorical, but a *real tumble*, by which the whole body of humanity became, as it were, lame to the performance of good works. Pride he will have to be nothing but a stiff neck; irresolution, the nerves shaken; an inclination to sinister paths, crookedness of the joints; spiritual deadness, a paralysis; want of charity, a contraction in the fingers; despising of government, a broken head; the plaster, a sermon; the lint to bind it up, the text; the probers, the preachers; a pair of crutches, the old and new law; a bandage, religious obligation: a fanciful mode of illustration, derived from the accidents and habits of his past calling *spiritualized*, rather than from any accurate acquaintance with the Hebrew text, in which report speaks him but a raw scholar. Mr. Elliston, from all that we can learn, has his religion yet to choose; though some think him a Muggletonian.

THE ASS.*

Mr. Collier, in his "Poetical Decameron" (Third Conversation), notices a tract printed in 1595, with the author's initials only, A. B., entitled "The Noblenesse of the Asse; a work rare, learned, and excellent." He has selected the following pretty passage from it: "He (the ass) refuseth no burden: he goes whither he is sent, without any contradiction. He lifts not his foote against any one; he bytes not; he is no fugitive, nor malicious affected. He doth all things in good sort, and to his liking that hath cause to employ him. If strokes be given him, he cares not for them; and, as our modern poet singeth, —

> 'Thou wouldst (perhaps) he should become thy foe,
> And to that end dost beat him many times:
> He cares not for himselfe, much less thy blow.' "†

Certainly Nature, foreseeing the cruel usage which this useful servant to man should receive at man's hand,

* From Hone's "Every-day Book."

† "Who this modern poet was," says Mr. Collier, "is a secret worth discovering." The wood-cut on the title of the pamphlet is — an ass, with a wreath of laurel round his neck.

did prudently in furnishing him with a tegument impervious to ordinary stripes. The malice of a child or a weak hand can make feeble impressions on him. His back offers no mark to a puny foeman. To a common whip or switch his hide presents an absolute insensibility. You might as well pretend to scourge a schoolboy with a tough pair of leather breeches on. His jerkin is well fortified; and therefore the costermongers, "between the years 1790 and 1800," did more politicly than piously in lifting up a part of his upper garment. I well remember that beastly and bloody custom. I have often longed to see one of those refiners in discipline himself at the cart's tail, with just such a convenient spot laid bare to the tender mercies of the whipster. But, since Nature has resumed her rights, it is to be hoped that this patient creature does not suffer to extremities; and that, to the savages who still belabor his poor carcass with their blows (considering the sort of anvil they are laid upon), he might in some sort, if he could speak, exclaim with the philosopher, "Lay on: you beat but upon the case of Anaxarchus."

Contemplating this natural safe-guard, this fortified exterior, it is with pain I view the sleek, foppish, combed, and curried person of this animal as he is disnaturalized at watering-places, &c., where they affect to make a palfrey of him. Fie on all such sophistications! It will never do, master groom. Something of his honest, shaggy exterior will still peep up in spite of you, — his good, rough, native, pine-apple coating. You cannot "refine a scorpion into a fish, though you rinse it and scour it with ever so cleanly cookery."*

* Milton, *from memory.*

The modern poet quoted by A. B. proceeds to celebrate a virtue for which no one to this day had been aware that the ass was remarkable: —

> "One other gift this beast hath as his owne,
> Wherewith the rest could not be furnishèd;
> On man himself the same was not bestowne:
> To wit, on him is ne'er engenderèd
> The hateful vermine that doth teare the skin,
> And to the bode [body] doth make his passage in."

And truly, when one thinks on the suit of impenetrable armor with which Nature (like Vulcan to another Achilles) has provided him, these subtile enemies to *our* repose would have shown some dexterity in getting into *his* quarters. As the bogs of Ireland by tradition expel toads and reptiles, he may well defy these small deer in his fastnesses. It seems the latter had not arrived at the exquisite policy adopted by the human vermin "between 1790 and 1800."

But the most singular and delightful gift of the ass, according to the writer of this pamphlet, is his *voice*, the "goodly, sweet, and continual brayings" of which, "whereof they forme a melodious and proportionable kinde of musicke," seem to have affected him with no ordinary pleasure. "Nor thinke I," he adds, "that any of our immoderate musitians can deny but that their song is full of exceeding pleasure to be heard; because therein is to be discerned both concord, discord, singing in the meane, the beginning to sing in large compasse, then following into rise and fall, the halfe-note, whole note, musicke of five voices, firme singing by four voices, three together, or one voice and a halfe. Then their variable contrarieties amongst them, when one delivers forth a long tenor or a short, the pausing for time, breathing in measure, breaking the minim or very least moment of time. Last of all, to heare the musicke of five or six voices chaunged to so many of asses is amongst them to heare a song of world without end."

There is no accounting for ears, or for that laudable enthusiasm with which an author is tempted to invest a favorite subject with the most incompatible perfections: I should otherwise, for my own taste, have been inclined rather to have given a place to these extraordinary musicians at that banquet of nothing-less-than-sweet-sounds, imagined by old Jeremy Collier (Essays, 1698, part ii. on Music), where, after describing the inspirating effects of martial music in a battle, he hazards an ingenious conjecture, whether a sort of *anti-music* might not be invented, which should have quite the contrary effect of "sinking the spirits, shaking the nerves, curdling the blood, and inspiring despair and cowardice and consternation. 'Tis probable," he says, "the roaring of lions, the warbling of cats and screech-owls, together with a mixture of the howling of dogs, judiciously imitated and compounded, might go a great way in this invention." The dose, we confess, is pretty potent, and skilfully enough prepared. But what shall we say to the Ass of Silenus, who, if we may trust to classic lore, by his own proper sounds, without thanks to cat or screech-owl, dismayed and put to rout a whole army of giants? Here was *anti-music* with a vengeance; a whole *Pan-Dis-Harmonicon* in a single lungs of leather!

But I keep you trifling too long on this asinine subject. I have already passed the *Pons Asinorum*, and will desist, remembering the old pedantic pun of Jem Boyer, my schoolmaster: —

"Ass *in præsenti* seldom makes a WISE MAN *in futuro*."

IN RE SQUIRRELS.*

WHAT is gone with the cages with the climbing squirrel, and bells to them, which were formerly the indispensable appendage to the outside of a tinman's shop, and were, in fact, the only live signs? One, we believe, still hangs out on Holborn; but they are fast vanishing with the good old modes of our ancestors.† They seem to have been superseded by that still more ingenious refinement of modern humanity,—the tread-mill; in which

* From Hone's "Every-day Book."

† Lamb not only had a passionate fondness for old books and —

"The old familiar faces,"

but he loved the old associations. He was no admirer of your modern improvements. Unlike Dr. Johnson, he did not go into the "most stately shops," but purchased his books and engravings at the stalls and from second-hand dealers. In his eyes, the old Inner-Temple Church was a handsomer and statelier structure than the finest cathedral in England; and to his ear, as well as to the ear of Will Honeycomb, the old familiar cries of the peripatetic London merchants were more musical than the songs of larks and nightingales. It grieved him sorely to see an old building demolished which he had passed and repassed for years, in his daily walks to and from his business; or an old custom abolished whose observance he had witnessed when a child. "The disappearance of the old clock from St. Dunstan's Church," says Moxon in his pleasant tribute to Lamb's memory in Leigh Hunt's Journal, "drew tears from his eyes; nor could he ever pass without emotion the place where Exeter 'Change once stood. The removal had spoiled a reality in Gay. 'The passer-by,' he said, 'no longer saw the combs dangle in his face.' This almost broke his heart." — EDITOR.

human squirrels still perform a similar round of ceaseless, improgressive clambering, which must be nuts to them.

We almost doubt the fact of the teeth of this creature being so purely orange-colored as Mr. Urban's correspondent gives out. One of our old poets — and they were pretty sharp observers of Nature — describes them as brown. But perhaps the naturalist referred to meant "of the color of a Maltese orange,"* which is rather more obfuscated than your fruit of Seville or St. Michael's, and may help to reconcile the difference. We cannot speak from observation; but we remember at school getting our fingers into the orangery of one of these little gentry (not having a due caution of the traps set there), and the result proved sourer than lemons. The author of the "Task" somewhere speaks of their anger as being "insignificantly fierce;" but we found the demonstration of it on this occasion quite as significant as we desired, and have not been disposed since to look any of these "gift horses" in the mouth. Maiden aunts keep these "small deer," as they do parrots, to bite people's fingers, on purpose to give them good advice "not to adventure so near the cage another time." As for their "six quavers divided into three quavers and a dotted crotchet," I suppose they may go into Jeremy Bentham's next budget of fallacies, along with the "melodious and proportionable kinde of musicke" recorded, in your last number, of an highly gifted animal.

* Fletcher in the "Faithful Shepherdess." The satyr offers to Clorin —

"Grapes whose lusty blood
Is the learned poet's good, —
Sweeter yet did never crown
The head of Bacchus; nuts more brown
Than the *squirrels'* teeth that crack them."

ESTIMATE OF DE FOE'S SECONDARY NOVELS.*

It has happened not seldom that one work of some author has so transcendently surpassed in execution the rest of his compositions, that the world has agreed to pass a sentence of dismissal upon the latter, and to consign them to total neglect and oblivion. It has done wisely in this not to suffer the contemplation of excellences of a lower standard to abate or stand in the way of the pleasure it has agreed to receive from the masterpiece.

Again: it has happened, that from no inferior merit of execution in the rest, but from superior good fortune in the choice of its subject, some single work shall have been suffered to eclipse, and cast into shade, the deserts of its less fortunate brethren. This has been done with more or less injustice in the case of the popular allegory of Bunyan, in which the beautiful and scriptural image of a pilgrim or wayfarer (we are all such upon earth), addressing itself intelligibly and feelingly to the bosoms of all, has silenced, and made almost to be forgotten, the more awful and scarcely less tender beauties of the "Holy War made by Shaddai upon Diabolus," of the same author, — a romance less happy in its subject, but surely well worthy of a secondary immortality. But in no instance has this excluding partiality been exerted with more unfairness than against what may be termed the secondary novels or romances of De Foe.

* From Walter Wilson's Life of De Foe.

While all ages and descriptions of people hang delighted over the "Adventures of Robinson Crusoe," and shall continue to do so, we trust, while the world lasts, how few comparatively will bear to be told that there exist other fictitious naratives by the same writer, — four of them at least of no inferior interest, except what results from a less felicitous choice of situation! "Roxana," "Singleton," "Moll Flanders," "Colonel Jack," are all genuine offspring of the same father. They bear the veritable impress of De Foe. An unpractised midwife that would not swear to the nose, lip, forehead, and eye of every one of them! They are, in their way, as full of incident, and some of them every bit as romantic; only they want the uninhabited island, and the charm that has bewitched the world, of the striking solitary situation.

But are there no solitudes out of the cave and the desert? or cannot the heart in the midst of crowds feel frightfully alone? Singleton on the world of waters, prowling about with pirates less merciful than the creatures of any howling wilderness, — is he not alone, with the faces of men about him, but without a guide that can conduct him through the mists of educational and habitual ignorance, or a fellow-heart that can interpret to him the new-born yearnings and aspirations of unpractised penitence? Or when the boy Colonel Jack, in the loneliness of the heart (the worst solitude), goes to hide his ill-purchased treasure in the hollow tree by night, and miraculously loses, and miraculously finds it again, — whom hath he there to sympathize with him? or of what sort are his associates?

The narrative manner of De Foe has a naturalness

about it beyond that of any other novel or romance writer. His fictions have all the air of true stories. It is impossible to believe, while you are reading them, that a real person is not narrating to you everywhere nothing but what really happened to himself. To this the extreme *homeliness* of their style mainly contributes. We use the word in its best and heartiest sense, — that which comes *home* to the reader. The narrators everywhere are chosen from low life, or have had their origin in it: therefore they tell their own tales (Mr. Coleridge has anticipated us in this remark), as persons in their degree are observed to do, with infinite repetition, and an overacted exactness, lest the hearer should not have minded, or have forgotten, some things that had been told before. Hence the emphatic sentences marked in the good old (but deserted) Italic type; and hence, too, the frequent interposition of the reminding old colloquial parenthesis, "I say," "Mind," and the like, when the story-teller repeats what, to a practised reader, might appear to have been sufficiently insisted upon before: which made an ingenious critic observe, that his works, in this kind, were excellent reading for the kitchen. And, in truth, the heroes and heroines of De Foe can never again hope to be popular with a much higher class of readers than that of the servant-maid or the sailor. Crusoe keeps its rank only by tough prescription. Singleton, the pirate; Colonel Jack, the thief; Moll Flanders, both thief and harlot; Roxana, harlot and something worse, — would be startling ingredients in the bill-of-fare of modern literary delicacies. But, then, what pirates, what thieves, and what harlots, is *the thief*, *the harlot*, and *the pirate* of De Foe!

We would not hesitate to say, that in no other book of fiction, where the lives of such characters are described, is guilt and delinquency made less seductive, or the suffering made more closely to follow the commission, or the penitence more earnest or more bleeding, or the intervening flashes of religious visitation upon the rude and uninstructed soul more meltingly and fearfully painted. They, in this, come near to the tenderness of Bunyan; while the livelier pictures and incidents in them, as in Hogarth or in Fielding, tend to diminish that fastidiousness to the concerns and pursuits of common life which an unrestrained passion for the ideal and the sentimental is in danger of producing.

POSTSCRIPT TO THE "CHAPTER ON EARS." *

A WRITER, whose real name, it seems, is *Boldero*, but who has been entertaining the town for the last twelve months with some very pleasant lucubrations under the assumed signature of *Leigh Hunt*,† in his "Indicator" of the 31st January last has thought fit to insinuate that I, *Elia*, do not write the little sketches which bear my signature in this magazine, but that the true author of them is a Mr. L——b. Observe the critical period

* From the "London Magazine," 1821.

† Clearly a fictitious appellation; for, if we admit the latter of these names to be in a manner English, what is *Leigh?* Christian nomenclature knows no such.

at which he has chosen to impute the calumny,—on the very eve of the publication of our last number,—affording no scope for explanation for a full month; during which time I must needs lie writhing and tossing under the cruel imputation of nonentity. Good Heavens! that a plain man must not be allowed *to be*—

They call this an age of personality; but surely this spirit of anti-personality (if I may so express it) is something worse.

Take away my moral reputation,—I may live to discredit that calumny; injure my literary fame,—I may write that up again: but, when a gentleman is robbed of his identity, where is he?

Other murderers stab but at our existence, a frail and perishing trifle at the best: but here is an assassin who aims at our very essence; who not only forbids us *to be* any longer, but *to have been* at all. Let our ancestors look to it.

Is the parish register nothing? Is the house in Princes Street, Cavendish Square, where we saw the light six and forty years ago, nothing? Were our progenitors from stately Genoa, where we flourished four centuries back, before the barbarous name of Boldero* was known to a European mouth, nothing? Was the goodly scion of our name, transplanted into England in the reign of the seventh Henry, nothing? Are the archives of the steelyard, in succeeding reigns (if haply they survive the fury of our envious enemies), showing that we flourished in prime repute, as merchants, down to the period of the Commonwealth, nothing?

* It is clearly of transatlantic origin.

"Why, then the world, and all that's in't, is nothing;
The covering sky is nothing; Bohemia nothing."

I am ashamed that this trifling writer should have power to move me so.

ELIA TO HIS CORRESPONDENTS.*

A CORRESPONDENT, who writes himself Peter Ball, or Bell, — for his handwriting is as ragged as his manners, — admonishes me of the old saying, that some people (under a courteous periphrasis, I slur his less ceremonious epithet) had need have good memories. In my "Old Benchers of the Inner Temple," I have delivered myself, and truly, a templar born. Bell clamors upon this, and thinketh that he hath caught a fox. It seems that in a former paper, retorting upon a weekly scribbler who had called my good identity in question (see Postscript to my "Chapter on Ears"), I profess myself a native of some spot near Cavendish Square, deducing my remoter origin from Italy. But who does not see, except this tinkling cymbal, that, in that idle fiction of Genoese ancestry, I was answering a fool according to his folly, — that Elia there expresseth himself ironically as to an approved slanderer, who hath no right to the truth, and can be no fit recipient of it? Such a one it is usual to leave to his delusions; or, leading him from error still to contradictory error, to plunge him (as we say) deeper in the

* From the "London Magazine," 1821.

mire, and give him line till he suspend himself. No understanding reader could be imposed upon by such obvious rodomontade to suspect me for an alien, or believe me other than English.

To a second correspondent, who signs himself "A Wiltshire Man," and claims me for a countryman upon the strength of an equivocal phrase in my "Christ's Hospital," a more mannerly reply is due. Passing over the Genoese fable, which Bell makes such a ring about, he nicely detects a more subtle discrepancy, which Bell was too obtuse to strike upon. Referring to the passage, I must confess, that the term "native town," applied to Calne, *primâ facie* seems to bear out the construction which my friendly correspondent is willing to put upon it. The context too, I am afraid, a little favors it. But where the words of an author, taken literally, compared with some other passage in his writings, admitted to be authentic, involve a palpable contradiction, it hath been the custom of the ingenuous commentator to smooth the difficulty by the supposition that in the one case an allegorical or tropical sense was chiefly intended. So, by the word "native," I may be supposed to mean a town where I might have been born, or where it might be desirable that I should have been born, as being situate in wholesome air, upon a dry, chalky soil, in which I delight; or a town with the inhabitants of which I passed some weeks, a summer or two ago, so agreeably, that they and it became in a manner native to me. Without some such latitude of interpretation in the present case, I see not how we can avoid falling into a gross error in physics, as to conceive that a gentleman may be born in two places, from which all modern and ancient testimony is alike abhorrent. Bacchus cometh the nearest to it, whom I remember Ovid to have honored with the epithet "twice born." * But, not to mention that he is so called (we conceive) in reference to the places *whence* rather than the places *where* he was delivered, — for, by either birth, he may probably be challenged for a Theban, — in a strict way of speaking, he was a *filius femoris* by no means in the same sense as he had been before a *filius alvi;* for that latter was but a secondary and tralatitious way of being born, and he but a denizen of the second house of his geniture. Thus much by way of explanation was thought due to the courteous "Wiltshire Man."

To "Indagator," "Investigator," "Incertus," and the rest of the pack, that are so importunate about the true localities of his birth, — as if, forsooth, Elia were presently about to be passed to his parish, — to all such church-warden critics he answereth, that, any explanation here given notwithstanding, he hath not so fixed his nativity (like a rusty vane) to one dull spot, but that, if he seeth occasion, or the argument shall demand it, he will be born again, in future papers, in whatever place, and at whatever period, shall seem good unto him.

"Modò me Thebis, modò Athenis."

---

* "Imperfectus adhuc infans genetricis abalvo
Eripitur, patrioque tener (si credere dignum)
Insuitur femori. . . .
Tutaque bis geniti sunt incunabula Bacchi."

Metamorph., lib. iii.

UNITARIAN PROTESTS;*

IN A LETTER TO A FRIEND OF THAT PERSUASION NEWLY MARRIED.

DEAR M——, — Though none of your acquaintance can with greater sincerity congratulate you upon this happy conjuncture than myself, one of the oldest of them, it was with pain I found you, after the ceremony, depositing in the vestry-room what is called a Protest. I thought you superior to this little sophistry. What! after submitting to the service of the Church of England; after consenting to receive a boon from her, in the person of your amiable consort, — was it consistent with sense, or common good manners, to turn round upon her, and flatly taunt her with false worship? This language is a little of the strongest in your books and from your pulpits, though there it may well enough be excused from religious zeal and the native warmth of nonconformity. But at the altar, — the Church-of-England altar, — adopting her forms, and complying with her requisitions to the letter, — to be consistent, together with the practice, I fear, you must drop the language of dissent. You are no longer sturdy non-cons: you are there occasional conformists. You submit to accept the privileges communicated by a form of words, exceptionable, and perhaps justly, in your view; but, so submitting, you have no right to quarrel with the

* From the "London Magazine," 1825.

ritual which you have just condescended to owe an obligation to. They do not force you into their churches. You come voluntarily, knowing the terms. You marry in the name of the Trinity. There is no evading this by pretending that you take the formula with your own interpretation: (and, so long as you can do this, where is the necessity of protesting?) for the meaning of a vow is to be settled by the sense of the imposer, not by any forced construction of the taker; else might all vows, and oaths too, be eluded with impunity. You marry, then, essentially as Trinitarians; and the altar no sooner satisfied than, hey, presto! with the celerity of a juggler, you shift habits, and proceed pure Unitarians again in the vestry. You cheat the church out of a wife, and go home smiling in your sleeves that you have so cunningly despoiled the Egyptians. In plain English, the Church has married you in the name of so and so, assuming that you took the words in her sense: but you outwitted her; you assented to them in your sense only, and took from her what, upon a right understanding, she would have declined giving you.

This is the fair construction to be put upon all Unitarian marriages, as at present contracted; and, so long as you Unitarians could salve your consciences with the *équivoque*, I do not see why the Established Church should have troubled herself at all about the matter. But the protesters necessarily see further. They have some glimmerings of the deception; they apprehend a flaw somewhere; they would fain be honest, and yet they must marry notwithstanding; for honesty's sake, they are fain to dehonestate themselves a little. Let me try the very words of your own protest, to see what confessions we can pick out of them.

"As Unitarians, therefore, we" (you and your newly espoused bride) "most solemnly protest against the service" (which yourselves have just demanded), "because we are thereby called upon not only tacitly to acquiesce, but to profess a belief, in a doctrine which is a dogma, as we believe, totally unfounded." But do you profess that belief during the ceremony? or are you only called upon for the profession, but do not make it? If the latter, then you fall in with the rest of your more consistent brethren who waive the protest; if the former, then, I fear, your protest cannot save you.

Hard and grievous it is, that, in any case, an institution so broad and general as the union of man and wife should be so cramped and straitened by the hands of an imposing hierarchy, that, to plight troth to a lovely woman, a man must be necessitated to compromise his truth and faith to Heaven; but so it must be, so long as you choose to marry by the forms of the church over which that hierarchy presides.

"Therefore," say you, "we protest." Oh poor and much fallen word, Protest! It was not so that the first heroic reformers protested. They departed out of Babylon once for good and all; they came not back for an occasional contact with her altars, — a dallying, and then a protesting against dalliance; they stood not shuffling in the porch, with a Popish foot within, and its lame Lutheran fellow without, halting betwixt. These were the true Protestants. You are — protesters.

Besides the inconsistency of this proceeding, I must think it a piece of impertinence, unseasonable at least, and out of place, to obtrude these papers upon the officiating clergyman; to offer to a public functionary an instrument which by the tenor of his function he is not obliged to accept, but rather he is called upon to reject. Is it done in his clerical capacity? He has no power of redressing the grievance. It is to take the benefit of his ministry, and then insult him. If in his capacity of fellow-Christian only, what are your scruples to him, so long as you yourselves are able to get over them, and do get over them by the very fact of coming to require his services? The thing you call a Protest might with just as good a reason be presented to the church-warden for the time being, to the parish-clerk, or the pew-opener.

The Parliament alone can redress your grievance, if any. Yet I see not how with any grace your people can petition for relief, so long as, by the very fact of your coming to church to be married, they do *bonâ fide* and strictly relieve themselves. The Upper House, in particular, is not unused to these same things, called Protests, among themselves. But how would this honorable body stare to find a noble lord conceding a measure, and in the next breath, by a solemn protest, disowning it! A protest there is a reason given for non-compliance, not a subterfuge for an equivocal occasional compliance. It was reasonable in the primitive Christians to avert from their persons, by whatever lawful means, the compulsory eating of meats which had been offered unto idols. I dare say, the Roman prefects and exarchates had plenty of petitioning in their days. But what would a Festus or Agrippa have replied to a petition to that effect, presented to him by some evasive Laodicean, with the very meat between his teeth, which he had been chewing voluntarily, rather than abide the penalty? Relief for tender consciences means nothing, where the conscience has previously relieved itself; that is, has complied with the injunctions which it seeks preposterously to be rid of. Relief for conscience there is properly none, but what by better information makes an act appear innocent and lawful with which the previous conscience was not satisfied to comply. All else is but relief from penalties, from scandal incurred by a complying practice, where the conscience itself is not fully satisfied.

"But," say you, "we have hard measure: the Quakers are indulged with the liberty denied to us." They are; and dearly have they earned it. You have come in (as a sect at least) in the cool of the evening, — at the eleventh hour. The Quaker character was hardened in the fires of persecution in the seventeenth century; not quite to the stake and fagot, but little short of that: they grew up and thrived against noisome prisons, cruel beatings, whippings, stockings. They have since endured a century or two of scoffs, contempts; they have been a by-word and a nay-word; they have stood unmoved: and the consequence of long conscientious resistance on one part is invariably, in the end, remission on the other. The legislature, that denied you the tolerance, which I do not know that at that time you even asked, gave them the liberty, which, without granting, they would have assumed. No penalties could have driven them into the churches. This is the consequence of entire measures. Had the early Quakers consented to take oaths, leaving a protest with the clerk of the court against them in the same breath with which they had taken them, do you in your conscience think that they would have been indulged at this day in their exclusive privilege of affirming? Let your people go on for a century or so, marrying in your own fashion, and I will warrant them, before the end of it, the legislature will be willing to concede to them more than they at present demand.

Either the institution of marriage depends not for its validity upon hypocritical compliances with the ritual of an alien church (and then I do not see why you cannot marry among yourselves, as the Quakers, without their indulgence, would have been doing to this day), or it does depend upon such ritual compliance. And then, in your protests, you offend against a divine ordinance. I have read in the Essex-street Liturgy a form for the celebration of marriage. Why is this become a dead letter? Oh! it has never been legalized; that is to say, in the law's eye, it is no marriage. But do you take upon you to say, in the view of the gospel it would be none? Would your own people, at least, look upon a couple so paired to be none? But the case of dowries, alimonies, inheritances, &c., which depend for their validity upon the ceremonial of the church by law established, — are these nothing? That our children are not legally *Filii Nullius*, — is this nothing? I answer, Nothing; to the preservation of a good conscience, nothing; to a consistent Christianity, less than nothing. Sad worldly thorns they are indeed, and stumbling-blocks well worthy to be set out of the way by a legislature calling itself Christian; but not likely to be removed in a hurry by any shrewd legislators who perceive that the petitioning complainants have not so much as bruised a shin in the resistance, but, prudently declining the briers and the prickles, nestle quietly down in the smooth two-sided velvet of a protesting occasional conformity.

I am, dear sir,

With much respect, yours, &c.,

ELIA.

ON

THE CUSTOM OF HISSING AT THE THEATRES;

WITH SOME ACCOUNT OF A CLUB OF DAMNED AUTHORS.*

MR. REFLECTOR,—I am one of those persons whom the world has thought proper to designate by the title of Damned Authors. In that memorable season of dramatic failures, 1806–7,—in which no fewer, I think, than two tragedies, four comedies, one opera, and three farces, suffered at Drury-lane Theatre,—I was found guilty of constructing an afterpiece, and was *damned*.

Against the decision of the public in such instances there can be no appeal. The clerk of Chatham might as well have protested against the decision of Cade and his followers, who were then *the public*. Like him, I was condemned because I could write.

* From the "Reflector," No. 3.

Not but it did appear to some of us that the measures of the popular tribunal at that period savored a little of harshness and of the *summum jus*. The public mouth was early in the season fleshed upon the "Vindictive Man," and some pieces of that nature; and it retained, through the remainer of it, a relish of blood. As Dr. Johnson would have said, "Sir, there was a habit of sibilation in the house."

Still less am I disposed to inquire into the reason of the comparative lenity, on the other hand, with which some pieces were treated, which, to indifferent judges, seemed at least as much deserving of condemnation as some of those which met with it. I am willing to put a favorable construction upon the votes that were given against us; I believe that there was no bribery or designed partiality in the case: only "our nonsense did not happen to suit their nonsense;" that was all.

But against the *manner* in which the public, on these occasions, think fit to deliver their disapprobation, I must and ever will protest.

Sir, imagine — but you have been present at the damning of a piece (those who never had that felicity, I beg them to imagine) — a vast theatre, like that which Drury Lane was before it was a heap of dust and ashes (I insult not over its fallen greatness; let it recover itself when it can for me, let it lift up its towering head once more, and take in poor authors to write for it; *hic cæstus artemque repono*), — a theatre like that, filled with all sorts of disgusting sounds, — shrieks, groans, hisses, but chiefly the last, like the noise of many waters, or that which Don Quixote heard from the fulling-mills, or that wilder combination of devilish sounds which St. Anthony listened to in the wilderness.

Oh! Mr. Reflector, is it not a pity, that the sweet human voice, which was given man to speak with, to sing with, to whisper tones of love in, to express compliance, to convey a favor, or to grant a suit, — that voice, which in a Siddons or a Braham rouses us, in a siren Catalani charms and captivates us, — that the musical, expressive human voice should be converted into a rival of the noises of silly geese, and irrational, venomous snakes?

I never shall forget the sounds on *my night*. I never before that time fully felt the reception which the Author of All Ill, in the "Paradise Lost," meets with from the critics in the *pit*, at the final close of his "Tragedy upon the Human Race," — though that, alas! met with too much success: —

> "From innumerable tongues
> A dismal universal *hiss*, the sound
> Of public scorn. Dreadful was the din
> Of *hissing* through the hall, thick swarming now
> With complicated monsters, head and tail,
> Scorpion and asp, and Amphisbæna dire,
> Cerastes horned, Hydrus, and Elops drear,
> And Dipsas."

For *hall* substitute *theatre*, and you have the very image of what takes place at what is called the *damnation* of a piece, — and properly so called; for here you see its origin plainly, whence the custom was derived, and what the first piece was that so suffered. After this, none can doubt the propriety of the appellation.

But, sir, as to the justice of bestowing such appalling, heart-withering denunciations of the popular obloquy upon the venial mistake of a poor author, who thought to please us in the act of filling his pockets, — for the sum of his demerits amounts to no more than that, — it does, I own, seem to me a species of retributive justice far too severe for the offence. A culprit in the pillory (bate the eggs) meets with no severer exprobration.

Indeed, I have often wondered that some modest critic has not proposed that there should be a wooden machine to that effect erected in some convenient part of the *proscenium*, which an unsuccessful author should be required to mount, and stand his hour, exposed to the apples and oranges of the pit. This *amende honorable* would well suit with the meanness of some authors, who, in their prologues, fairly prostrate their skulls to the audience, and seem to invite a pelting.

Or why should they not have their pens publicly broke over their heads, as the swords of recreant knights in old times were, and an oath administered to them that they should never write again?

Seriously, *Messieurs the Public*, this outrageous way which you have got of expressing your displeasures is too much for the occasion. When I was deafening under the effects of it, I could not help asking what crime of great moral turpitude I had committed: for every man about me seemed to feel the offence as personal to himself; as something which public interest and private feelings alike called upon him, in the strongest possible manner, to stigmatize with infamy.

The Romans, it is well known to you, Mr. Reflector, took a gentler method of marking their disapprobation of an author's work. They were a humane and equitable nation. The left the *furca* and the *patibulum*, the axe and the rods, to great offenders: for these minor and (if I may so term them) extra-moral offences, *the bent thumb* was considered as a sufficient sign of disapprobation, — *vertere pollicem;* as *the pressed thumb*, *premere pollicem*, was a mark of approving.

And really there seems to have been a sort of fitness in this method, a correspondency of sign in the punishment to the offence. For, as the action of writing is performed by bending the thumb forward, the retroversion or bending back of that joint did not unaptly point to the opposite of that action; implying that it was the will of the audience that the author should *write no more:* a much more significant as well as more humane way of expressing that desire than our custom of hissing, which is altogether senseless and indefensible. Nor do we find that the Roman audiences deprived themselves, by this lenity, of any tittle of that supremacy which audiences in all ages have thought themselves bound to maintain over such as have been candidates for their applause. On the contrary, by this method they seem to have had the author, as we should express it, completely *under finger and thumb*.

The provocations to which a dramatic genius is exposed from the public are so much the more vexatious as they are removed from any possibility of retaliation, the hope of which sweetens most other injuries; for the public *never writes itself*. Not but something very like it took place at the time of the O. P. differences. The placards which were nightly exhibited, were, properly speaking, the composition of the public. The public wrote them, the public applauded them; and precious morceaux of wit and eloquence they were, — except some few, of a better quality, which it is well known were furnished by professed dramatic writers. After this specimen of what the public can do for itself, it should be a little slow in condemning what others do for it.

As the degrees of malignancy vary in people according as they have more or less of the Old Serpent (the father of hisses) in their composition, I have sometimes amused myself with analyzing this many-headed hydra, which calls itself the public, into the component parts of which it is "complicated, head and tail," and seeing how many varieties of the snake kind it can afford.

First, there is the Common English Snake. — This is that part of the auditory who are always the majority at damnations; but who, having no critical venom in themselves to sting them on, stay till they hear others hiss, and then join in for company.

The Blind Worm, is a species very nearly allied to the foregoing. Some naturalists have doubted whether they are not the same.

The Rattlesnake. — These are your obstreperous talking critics, — the impertinent guides of the pit, — who will not give a plain man leave to enjoy an evening's entertainment; but, with their frothy jargon and incessant finding of faults, either drown his pleasure quite, or force him, in his own defence, to join in their clamorous censure. The hiss always originates with these. When this creature springs his *rattle*, you would think, from the noise it makes, there was something in it; but you have only to examine the instrument from which the noise proceeds, and you will find it typical of a critic's tongue, — a shallow membrane, empty, voluble, and seated in the most contemptible part of the creature's body.

The Whipsnake. — This is he that lashes the poor author the next day in the newspapers.

The Deaf Adder, or *Surda Echidna* of Linnæus. — Under this head may be classed all that portion of the spectators (for audience they properly are not), who, not finding the first act of a piece answer to their preconceived notions of what a first act should be, like Obstinate in John Bunyan, positively thrust their fingers in their ears, that they may not hear a word of what is coming, though perhaps the very next act may be composed in a style as different as possible, and be written quite to their own tastes. These adders refuse to hear the voice of the charmer, because the tuning of his instrument gave them offence.

I should weary you, and myself too, if I were to go through all the classes of the serpent kind. Two qualities are common to them all. They are creatures of remarkably cold digestions, and chiefly haunt *pits* and low grounds.

I proceed with more pleasure to give you an account of a club to which I have the honor to belong. There are fourteen of us, who are all authors that have been once in our lives what is called *damned*. We meet on the anniversaries of our respective nights, and make ourselves merry at the expense of the public. The chief tenets which distinguish our society, and which every man among us is bound to hold for gospel, are, —

That the public, or mob, in all ages, have been a set of blind, deaf, obstinate, senseless, illiterate savages. That no man of genius, in his senses, would be ambitious of pleasing such a capricious, ungrateful rabble. That the only legitimate end of writing for them is to pick their pockets; and, that failing, we are at full liberty to vilify and abuse them as much as ever we think fit.

That authors, by their affected pretences to humility, which they made use of as a cloak to insinuate their writings into the callous senses of the multitude, obtuse to every thing but the grossest flattery, have by degrees made that great beast their master; as we may act submission to children till we are obliged to practise it in earnest. That authors are and ought to be considered the masters and preceptors of the public, and not *vice versâ*. That it was so in the days of Orphèus, Linus, and Musæus; and would be so again, if it were not that writers prove traitors to themselves. That, in particular, in the days of the first of those three great authors just mentioned, audiences appear to have been perfect models of what audiences should be; for though, along with the trees and the rocks and the wild creatures which he drew after him to listen to his strains, some serpents doubtless came to hear his music, it does not appear that any one among them ever lifted up *a dissentient voice*. They knew what was due to authors in those days. Now every stock and stone turns into a serpent, and has a voice.

That the terms "courteous reader" and "candid auditors," as having given rise to a false notion in those to whom they were applied, as if they conferred upon them some right, *which they cannot have*, of exercising their judgments, ought to be utterly banished and exploded.

These are our distinguishing tenets. To keep up the memory of the cause in which we suffered, as the ancients sacrificed a goat, a supposed unhealthy animal, to Æsculapius, on our feast-nights we cut up a goose, an animal typical of *the popular voice*, to the deities of Candor and Patient Hearing. A zealous member of the society once proposed that we should revive the obsolete luxury of viper-broth; but, the stomachs of some of the company rising at the proposition, we lost the benefit of that highly salutary and *antidotal dish*.

The privilege of admission to our club is strictly limited to such as have been fairly *damned*. A piece that has met with ever so little applause, that has but languished its night or two, and then gone out, will never entitle its author to a seat among us. An exception to our usual readiness in conferring this privilege is in the case of a writer, who, having been once condemned, writes again, and becomes candidate for a second martyrdom. Simple damnation we hold to be a merit; but to be twice damned we adjudge infamous. Such a one we utterly reject, and blackball without a hearing: —

"*The common damned shun his society.*"

Hoping that your publication of our regulations may be a means of inviting some more members into our society, I conclude this long letter.

I am, sir, yours,

SEMEL-DAMNATUS.*

* The germ of this article is contained in the following passage from a letter to Manning (then sojourning among the Mandarins), in which Lamb,

CHARLES LAMB'S AUTOBIOGRAPHY.*

Charles Lamb, born in the Inner Temple, 10th February, 1775; educated in Christ's Hospital; after-

half humorously, half pathetically, describes the reception the town gave his famous and unfortunate farce, "Mr. H.:" —

"So I go creeping on since I was lamed with that cursed fall from off the top of Drury-Lane Theatre into the pit, something more than a year ago. However, I have been free of the house ever since, and the house was pretty free with me upon that occasion. Hang 'em, how they hissed! It was not a hiss neither, but a sort of a frantic yell, like a congregation of mad geese; with roaring sometimes like bears; mows and mops like apes; sometimes snakes, that hissed me into madness. 'Twas like Saint Anthony's temptations. Mercy on us! that God should give his favorite children, men, mouths to speak with, to discourse rationally, to promise smoothly, to flatter agreeably, to encourage warmly, to counsel wisely, to sing with, to drink with, and to kiss with, and that they should turn them into mouths of adders, bears, wolves, hyenas, and whistle like tempests, and emit breath through them like distillations of aspic poison, to asperse and vilify the innocent labors of their fellow-creatures who are desirous to please them! Heaven be pleased to make the teeth rot out of them all, therefore! Make them a reproach, and all that pass by them to loll out their tongue at them! Blind mouths! as Milton somewhere calls them." — Editor.

* This, the briefest, and perhaps the wittiest and most truthful, autobiography in the language, was published in the "New Monthly Magazine" a few months after its author's death, with the following preface or introduction from the pen of some unknown admirer of Elia: —

"We have been favored, by the kindness of Mr. Upcott, with the following sketch, written in one of his manuscript collections, by Charles Lamb. It will be read with deep interest by all, but with the deepest interest by those who had the honor and the happiness of knowing the writer. It is so singularly characteristic, that we can scarcely persuade ourselves we do not hear it, as we read, spoken from his living lips. Slight as it is, it conveys the most exquisite and perfect notion of the personal manner and habits of our friend. For the intellectual rest, we lift the veil of its noble modesty, and can even here discern them. Mark its humor, crammed into a few thinking words, — its pathetic sensibility in the midst of contrast, — its wit, truth, and feeling, — and, above all, its fanciful retreat at the close, under a phantom cloud of death." — Editor.

wards a clerk in the Accountants' Office, East-India House; pensioned off from that service, 1825, after thirty-three years' service; is now a gentleman at large; can remember few specialities in his life worth noting, except that he once caught a swallow flying (*teste suâ manu*). Below the middle stature; cast of face slightly Jewish, with no Judaic tinge in his complexional religion; stammers abominably, and is therefore more apt to discharge his occasional conversation in a quaint aphorism, or a poor quibble, than in set and edifying speeches; has consequently been libelled as a person always aiming at wit; which, as he told a dull fellow that charged him with it, is at least as good as aiming at dulness. A small eater, but not drinker; confesses a partiality for the production of the juniper-berry; was a fierce smoker of tobacco, but may be resembled to a volcano burnt out, emitting only now and then a casual puff. Has been guilty of obtruding upon the public a tale, in prose, called "Rosamund Gray;" a dramatic sketch, named "John Woodvil;" a "Farewell Ode to Tobacco," with sundry other poems, and light prose matter, collected in two slight crown octavos, and pompously christened his works, though in fact they were his recreations; and his true works may be found on the shelves of Leadenhall Street, filling some hundred folios. He is also the true Elia, whose Essays are extant in a little volume, published a year or two since, and rather better known from that name without a meaning than from any thing he has done, or can hope to do, in his own. He was also the first to draw the public attention to the old English dramatists, in a work called "Specimens of English Dramatic Writers who lived about the Time of Shakspeare," published about fifteen years since. In short, all his merits and demerits to set forth would take to the end of Mr. Upcott's book, and then not be told truly.

He died 18 , much lamented.*

Witness his hand,

CHARLES LAMB.

18th April, 1827.

ON THE DEATH OF COLERIDGE.†

WHEN I heard of the death of Coleridge, it was without grief. It seemed to me that he long had been on the confines of the next world, — that he had a

* *To anybody.* — Please to fill up these blanks.

† Disraeli wrote a book on the Quarrels of Authors. Somebody should write one on the Friendships of Literary Men. If such a work is ever written, Charles Lamb and Samuel Taylor Coleridge will be honorably mentioned therein. Among all the friendships celebrated in tale or history, there is none more admirable than that which existed between these two eminent men. The "golden thread that tied their hearts together" was never broken. Their friendship was never "chipt or diminished;" but, the longer they lived, the stronger it grew. Death could not destroy it.

Lamb, after Coleridge's death, as if weary of "this green earth," as if not caring if "sun and sky and breeze, and solitary walks, and summer holidays, and the greenness of fields, and the delicious juices of meats and fishes, and society, and the cheerful glass, and candle-light, and fireside conversations, and innocent vanities, and jests, and irony itself," went out with life, willingly sought "Lavinian shores."

"Lamb," as Mr. John Forster says in his beautiful tribute to his memory, "never fairly recovered the death of Coleridge. He thought of little else (his sister was but another portion of himself) until his own great spirit joined his friend. He had a habit of venting his melancholy in a sort of mirth. He would, with nothing graver than a pun, 'cleanse his bosom of the perilous stuff that weighed' upon it. In a jest, or a few light phrases, he would lay open the last recesses of his heart. So in respect of the death of hunger for eternity. I grieved then that I could not grieve. But, since, I feel how great a part he was of me. His great and dear spirit haunts me. I cannot think a thought, I cannot make a criticism on men or books, without an ineffectual turning and reference to him. He was the proof and touchstone of all my cogitations. He was a Grecian (or in the first form) at Christ's Hospital, where I was Deputy-Grecian; and the same subordination and deference to him I have preserved through a life-long acquaintance. Great in his writings, he was greatest in his conversation. In him was disproved that old maxim, that we should allow every one his share of talk. He would talk from morn to dewy eve, nor cease till far midnight; yet who ever would interrupt him? who would obstruct that continuous flow of converse, fetched from Helicon or Zion? He had the tact of making the unintelligible seem plain. Many who read the abstruser parts of his "Friend" would complain that his works did not answer to his spoken wisdom. They were identical. But he had a tone in oral delivery which seemed to convey sense to those who were otherwise imperfect recipients. He was my fifty-years-old friend without a dissension. Never saw I his likeness, nor probably the world can

Coleridge. Some old friends of his saw him two or three weeks ago, and remarked the constant turning and reference of his mind. He interrupted himself and them almost every instant with some play of affected wonder or astonishment, or humorous melancholy, on the words, '*Coleridge is dead.*' Nothing could divert him from that; for the thought of it never left him. About the same time, we had written to him to request a few lines for the literary album of a gentleman who entertained a fitting admiration of his genius. It was the last request we were destined to make, the last kindness we were allowed to receive. He wrote in Mr. Keymer's volume, — and wrote of Coleridge." — EDITOR.

see again. I seem to love the house he died at more passionately than when he lived. I love the faithful Gilmans more than while they exercised their virtues towards him living. What was his mansion is consecrated to me a chapel.

EDMONTON, Nov. 21, 1834.

THE OLD ACTORS.*

I DO not know a more mortifying thing than to be conscious of a foregone delight, with a total oblivion of the person and manner which conveyed it. In dreams I often stretch and strain after the countenance of Edwin whom I once saw in "Peeping Tom." I cannot catch a feature of him. He is no more to me than Nokes or Pinkethman. Parsons, and, still more, Dodd, were near being lost to me till I was refreshed with their portraits (fine treat) the other day at Mr. Matthews's gallery at Highgate; which, with the exception of the Hogarth pictures a few years since exhibited in Pall Mall, was the most delightful collection I ever gained admission to. There hang the players, in their single persons and in grouped scenes, from the Restoration, — Bettertons, Booths, Garricks, —justifying the prejudices which we entertain for them; the Bracegirdles, the Mountforts, and the Oldfields, fresh as Cibber has described them; the Woffington (a true Hogarth) upon a couch, dallying and dangerous; the screen scene in Brinsley's famous comedy; with Smith and Mrs. Abingdon whom I have

* From the "London Magazine," 1822.

not seen; and the rest, whom, having seen, I see still there. There is Henderson, unrivalled in Comus, whom I saw at second-hand in the elder Harley; Harley, the rival of Holman, in Horatio; Holman, with the bright glittering teeth, in Lothario, and the deep pavior's sighs in Romeo, the jolliest person ("our son is fat") of any Hamlet I have yet seen, with the most laudable attempts (for a personable man) at looking melancholy; and Pope, the abdicated monarch of tragedy and comedy, in Harry the Eighth; and Lord Townley. There hang the two Aickins, brethren in mediocrity; Wroughton, who in Kitely seemed to have forgotten that in prouder days he had personated Alexander; the specious form of John Palmer, with the special effrontery of Bobby; Bensley, with the trumpet-tongue; and little Quick (the retired Dioclesian of Islington), with his squeak like a Bart'lemew fiddle. There are fixed, cold as in life, the immovable features of Moody, who, afraid of o'erstepping Nature, sometimes stopped short of her; and the restless fidgetiness of Lewis, who, with no such fears, not seldom leaped o' the other side. There hang Farren and Whitfield, and Burton and Phillimore, names of small account in those times, but which, remembered now, or casually recalled by the sight of an old play-bill, with their associated recordations, can "drown an eye unused to flow." There too hangs, not far removed from them in death, the graceful plainness of the first Mrs. Pope, with a voice unstrung by age, but which in her better days must have competed with the silver tones of Barry himself, so enchanting in decay do I remember it, — of all her lady parts, exceeding herself in the "Lady Quakeress" (there earth touched heaven) of O'Keefe, when she played it to the "merry cousin" of Lewis; and Mrs. Mattocks, the sensiblest of viragos; and Miss Pope, a gentlewoman ever, to the verge of ungentility, with Churchill's compliment still burnishing upon her gay honeycomb lips. There are the two Bannisters, and Sedgwick, and Kelly, and Dignum (Diggy), and the by-gone features of Mrs. Ward, matchless in Lady Loverule; and the collective majesty of the whole Kemble family; and (Shakspeare's woman) Dora Jordan; and, by her, *two antics*, who, in former and in latter days, have chiefly beguiled us of our griefs; whose portraits we shall strive to recall, for the sympathy of those who may not have had the benefit of viewing the matchless Highgate collection.*

CAPTAIN STARKEY.

To the Editor of the "Every-day Book:"—

DEAR SIR, —I read your account of this unfortunate being, and his forlorn piece of self-history,† with that smile of half-interest which the annals of insignificance excite, till I came to where he says, "I was bound ap-

* Here follows, in the article as originally published, the well-known masterly pen-and-ink portraits of Suett and Munden. The article on Suett, Lamb incorporated into the "Essay on some of the old Actors:" that on Munden, he reprinted as a separate chapter in the first series of the Essays of Elia. — EDITOR.

† "Memoirs of the Life of Benjamin Starkey, late of London, but now an inmate of the Freemen's Hospital in Newcastle. Written by himself. With a portrait of the author, and a fac-simile of his handwriting. Printed and sold by William Hall, Great Market, Newcastle." 1818. 12mo, pp. 14.

prentice to Mr. William Bird, an eminent writer, and teacher of languages and mathematics," &c.; when I started as one does in the recognition of an old acquaintance in a supposed stranger. This, then, was that Starkey of whom I have heard my sister relate so many pleasant anecdotes; and whom, never having seen, I yet seem almost to remember. For nearly fifty years, she had lost all sight of him; and, behold! the gentle usher of her youth, grown into an aged beggar, dubbed with an opprobrious title to which he had no pretensions; an object and a May-game! To what base purposes may we not return! What may not have been the meek creature's sufferings, what his wanderings, before he finally settled down in the comparative comfort of an old hospitaller of the almonry of Newcastle? And is poor Starkey dead?

I was a scholar of that "eminent writer" that he speaks of; but Starkey had quitted the school about a year before I came to it. Still the odor of his merits had left a fragrancy upon the recollection of the elder pupils. The schoolroom stands where it did, looking into a discolored, dingy garden in the passage leading from Fetter Lane into Bartlett's Buildings. It is still a school, though the main prop, alas! has fallen so ingloriously; and bears a Latin inscription over the entrance in the lane, which was unknown in our humbler times. Heaven knows what "languages" were taught in it then! I am sure that neither my sister nor myself brought any out of it but a little of our native English. By "mathematics," reader, must be understood "ciphering." It was, in fact, a humble day-school, at which reading and writing were taught to us boys in the morning; and the same slender erudition was communicated to the girls, our sisters, &c., in the evening. Now, Starkey presided, under Bird, over both establishments. In my time, Mr. Cook, now or lately a respectable singer and performer at Drury-Lane Theatre, and nephew to Mr. Bird, had succeeded to him. I well remember Bird. He was a squat, corpulent, middle-sized man, with something of the gentleman about him, and that peculiar mild tone — especially while he was inflicting punishment — which is so much more terrible to children than the angriest looks and gestures. Whippings were not frequent; but, when they took place, the correction was performed in a private room adjoining, where we could only hear the plaints, but saw nothing. This heightened the decorum and the solemnity. But the ordinary chastisement was the bastinado, a stroke or two on the palm with that almost obsolete weapon now, — the ferule. A ferule was a sort of flat ruler, widened, at the inflicting end, into a shape resembling a pear, — but nothing like so sweet, — with a delectable hole in the middle to raise blisters, like a cupping-glass. I have an intense recollection of that disused instrument of torture, and the malignancy, in proportion to the apparent mildness, with which its strokes were applied. The idea of a rod is accompanied with something ludicrous; but by no process can I look back upon this blister-raiser with any thing but unmingled horror. To make him look more formidable, — if a pedagogue had need of these heightenings, — Bird wore one of those flowered Indian gowns formerly in use with school-masters, the strange figures upon which we used to interpret into hieroglyphics of

10

pain and suffering. But, boyish fears apart, Bird, I believe, was, in the main, a humane and judicious master.

Oh, how I remember our legs wedged into those uncomfortable sloping desks, where we sat elbowing each other; and the injunctions to attain a free hand, unattainable in that position; the first copy I wrote after, with its moral lesson, "Art improves Nature;" the still earlier pot-hooks and the hangers, some traces of which I fear may yet be apparent in this manuscript; the truant looks side-long to the garden, which seemed a mockery of our imprisonment; the prize for best spelling which had almost turned my head, and which, to this day, I cannot reflect upon without a vanity, which I ought to be ashamed of; our little leaden inkstands, not separately subsisting, but sunk into the desks; the bright, punctually-washed morning fingers, darkening gradually with another and another ink-spot! What a world of little associated circumstances, pains, and pleasures, mingling their quotas of pleasure, arise at the reading of those few simple words, — "Mr. William Bird, an eminent writer, and teacher of languages and mathematics in Fetter Lane, Holborn"!

Poor Starkey, when young, had that peculiar stamp of old-fashionedness in his face which makes it impossible for a beholder to predicate any particular age in the object. You can scarce make a guess between seventeen and seven and thirty. This antique cast always seems to promise ill-luck and penury. Yet it seems he was not always the abject thing he came to. My sister, who well remembers him, can hardly forgive Mr. Thomas Ranson for making an etching so unlike her idea of him when he was a youthful teacher at Mr. Bird's school. Old age and poverty — a life-long poverty, she thinks — could at no time have so effaced the marks of native gentility which were once so visible in a face otherwise strikingly ugly, thin, and care-worn. From her recollections of him, she thinks that he would have wanted bread before he would have begged or borrowed a half-penny. "If any of the girls," she says, "who were my school-fellows, should be reading, through their aged spectacles, tidings, from the dead, of their youthful friend Starkey, they will feel a pang, as I do, at having teased his gentle spirit." They were big girls, it seems, too old to attend his instructions with the silence necessary; and, however old age and a long state of beggary seem to have reduced his writing faculties to a state of imbecility, in those days his language occasionally rose to the bold and figurative: for, when he was in despair to stop their chattering, his ordinary phrase was, "Ladies, if you will not hold your peace, not all the powers in heaven can make you." Once he was missing for a day or two: he had run away. A little, old, unhappy-looking man brought him back, — it was his father, — and he did no business in the school that day, but sat moping in a corner, with his hands before his face; and the girls, his tormentors, in pity for his case, for the rest of that day forbore to annoy him. "I had been there but a few months," adds she, "when Starkey, who was the chief instructor of us girls, communicated to us a profound secret, — that the tragedy of 'Cato' was shortly to be acted by the elder boys, and that we were to be invited to the representation." That Starkey lent a helping hand in fashioning the actors, she remembers; and, but for his unfortunate person, he might have had some distinguished part in the scene to enact. As it was, he had the arduous task of prompter assigned to him ; and his feeble voice was heard clear and distinct, repeating the text during the whole performance. She describes her recollection of the cast of characters, even now, with a relish. Martia, by the handsome Edgar Hickman, who afterwards went to Africa, and of whom she never afterwards heard tidings ; Lucia, by Master Walker, whose sister was her particular friend ; Cato, by John Hunter, a masterly declaimer, but a plain boy, and shorter by the head than his two sons in the scene, &c. In conclusion, Starkey appears to have been one of those mild spirits, which, not originally deficient in understanding, are crushed by penury into dejection and feebleness. He might have proved a useful adjunct, if not an ornament, to society, if Fortune had taken him into a very little fostering ; but, wanting that, he became a captain, — a by-word, — and lived and died a broken bulrush.

A POPULAR FALLACY,*

THAT A DEFORMED PERSON IS A LORD.

AFTER a careful perusal of the most approved works that treat of nobility, and of its origin in these realms in particular, we are left very much in the dark as to the original patent in which this branch of it is recognized. Neither Camden in his "Etymologie and Original of Barons," nor Dugdale in his "Baronage of England,"

* From the "New Monthly Magazine," 1826.

nor Selden (a more exact and laborious inquirer than either) in his "Titles of Honor," afford a glimpse of satisfaction upon the subject. There is an heraldic term, indeed, which seems to imply gentility, and the right to coat armor (but nothing further), in persons thus qualified. But the *sinister bend* is more probably interpreted by the best writers on this science, of some irregularity of birth than of bodily conformation. Nobility is either hereditary or by creation, commonly called patent. Of the former kind, the title in question cannot be, seeing that the notion of it is limited to a personal distinction which does not necessarily follow in the blood. Honors of this nature, as Mr. Anstey very well observes, descend, moreover, in a *right line*. It must be by patent, then, if any thing. But who can show it? How comes it to be dormant? Under what king's reign is it patented? Among the grounds of nobility cited by the learned Mr. Ashmole, after "Services in the Field or in the Council Chamber," he judiciously sets down "Honors conferred by the sovereign out of mere benevolence, or as favoring one subject rather than another for some likeness or conformity observed (or but supposed) in him to the royal nature;" and instances the graces showered upon Charles Brandon, who, "in his goodly person being thought not a little to favor the port and bearing of the king's own majesty, was by that sovereign, King Henry the Eighth, for some or one of these respects, highly promoted and preferred." Here, if anywhere, we thought we had discovered a clew to our researches. But after a painful investigation of the rolls and records under the reign of Richard the Third, or "Richard Crouchback," as he is more usually designated in the chronicles, — from a traditionary stoop or gibbosity in that part, — we do not find that that monarch conferred any such lordships as are here pretended, upon any subject or subjects, on a simple plea of "conformity" in that respect to the "royal nature." The posture of affairs, in those tumultuous times preceding the battle of Bosworth, possibly left him at no leisure to attend to such niceties. Further than his reign, we have not extended our inquiries; the kings of England who preceded or followed him being generally described by historians to have been of straight and clean limbs, the "natural derivative," says Daniel,* "of high blood, if not its primitive recommendation to such ennoblement, as denoting strength and martial prowess, — the qualities set most by in that fighting age." Another motive, which inclines us to scruple the validity of this claim, is the remarkable fact, that none of the persons in whom the right is supposed to be vested do ever insist upon it themselves. There is no instance of any of them "suing his patent," as the law-books call it; much less of his having actually stepped up into his proper seat, as, so qualified, we might expect that some of them would have had the spirit to do, in the House of Lords. On the contrary, it seems to be a distinction thrust upon them. "Their title of 'lord,'" says one of their own body, speaking of the common people, "I never much valued, and now I entirely despise; and yet they will force it upon me as an honor which they have a right to bestow, and which I have none to refuse." † Upon a dispassionate review of the subject, we are disposed to believe that there is no right to the

* History of England, "Temporibus Edwardi Primi et sequentibus."

† Hay on Deformity.

peerage incident to mere bodily configuration; that the title in dispute is merely honorary, and depending upon the breath of the common people, which in these realms is so far from the power of conferring nobility, that the ablest constitutionalists have agreed in nothing more unanimously than in the maxim, that "the king is the sole fountain of honor."

LETTER TO AN OLD GENTLEMAN WHOSE EDUCATION HAS BEEN NEGLECTED.*

To the Editor of the "London Magazine:" —

DEAR SIR, — I send you a bantering "Epistle to an Old Gentleman whose Education is supposed to have been neglected." Of course, it was *suggested* by some letters of your admirable Opium-Eater, the discontinuance of which has caused so much regret to myself in common with most of your readers. You will do me injustice by supposing, that, in the remotest degree, it was my intention to ridicule those papers. The fact is, the most serious things may give rise to an innocent burlesque; and, the more serious they are, the fitter they become for that purpose. It is not to be supposed that Charles Cotton did not entertain a very high regard for Virgil, notwithstanding he travestied that poet. Yourself can testify the deep respect I have always held for the profound learning and penetrating genius of our friend. Nothing upon earth would give me greater pleasure than to find that he has not lost sight of his entertaining and instructive purpose.

I am, dear sir, yours and *his* sincerely, ELIA.

MY DEAR SIR, — The question which you have done me the honor to propose to me, through the medium of our common friend, Mr. Grierson, I shall endeavor to answer with as much exactness as a limited observation and experience can warrant.

You ask, — or rather Mr. Grierson, in his own interesting language, asks for you, — "Whether a person at the age of sixty-three, with no more proficiency than a

* From the "London Magazine," 1825.

tolerable knowledge of most of the characters of the English alphabet at first sight amounts to, by dint of persevering application and good masters, — a docile and ingenuous disposition on the part of the pupil always presupposed, — may hope to arrive, within a presumable number of years, at that degree of attainments which shall entitle the possessor to the character, which you are on so many accounts justly desirous of acquiring, of a *learned man*."

This is fairly and candidly stated, — only I could wish that on one point you had been a little more explicit. In the mean time, I will take it for granted, that by a "knowledge of the alphabetic characters" you confine your meaning to the single powers only, as you are silent on the subject of the diphthongs and harder combinations.

Why, truly, sir, when I consider the vast circle of sciences, — it is not here worth while to trouble you with the distinction between learning and science, which a man must be understood to have made the tour of in these days, before the world will be willing to concede to him the title which you aspire to, — I am almost disposed to reply to your inquiry by a direct answer in the negative.

However, where all cannot be compassed, a great deal that is truly valuable may be accomplished. I am unwilling to throw out any remarks that should have a tendency to damp a hopeful genius; but I must not, in fairness, conceal from you that you have much to do. The consciousness of difficulty is sometimes a spur to exertion. Rome — or rather, my dear sir, to borrow an illustration from a place as yet more familiar to you, Rumford — Rumford was not built in a day.

Your mind as yet, give me leave to tell you, is in the state of a sheet of white paper. We must not blot or blur it over too hastily. Or, to use an opposite simile, it is like a piece of parchment all bescrawled and bescribbled over with characters of no sense or import, which we must carefully erase and remove before we can make way for the authentic characters or impresses which are to be substituted in their stead by the corrective hand of science.

Your mind, my dear sir, again, resembles that same parchment, which we will suppose a little hardened by time and disuse. We may apply the characters; but are we sure that the ink will sink?

You are in the condition of a traveller that has all his journey to begin. And, again, you are worse off than the traveller which I have supposed; for you have already lost your way.

You have much to learn, which you have never been taught; and more, I fear, to unlearn, which you have been taught erroneously. You have hitherto, I dare say, imagined that the sun moves round the earth. When you shall have mastered the true solar system, you will have quite a different theory upon that point, I assure you. I mention but this instance. Your own experience, as knowledge advances, will furnish you with many parallels.

I can scarcely approve of the intention, which Mr. Grierson informs me you had contemplated, of entering yourself at a common seminary, and working your way up from the lower to the higher forms with the children. I see more to admire in the modesty than in the expediency of such a resolution. I own I cannot reconcile myself to the spectacle of a gentleman at your time of life, seated, as must be your case at first, below a tyro of four or five; for at that early age the rudiments of education usually commence in this country. I doubt whether more might not be lost in the point of fitness than would be gained in the advantages which you propose to yourself by this scheme.

You say you stand in need of emulation; that this incitement is nowhere to be had but at a public school; that you should be more sensible of your progress by comparing it with the daily progress of those around you. But have you considered the nature of emulation, and how it is sustained at those tender years which you would have to come in competition with? I am afraid you are dreaming of academic prizes and distinctions. Alas! in the university for which you are preparing, the highest medal would be a silver penny; and you must graduate in nuts and oranges.

I know that Peter, the great Czar — or Emperor — of Muscovy, submitted himself to the discipline of a dock-yard at Deptford, that he might learn, and convey to his countrymen, the noble art of ship-building. You are old enough to remember him, or at least the talk about him. I call to mind also other great princes, who, to instruct themselves in the theory and practice of war, and set an example of subordination to their subjects, have condescended to enroll themselves as private soldiers; and, passing through the successive ranks of corporal, quarter-master, and the rest, have served their way up to the station at which most princes are willing enough to set out, — of general and commander-in-chief over their own forces. But — besides that there is oftentimes great sham and pretence in their show of mock humility — the competition which they stooped to was with their co-evals, however inferior to them in birth. Between ages so very disparate as those which you contemplate, I fear there can no salutary emulation subsist.

Again: in the other alternative, could you submit to the ordinary reproofs and discipline of a day-school? Could you bear to be corrected for your faults? Or how would it look to see you put to stand, as must be the case sometimes, in a corner?

I am afraid the idea of a public school in your circumstances must be given up.

But is it impossible, my dear sir, to find some person of your own age, — if of the other sex, the more agreeable, perhaps, — whose information, like your own, has rather lagged behind their years, who should be willing to set out from the same point with yourself? to undergo the same tasks? — thus at once inciting and sweetening each other's labors in a sort of friendly rivalry. Such a one, I think, it would not be difficult to find in some of the western parts of this island, — about Dartmoor, for instance.

Or what if, from your own estate, — that estate, which, unexpectedly acquired so late in life, has inspired into you this generous thirst after knowledge, — you were to select some elderly peasant, that might best be spared from the land, to come and begin his education with you, that you might till, as it were, your minds together, — one whose heavier progress might invite, without a fear of discouraging, your emulation? We might then see — starting from an equal post — the difference of the clownish and the gentle blood.

A private education, then, or such a one as I have been describing, being determined on, we must in the next place look out for a preceptor; for it will be some time before either of you, left to yourselves, will be able to assist the other to any great purpose in his studies.

And now, my dear sir, if, in describing such a tutor as I have imagined for you, I use a style a little above the familiar one in which I have hitherto chosen to address you, the nature of the subject must be my apology. *Difficile est de scientiis inscienter loqui;* which is as much as to say, that, "in treating of scientific matters, it is difficult to avoid the use of scientific terms." But I shall endeavor to be as plain as possible. I am not going to present you with the *ideal* of a pedagogue as it may exist in my fancy, or has possibly been realized in the persons of Buchanan and Busby. Something less than perfection will serve our turn. The scheme which I propose in this first or introductory letter has reference to the first four or five years of your education only; and, in enumerating the qualifications of him that should undertake the direction of your studies, I shall rather point out the *minimum*, or *least*, that I shall require of him, than trouble you in the search of attainments neither common nor necessary to our immediate purpose.

He should be a man of deep and extensive knowledge. So much at least is indispensable. Something older than yourself, I could wish him, because years add reverence.

To his age and great learning, he should be blessed

with a temper and a patience willing to accommodate itself to the imperfections of the slowest and meanest capacities. Such a one, in former days, Mr. Hartlib appears to have been; and such, in our days, I take Mr. Grierson to be: but our friend, you know, unhappily has other engagements. I do not demand a consummate grammarian; but he must be a thorough master of vernacular orthography, with an insight into the accentualities and punctualities of modern Saxon, or English. He must be competently instructed (or how shall he instruct you?) in the tetralogy, or four first rules, upon which not only arithmetic, but geometry, and the pure mathematics themselves, are grounded. I do not require that he should have measured the globe with Cook or Ortelius; but it is desirable that he should have a general knowledge (I do not mean a very nice or pedantic one) of the great division of the earth into four parts, so as to teach you readily to name the quarters. He must have a genius capable in some degree of soaring to the upper element, to deduce from thence the not much dissimilar computation of the cardinal points, or hinges, upon which those invisible phenomena, which naturalists agree to term *winds*, do perpetually shift and turn. He must instruct you, in imitation of the old Orphic fragments (the mention of which has possibly escaped you), in numeric and harmonious responses, to deliver the number of solar revolutions within which each of the twelve periods, into which the *Annus Vulgaris*, or common year, is divided, doth usually complete and terminate itself. The intercalaries, and other subtle problems, he will do well to omit, till riper years, and course of study, shall have rendered you more capable thereof. He must be capable of embracing all history, so as, from the countless myriads of individual men who have peopled this globe of earth, —*for it is a globe*, — by comparison of their respective births, lives, deaths, fortunes, conduct, prowess, &c., to pronounce, and teach you to pronounce, dogmatically and catechetically, who was the richest, who was the strongest, who was the wisest, who was the meekest, man that ever lived; to the facilitation of which solution, you will readily conceive, a smattering of biography would in no inconsiderable degree conduce. Leaving the dialects of men (in one of which I shall take leave to suppose you by this time at least superficially instituted), you will learn to ascend with him to the contemplation of that unarticulated language which was before the written tongue; and, with the aid of the elder Phrygian or Æsopic key, to interpret the sounds by which the animal tribes communicate their minds, evolving moral instruction with delight from the dialogue of cocks, dogs, and foxes. Or, marrying theology with verse, from whose mixture a beautiful and healthy offspring may be expected, in your own native accents (but purified), you will keep time together to the profound harpings of the more modern or Wattsian hymnics.

Thus far I have ventured to conduct you to a " hill-side, whence you may discern the right path of a virtuous and noble education; laborious indeed at the first ascent, but else so smooth, so green, so full of goodly prospects and melodious sounds on every side, that the harp of Orpheus was not more charming." *

* Milton's " Tracate on Education," addressed to Mr. Hartlib.

With my best respects to Mr. Grierson, when you see him,

I remain, dear sir, your obedient servant,

ELIA.

ON THE AMBIGUITIES ARISING FROM PROPER NAMES.*

How oddly it happens that the same sound shall suggest to the minds of two persons hearing it ideas the most opposite! I was conversing, a few years since, with a young friend upon the subject of poetry, and particularly that species of it which is known by the name of the epithalamium. I ventured to assert that the most perfect specimen of it in our language was the "Epithalamium" of Spenser upon his own marriage.

My young gentleman, who has a smattering of taste, and would not willingly be thought ignorant of any thing remotely connected with the *belles-lettres*, expressed a degree of surprise, mixed with mortification, that he should never have heard of this poem; Spenser being an author with whose writings he thought himself peculiarly conversant.

I offered to show him the poem in the fine folio copy of the poet's works which I have at home. He seemed pleased with the offer, though the mention of the folio seemed again to puzzle him. But, presently after,

* From "The Reflector," No. 2. All the facts (and fictions too, if there be any) in this article will be found in one of Lamb's early letters to Wordsworth. — EDITOR.

assuming a grave look, he compassionately muttered to himself, "Poor Spencer!"

There was something in the tone with which he spoke these words that struck me not a little. It was more like the accent with which a man bemoans some recent calamity that has happened to a friend, than that tone of sober grief with which we lament the sorrows of a person, however excellent and however grievous his afflictions may have been, who has been dead more than two centuries. I had the curiosity to inquire into the reasons of so uncommon an ejaculation. My young gentleman, with a more solemn tone of pathos than before, repeated, "Poor Spencer!" and added, "He has lost his wife!"

My astonishment at this assertion rose to such a height, that I began to think the brain of my young friend must be cracked, or some unaccountable revery had gotten possession of it. But, upon further explanation, it appeared that the word "Spenser" — which to you or me, reader, in a conversation upon poetry too, would naturally have called up the idea of an old poet in a ruff, one Edmund Spenser, that flourished in the days of Queen Elizabeth, and wrote a poem called "The Fairy Queen," with "The Shepherd's Calendar," and many more verses besides — did, in the mind of my young friend, excite a very different and quite modern idea; namely, that of the Honorable William Spencer, one of the living ornaments, if I am not misinformed, of this present poetical era, A.D. 1811.

ELIA ON HIS "CONFESSIONS OF A DRUNKARD."*

MANY are the sayings of Elia, painful and frequent his lucubrations, set forth for the most part (such his modesty!) without a name; scattered about in obscure periodicals and forgotten miscellanies. From the dust of some of these it is our intention occasionally to revive a tract or two that shall seem worthy of a better fate, especially at a time like the present, when the pen of our industrious contributor, engaged in a laborious

* From the "London Magazine," 1822.

Willis, in his "Pencillings by the Way," describing his interview with Charles and Mary Lamb, says, "Nothing could be more delightful than the kindness and affection between the brother and the sister; though Lamb was continually taking advantage of her deafness to mystify her with the most singular gravity upon every topic that was started. 'Poor Mary!' said he: 'she hears all of an epigram but the point.' — 'What are you saying of me, Charles?' she asked. 'Mr. Willis,' said he, raising his voice, 'admires *your* "Confessions of a Drunkard" very much, and I was saying it was no merit of yours that you understood the subject.' We had been speaking of this admirable essay (which is his own) half an hour before."

That essay has been strangely and purposely misunderstood. Elia, albeit he loved the cheerful glass, was not a drunkard. The "poor nameless egotist" of the Confessions is not Charles Lamb. In printing the article in the "London Magazine" (it was originally contributed to a collection of tracts published by Basil Montagu), Elia introduced it to the readers of that periodical in the above explanatory paragraphs. They should be printed in all editions of Elia as a note to the article they explain and comment on; for many persons, like the writer in the London "Quarterly Review," believe, or profess to believe, that this "fearful picture of the consequences of intemperance" is a true tale. "How far it was from actual truth," says Talfourd, "the Essays of Elia, the production of a later day, in which the maturity of his feeling, humor, and reason, is exhibited, may sufficiently show." — EDITOR.

digest of his recent Continental tour, may haply want the leisure to expatiate in more miscellaneous speculations. We have been induced, in the first instance, to reprint a thing which he put forth in a friend's volume some years since, entitled "The Confessions of a Drunkard," seeing that Messieurs the Quarterly Reviewers have chosen to embellish their last dry pages with fruitful quotations therefrom; adding, from their peculiar brains, the gratuitous affirmation, that they have reason to believe that the describer (in his delineations of a drunkard, forsooth!) partly sat for his own picture. The truth is, that our friend had been reading among the essays of a contemporary, who has perversely been confounded with him, a paper in which Edax (or the Great Eater) humorously complaineth of an inordinate appetite; and it struck him that a better paper — of deeper interest and wider usefulness — might be made out of the imagined experiences of a Great Drinker. Accordingly he set to work, and, with that mock fervor and counterfeit earnestness with which he is too apt to over-realize his descriptions, has given us — a frightful picture indeed, but no more resembling the man Elia than the fictitious Edax may be supposed to identify itself with Mr. L., its author. It is, indeed, a compound extracted out of his long observations of the effects of drinking upon all the world about him; and this accumulated mass of misery he hath centred (as the custom is with judicious essayists) in a single figure. We deny not that a portion of his own experiences may have passed into the picture; (as who, that is not a washy fellow, but must at some times have felt the after-operation of a too-generous cup?) but then how heightened! how exaggerated! how little within the sense of the Review, where a part, in their slanderous usage, must be understood to stand for the whole! But it is useless to expostulate with this Quarterly slime, brood of Nilus, watery heads with hearts of jelly, spawned under the sign of Aquarius, incapable of Bacchus, and therefore cold, washy, spiteful, bloodless. Elia shall string them up one day, and show their colors, — or, rather, how colorless and vapid the whole fry, — when he putteth forth his long-promised, but unaccountably hitherto delayed, "Confessions of a Water-drinker."

THE LAST PEACH.*

I AM the miserablest man living. Give me counsel, dear Editor. I was bred up in the strictest principles of honesty, and have passed my life in punctual adherence to them. Integrity might be said to be ingrained in our family. Yet I live in constant fear of one day coming to the gallows.

Till the latter end of last autumn, I never experienced these feelings of self-mistrust, which ever since have imbittered my existence. From the apprehension of that unfortunate man,† whose story began to make so great an impression upon the public about that time, I date my horrors. I never can get it out of my head

* From the "London Magazine" [illegible]25.

† Fauntleroy.

that I shall some time or other commit a forgery, or do some equally vile thing. To make matters worse, I am in a banking-house. I sit surrounded with a cluster of bank-notes. These were formerly no more to me than meat to a butcher's dog. They are now as toads and aspics. I feel all day like one situated amidst gins and pitfalls. Sovereigns, which I once took such pleasure in counting out, and scraping up with my little tin shovel (at which I was the most expert in the banking-house), now scald my hands. When I go to sign my name, I set down that of another person, or write my own in a counterfeit character. I am beset with temptations without motive. I want no more wealth than I possess. A more contended being than myself, as to money matters, exists not. What should I fear?

When a child, I was once let loose, by favor of a nobleman's gardener, into his lordship's magnificent fruit-garden, with full leave to pull the currants and the gooseberries; only I was interdicted from touching the wall-fruit.* Indeed, at that season (it was the end

* This garden belonged to "Blakesmoor," the fine old family mansion of the Plummers of Hertfordshire, in whose family Lamb's maternal grandmother — the "grandame" of his poem of that name, and the "great-grandmother Field" of Elia's "Dream Children" — was housekeeper for many years.

About this great house, where he passed so many happy holidays when a boy, and of which he writes so beautifully in two of the Essays of Elia, Lamb thus speaks in one of his letters to Barton: —

"You have well described your old, fashionable, grand, paternal hall. Is it not odd that every one's earliest recollections are of some such place? I had my Blakesware (Blakesmoor in the 'London'). Nothing fills a child's mind like a large old mansion: better if un — or partially — occupied, peopled with the spirits of deceased members for the county, and justices of the quorum. Would I were buried in the peopled solitude of one, with my feelings at seven years old! Those marble busts of the emperors — they seemed as if they were to stand for ever, as they had stood from the living of autumn), there was little left. Only on the south wall (can I forget the hot feel of the brick-work?) lingered the one last peach. Now, peaches are a fruit which I always had, and still have, an almost utter aversion to. There is something to my palate singularly harsh and repulsive in the flavor of them. I know not by what demon of contradiction inspired; but I was haunted with an irresistible desire to pluck it. Tear myself as often as I would from the spot, I found myself still recurring to it; till, maddening with desire (desire I cannot call it), with wilfulness rather, — without appetite, — against appetite, I may call it, — in an evil hour I reached out my hand, and plucked it. Some few raindrops just then fell; the sky (from a bright day) became overcast; and I was a type of our first parents, after the eating of that fatal fruit. I felt myself naked and ashamed, stripped of my virtue, spiritless. The downy fruit, whose sight rather than savor had tempted me, dropped from my hand, never to be tasted. All the commentators in the world cannot persuade me but that the Hebrew word, in the second chapter of Genesis, translated "apple," should be rendered "peach." Only this way can I reconcile that mysterious story.

Just such a child at thirty am I among the cash and valuables, longing to pluck, without an idea of enjoyment further. I cannot reason myself out of these fears: I dare not laugh at them. I was tenderly and

ages of Rome, in that old marble hall, and I to partake of their permanency. Eternity was, while I thought not of Time. But he thought of me, and they are toppled down, and corn covers the spot of the noble old dwelling and its princely gardens. I feel like a grasshopper, that, chirping about the ground, escapes his scythe only by my littleness. Even now he is whetting one of his smallest razors to clean wipe me out, perhaps. Well!" — EDITOR.

lovingly brought up. What then? Who that in life's entrance had seen the babe F——, from the lap stretching out his little fond mouth to catch the maternal kiss, could have predicted, or as much as imagined, that life's very different exit? The sight of my own fingers torments me; they seem so admirably constructed for — pilfering. Then that jugular vein, which I have in common ——; in an emphatic sense may I say with David, I am "fearfully made." All my mirth is poisoned by these unhappy suggestions. If, to dissipate reflection, I hum a tune, it changes to the "Lamentations of a Sinner." My very dreams are tainted. I awake with a shocking feeling of my hand in some pocket.

Advise me, dear Editor, on this painful heart-malady. Tell me, do you feel any thing allied to it in yourself? Do you never feel an itching, as it were, — a *dactylomania*, — or am I alone? You have my honest confession. My next may appear from Bow Street.

SUSPENSURUS.*

* The day after the execution of Fauntleroy, and some months before the publication of this little sketch, Lamb thus solemnly, yet humorously withal, writes to the Quaker poet: "And now, my dear sir, trifling apart, the gloomy catastrophe of yesterday morning prompts a sadder vein. The fate of the unfortunate Fauntleroy makes me, whether I will or no, to cast reflecting eyes around on such of my friends, as, by a parity of situation, are exposed to a similarity of temptation. My very style seems to myself to become more impressive than usual with the charge of them. Who that standeth knoweth but he may yet fall? Your hands as yet, I am most willing to believe, have never deviated into others' property. You think it impossible that you could ever commit so heinous an offence: but so thought Fauntleroy once; so have thought many besides him, who at last have expiated as he hath done. You are as yet upright; but you are a banker, or, at least, the next thing to it. I feel the delicacy of the subject; but cash must pass through your hands, sometimes to a great amount. If in an unguarded hour — but I will hope better. Consider the scandal it will bring upon those of your persuasion! Thousands would go to see

REFLECTIONS IN THE PILLORY.*

About the year 18—, one R——d, a respectable London merchant (since dead), stood in the pillory for some alleged fraud upon the revenue. Among his papers were found the following "Reflections," which we have obtained by favor of our friend Elia, who knew him well, and had heard him describe the train of his feelings, upon that trying occasion, almost in the words of the manuscript. Elia speaks of him as a man (with the exception of the peccadillo aforesaid) of singular integrity in all his private dealings, possessing great suavity of manner, with a certain turn for humor. As our object is to present human nature under every possible circumstance, we do not think that we shall sully our pages by inserting it. — EDITOR OF "LONDON MAGAZINE."

SCENE, — *Opposite the Royal Exchange.*
TIME, — *Twelve to one, noon.*

KETCH, my good fellow, you have a neat hand. Prithee, adjust this new collar to my neck gingerly. I am not used to these wooden cravats. There, softly, softly. That seems the exact point between ornament and strangulation. A thought looser on this side. Now it will do. And have a care in turning me,

a Quaker hanged that would be indifferent to the fate of a Presbyterian or an Anabaptist. Think of the effect it would have on the sale of your poems alone, not to mention higher considerations! I tremble, I am sure, at myself, when I think that so many poor victims of the law, at one time of their life, made as sure of never being hanged, as I, in my own presumption, am ready, too ready, to do myself. What are we better than they? Do we come into the world with different necks? Is there any distinctive mark under our left ears? Are we unstrangulable, I ask you? Think on these things. I am shocked sometimes at the shape of my own fingers; not for their resemblance to the ape tribe (which is something), but for the exquisite adaptation of them to the purposes of picking, fingering, &c." — EDITOR.

* From the "London Magazine," 1825.

that I present my aspect due vertically. I now face the orient. In a quarter of an hour I shift southward,—do you mind?—and so on till I face the east again, travelling with the sun. No half-points, I beseech you,—N. N. by W., or any such elaborate niceties. They become the shipman's card, but not this mystery. Now leave me a little to my own reflections.

Bless us, what a company is assembled in honor of me! How grand I stand here! I never felt so sensibly before the effect of solitude in a crowd. I muse in solemn silence upon that vast miscellaneous rabble in the pit there. From my private box, I contemplate, with mingled pity and wonder, the gaping curiosity of those underlings. There are my Whitechapel supporters. Rosemary Lane has emptied herself of the very flower of her citizens to grace my show. Duke's place sits desolate. What is there in my face, that strangers should come so far from the east to gaze upon it? [*Here an egg narrowly misses him.*] That offering was well meant, but not so cleanly executed. By the tricklings, it should not be either myrrh or frankincense. Spare your presents, my friends: I am noways mercenary. I desire no missive tokens of your approbation. I am past those valentines. Bestow these coffins of untimely chickens upon mouths that water for them. Comfort your addle spouses with them at home, and stop the mouths of your brawling brats with such Olla Podridas: they have need of them. [*A brick is let fly.*] Discase not, I pray you, nor dismantle your rent and ragged tenements, to furnish me with architectural decorations, which I can excuse. This fragment might have stopped a flaw against snow comes. [*A coal flies.*]

Cinders are dear, gentlemen. This nubbling might have helped the pot boil, when your dirty cuttings from the shambles at three-ha'pence a pound shall stand at a cold simmer. Now, south about, Ketch. I would enjoy Australian popularity.

What, my friends from over the water! Old benchers — flies of a day — ephemeral Romans — welcome! Doth the sight of me draw souls from limbo? can it dispeople purgatory? — Ha!

What am I, or what was my father's house, that I should thus be set up a spectacle to gentlemen and others? Why are all faces, like Persians at the sunrise, bent singly on mine alone? It was wont to be esteemed an ordinary visnomy, a quotidian merely. Doubtless these assembled myriads discern some traits of nobleness, gentility, breeding, which hitherto have escaped the common observation, — some intimations, as it were, of wisdom, valor, piety, and so forth. My sight dazzles; and, if I am not deceived by the too-familiar pressure of this strange neckcloth that envelops it, my countenance gives out lambent glories. For some painter now to take me in the lucky point of expression! — the posture so convenient! — the head never shifting, but standing quiescent in a sort of natural frame! But these artisans require a westerly aspect. Ketch, turn me.

Something of St. James's air in these my new friends. How my prospects shift and brighten! Now, if Sir Thomas Lawrence be anywhere in that group, his fortune is made for ever. I think I see some one taking out a crayon. I will compose my whole face to a smile, which yet shall not so predominate but that gravity and gayety shall contend, as it were, — you understand me? I will work up my thoughts to some mild rapture, — a gentle enthusiasm, — which the artist may transfer, in a manner, warm to the canvas. I will inwardly apostrophize my tabernacle.

Delectable mansion, hail! House not made of every wood! Lodging that pays no rent; airy and commodious; which, owing no window-tax, art yet all case ment, out of which men have such pleasure in peering and overlooking, that they will sometimes stand an hour together to enjoy thy prospects! Cell, recluse from the vulgar! Quiet retirement from the great Babel, yet affording sufficient glimpses into it! Pulpit, that instructs without note or sermon-book; into which the preacher is inducted without tenth or first-fruit! Throne, unshared and single, that disdainest a Brentford competitor! Honor without co-rival! Or hearest thou, rather, magnificent theatre, in which the spectator comes to see and to be seen? From thy giddy heights I look down upon the common herd, who stand with eyes upturned, as if a winged messenger hovered over them; and mouths open, as if they expected manna. I feel, I feel, the true episcopal yearnings. Behold in me, my flock, your true overseer! What though I cannot lay hands, because my own are laid; yet I can mutter benedictions. True *otium cum dignitate!* Proud Pisgah eminence! pinnacle sublime! O Pillory! 'tis thee I sing! Thou younger brother to the gallows, without his rough and Esau palms, that with ineffable contempt surveyest beneath thee the grovelling stocks, which claims presumptuously to be of thy great race! Let that low wood know that thou art far higher born. Let that domicile for groundling rogues and base earth-kissing varlets envy thy preferment, not seldom fated to be the wanton baiting-house, the temporary retreat, of poet and of patriot. Shades of Bastwick and of Prynne hover over thee,—Defoe is there, and more greatly daring Shebbeare, — from their (little more elevated) stations they look down with recognitions. Ketch, turn me.

I now veer to the north. Open your widest gates, thou proud Exchange of London, that I may look in as proudly! Gresham's wonder, hail! I stand upon a level with all your kings. They and I, from equal heights, with equal superciliousness, o'erlook the plodding money-hunting tribe below, who, busied in their sordid speculations, scarce elevate their eyes to notice your ancient, or my recent, grandeur. The second Charles smiles on me from three pedestals! * He closed the Exchequer: I cheated the Excise. Equal our darings, equal be our lot.

Are those the quarters? 'tis their fatal chime. That the ever-winged hours would but stand still! but I must descend, — descend from this dream of greatness. Stay, stay, a little while, importunate hour-hand! A moment or two, and I shall walk on foot with the undistinguished many. The clock speaks one. I return to common life. Ketch, let me out.

* A statue of Charles II., by the elder Cibber, adorns the front of the Exchange. He stands also on high, in the train of his crowned ancestors, in his proper order, *within* that building. But the merchants of London, in a superfetation of loyalty, have, within a few years, caused to be erected another effigy of him on the ground in the centre of the interior. We do not hear that a fourth is in contemplation.

A SATURDAY'S DINNER.*

"When a man keeps a constant table, he may be allowed sometimes to serve up a cold dish of meat, or toss up the fragments of a feast into a *ragoût*. I have sometimes, in a scarcity of provisions, been obliged to take the same kind of liberty, and to entertain my reader with the leavings of a former treat. I must this day have recourse to the same method, and beg my guests to sit down to a kind of Saturday's dinner." — *Tatler*, No. 258.

THE different way in which the same story may be told by different persons was never more strikingly illustrated than by the manner in which the celebrated Jeremy Collier has described the effects of Timotheus' music upon Alexander, in the second part of his Essays. We all know how Dryden has treated the subject. Let us now hear his great contemporary and antagonist: "Timotheus, a Grecian," says Collier, "was so great a master, that he could make a man storm and swagger like a tempest; and then, by altering the notes and the time, he could take him down again, and sweeten his humor in a trice. One time, when Alexander was at dinner, the man played him a Phrygian air. The prince immediately rises, snatches up his lance, and puts himself into a posture of fighting; and the retreat was no

* Under this heading, I have placed sundry scraps and fragments of Lamb's inditing, which are too short to be printed in distinct chapters, and too good (I think) to be left out of this collection. Mr. Moxon says that Elia had a strong aversion to roast beef and to fowl, and to any wines but port or sherry. "Tripe and cow-heel were to him delicacies, — rare dainties!" And I suspect, that, to a true lover of Lamb, our "Saturday's Dinner" will be better and more satisfactory than the costly and splendid banquets of some of the popular and fashionable literary caterers of the day. — EDITOR.

sooner sounded by the change of the harmony, but his arms were grounded, and his fire extinct; and he sat down as orderly as if he had come from one of Aristotle's lectures. I warrant you, Demosthenes would have been flourishing about such business a long hour, and may be not have done it neither. But Timotheus had a nearer cut to the soul: he could neck a passion at a stroke, and lay it asleep. Pythagoras once met with a parcel of drunken fellows, who were likely to be troublesome enough. He presently orders music to play grave, and chops into a Dorian. Upon this they all threw away their garlands, and were as sober and as shame-faced as one would wish." It is evident that Dryden in his inspired ode, and Collier in all this pudder of prose, meant the same thing. But what a work does the latter make with his "necking a passion at his stroke," "making a man storm and swagger like a tempest," and then "taking him down, and sweeting his humor in a trice"! What in Dryden is "softly sweet in Lydian measures," Collier calls "chopping into a Dorian." This Collier was the same, who, in his Biographical Dictionary, says of Shakspeare, that "though his genius generally was jocular, and inclining to festivity, yet *he could when he pleased be as serious as anybody*."

Oh the comfort of sitting down heartily to an old folio, and thinking surely that the next hour or two will be your own! — and the misery of being defeated by the useless call of somebody, who is come to tell you that he has just come from hearing Mr. Irving! What is that to you? Let him go home, and digest what the good man has said. You are at your chapel, in your oratory.

My friend Hume (not M.P.) has a curious manuscript in his possession, the original draught of the celebrated "Beggar's Petition," (who cannot say by heart the "Beggar's Petition"?) as it was written by some school-usher (as I remember), with corrections interlined from the pen of Oliver Goldsmith. As a specimen of the doctor's improvement, I recollect one most judicious alteration:—

"A pampered menial drove me from the door."

It stood originally,—

"A livery servant drove me," &c.

Here is an instance of poetical or artificial language properly substituted for the phrase of common conversation; against Wordsworth.

There is something to me repugnant, at any time, in a written hand. The text never seems determinate. Print settles it. I had thought of the "Lycidas" as of a full-grown beauty,—as springing up with all its parts absolute,—till, in an evil hour, I was shown the original copy of it, together with the other minor poems of its author, in the library of Trinity, kept like something to be proud of. I wish they had thrown them in the Cam, or sent them, after the latter cantos of Spenser, into the Irish Channel. How it staggered me to see the fine things in their ore!—interlined, corrected, as if their words were mortal, alterable, displaceable at pleasure; as if they might have been otherwise, and just as good; as if inspiration were made up of parts, and those fluctuating, successive, indifferent! I will never go into the workshop of any great artist again, nor desire a sight of his picture, till it is fairly off the easel; no, not if Raphael were to be alive again, and painting another Galatea.

Our ancestors, the noble old Puritans of Cromwell's day, could distinguish between a day of religious rest and a day of recreation; and while they exacted a vigorous abstinence from all amusements (even to walking out of nursery-maids with their charges in the fields) upon the sabbath, in lieu of the superstitious observance of the saints' days, which they abrogated, they humanely gave to the apprentices and poorer sort of people every alternate Thursday for a day of entire sport and recreation. A strain of piety and policy to be commended above the profane mockery of the Stuarts and their "Book of Sports."

I was once amused — there is a pleasure in *affecting* affectation — at the indignation of a crowd that was justling in with me at the pit-door of Covent-Garden Theatre to have a sight of Master Betty — then at once in his dawn and his meridian — in Hamlet. I had been invited quite unexpectedly to join a party whom I met near the door of the play-house; and I happened to have in my hand a large octavo of Johnson and Steeven's "Shakspeare," which, the time not admitting of my carrying it home, of course went with me to the theatre. Just in the very heat and pressure of the doors opening, — the rush, as they term it, — I deliberately held the volume over my head, open at the scene in which the young Roscius had been most cried up, and quietly read by the lamplight. The clamor became universal.

"The affectation of the fellow!" cried one. "Look at that gentleman *reading*, papa!" squeaked a young lady, who, in her admiration of the novelty, almost forgot her fears. I read on. "He ought to have his book knocked out of his hand!" exclaimed a pursy cit, whose arms were too fast pinioned to his side to suffer him to execute his kind intention. Still I read on, and, till the time came to pay my money, kept as unmoved as Saint Anthony at his holy offices, with the satyrs, apes, and hobgoblins moping, and making mouths at him, in the picture; while the good man sits as undisturbed at the sight as as if he were sole tenant of the desert. The individual rabble (I recognized more than one of their ugly faces) had damned a slight piece of mine but a few nights since; and I was determined the culprits should not a second time put me out of countenance.

Samuel Johnson, whom, to distinguish from the doctor, we may call the Whig, was a very remarkable writer. He may be compared to his contemporary, Dr. Fox, whom he resembled in many points. He is another instance of King William's discrimination, which was so superior to that of any of his ministers. Johnson was one of the most formidable of the advocates for the Exclusion Bill; and he suffered by whipping and imprisonment under James accordingly. Like Asgill, he argues with great apparent candor and clearness till he gets his opponent within reach; and then comes a blow as from a sledge-hammer. I do not know where I could put my hand on a book containing so much sense and constitutional doctrine as this thin folio of Johnson's Works; and what party in this country would read so severe a lecture in it as our modern Whigs? A close reasoner and a good writer in general may be known by his pertinent use of connections. Read any page of Johnson, you cannot alter one conjunction without spoiling the sense: it is a linked chain throughout. In your modern books, for the most part, the sentences in a page have the same connection with each other that marbles have in a bag: they touch without adhering.*

We are too apt to indemnify ourselves for some characteristic excellence we are kind enough to concede to a great author by denying him every thing else. Thus Donne and Cowley, by happening to possess more wit, and faculty of illustration, than other men, are supposed to have been incapable of nature or feeling: they are usually opposed to such writers as Shenstone and Parnell; whereas, in the very thickest of their conceits, — in the bewildering mazes of tropes and figures, — a warmth of soul and generous feeling shines through, the "sum" of which, "forty thousand" of those natural poets, as they are called, "with all their quantity," could not make up.

D.† commenced life, after a course of hard study, in the "House of pure Emanuel," as usher to a knavish, fanatic schoolmaster at ——, at a salary of eight pounds per annum, with board and lodging. Of this poor stipend he never received above half in all the laborious years he served this man. He tells a plea-

* This criticism was written by Lamb on the fly-leaf of his copy of "The Works of Mr. Samuel Johnson." — EDITOR.

† George Dyer.

sant anecdote, that when poverty, staring out at his ragged knees, has sometimes compelled him, against the modesty of his nature, to hint at arrears, Dr. —— would take no immediate notice; but after supper, when the school was called together to even-song, he would never fail to introduce some instructive homily against riches, and the corruption of the heart occasioned through the desire of them, — ending with, "Lord, keep thy servants, above all things, from the heinous sin of avarice. Having food and raiment, let us therewithal be content. Give me Agur's wish,"— and the like, — which, to the little auditory, sounded like a doctrine full of Christian prudence and simplicity, but, to poor D., was a receipt in full for that quarter's demands at least.

And D. has been under-working for himself ever since, — drudging at low rates for unappreciating booksellers, — wasting his fine erudition in silent corrections of the classics, and in those unostentatious but solid services to learning which commonly fall to the lot of laborious scholars who have not the art to sell themselves to the best advantage. He has published poems which do not sell, because their character is inobtrusive, like his own; and because he has been too much absorbed in ancient literature to know what the popular mark in poetry is, even if he could have hit it. And therefore his verses are properly what he terms them, —*crotchets;* voluntaries; odes to Liberty and Spring; effusions; little tributes and offerings, left behind him upon tables and window-seats, at parting from friends' houses, and from all the inns of hospitality, where he has been courteously (or but tolerably) received in his pilgrimage. If his Muse of kindness halt a little behind the strong lines, in fashion in this excitement-craving age, his prose is the best of the sort in the world, and exhibits a faithful transcript of his own healthy, natural mind, and cheerful, innocent tone of conversation.

"Pray God, your honor relieve me," said a poor beads-woman to my friend L—— one day: "I have seen better days."—"So have I, my good woman," retorted he, looking up at the welkin, which was just then threatening a storm; and the jest (he will have it) was as good to the beggar as a tester.

It was, at all events, kinder than consigning her to the stocks or the parish beadle.

But L—— has a way of viewing things in a paradoxical light on some occasions.

I have in my possession a curious volume of Latin verses, which I believe to be unique. It is entitled, *Alexandri Fultoni Scoti Epigrammatorum libri quinque.* It purports to be printed at Perth, and bears date 1679. By the appellation which the author gives himself in the preface, *hypodidasculus*, I suppose him to have been an usher at some school. It is no uncommon thing now-a-days for persons concerned in academies to affect a literary reputation in the way of their trade. The "master of a seminary for a limited number of pupils at Islington" lately put forth an edition of that scarce tract, "The Elegy in a Country Churchyard" (to use his own words), with notes and head-lines! But to our author. These epigrams of Alexander Fulton, Scotchman, have little remarkable in them besides extreme dulness and insipidity; but there is one, which, by its being marshalled in the front of the volume, seems to have been the darling of its parent, and for its exquisite flatness, and the surprising strokes of an anachronism with which it is pointed, deserves to be rescued from oblivion. It is addressed, like many of the others, to a fair one: —

AD MARIULAM SUAM AUTOR.

"Moserunt bella olim Helenæ decor atque venustas
Europen inter frugifer amque Asiam.
Tam bona, quam tu, tam prudens, sin illa fuisset,
Ad lites issent Africa et America!"

Which, in humble imitation of mine author's peculiar poverty of style, I have ventured thus to render into English: —

THE AUTHOR TO HIS MOGGY.

"For Love's illustrious cause, and Helen's charms,
All Europe and all Asia rushed to arms.
Had she with these thy polished sense combined,
All Afric and America had joined!"

The happy idea of an American war undertaken in the cause of beauty ought certainly to recommend the author's memory to the countrymen of Madison and Jefferson; and the bold anticipation of the discovery of that continent in the time of the Trojan War is a flight beyond the Sibyl's books.

A CHARACTER OF THE LATE ELIA.*

BY A FRIEND.

THIS gentleman, who for some months past had been in a declining way, hath at length paid his final tribute to nature. He just lived long enough (it was what he wished) to see his papers collected into a volume. The pages of the "London Magazine" will henceforth know him no more.

Exactly at twelve last night, his queer spirit departed; and the bells of Saint Bride's rang him out with the old year. The mournful vibrations were caught in the dining-room of his friends T. and H.; † and the company, assembled there to welcome in another 1st of January, checked their carousals in mid-mirth, and were silent. Janus wept. The gentle P——r,‡ in a whisper, signified his intention of devoting an elegy; and Allan C.,§ nobly forgetful of his countrymen's wrongs, vowed a memoir to his *manes* full and friendly as a "Tale of Lyddalcross."

To say truth, it is time he were gone. The humor of the thing, if there was ever much in it, was pretty well exhausted; and a two years' and a half existence has been a tolerable duration for a phantom.

* From the "London Magazine," 1823. A part of this article was republished by its author as a preface to "The Last Essays of Elia." — EDITOR.

† Taylor and Hessey, the publishers of the "London Magazine."

‡ Proctor, better known as Barry Cornwall.

§ Cunningham.

I am now at liberty to confess, that much which I have heard objected to my late friend's writings was well founded. Crude they are, I grant you, — a sort of unlicked, incondite things, — villanously pranked in an affected array of antique modes and phrases. They had not been *his* if they had been other than such; and better it is that a writer should be natural in a self-pleasing quaintness, than to affect a naturalness (so called) that should be strange to him. Egotistical they have been pronounced by some who did not know that what he tells us as of himself was often true only (historically) of another; as in his Third Essay (to save many instances), where, under the *first person* (his favorite figure), he shadows forth the forlorn estate of a country boy placed at a London school, far from his friends and connections, — in direct opposition to his own early history. If it be egotism to imply and twine with his own identity the griefs and affections of another, — making himself many, or reducing many unto himself, — then is the skilful novelist, who all along brings in his hero or heroine, speaking of themselves, the greatest egotist of all; who yet has never, therefore, been accused of that narrowness. And how shall the intenser dramatist escape being faulty, who doubtless, under cover of passion uttered by another, oftentimes gives blameless vent to his most inward feelings, and expresses his own story modestly?

My late friend was in many respects a singular character. Those who did not like him hated him; and some, who once liked him, afterwards became his bitterest haters. The truth is, he gave himself too little concern what he uttered, and in whose presence. He observed neither time nor place, and would even out with what came uppermost. With the severe religionist he would pass for a free-thinker; while the other faction set him down for a bigot, or persuaded themselves that he belied his sentiments. Few understood him; and I am not certain that at all times he quite understood himself. He too much affected that dangerous figure,— irony. He sowed doubtful speeches, and reaped plain, unequivocal hatred. He would interrupt the gravest discussion with some light jest; and yet, perhaps, not quite irrelevant in ears that could understand it. Your long and much talkers hated him. The informal habit of his mind, joined to an inveterate impediment of speech, forbade him to be an orator; and he seemed determined that no one else should play that part when he was present. He was *petit* and ordinary in his person and appearance. I have seen him sometimes in what is called good company, but, where he has been a stranger, sit silent, and be suspected for an odd fellow; till, some unlucky occasion provoking it, he would stutter out some senseless pun (not altogether senseless perhaps, if rightly taken), which has stamped his character for the evening. It was hit or miss with him; but, nine times out of ten, he contrived by this device to send away a whole company his enemies. His conceptions rose kindlier than his utterance, and his happiest *impromptus* had the appearance of effort. He has been accused of trying to be witty, when in truth he was but struggling to give his poor thoughts articulation. He chose his companions for some individuality of character which they manifested. Hence not many persons of science, and few professed *literati*, were of his councils. They were, for the most part, persons of an uncertain fortune; and, as to such people commonly nothing is more obnoxious than a gentleman of settled (though moderate) income, he passed with most of them for a great miser. To my knowledge, this was a mistake. His *intimados*, to confess a truth, were, in the world's eye, a ragged regiment. He found them floating on the surface of society; and the color, or something else, in the weed, pleased him. The burrs stuck to him; but they were good and loving burrs for all that. He never greatly cared for the society of what are called good people. If any of these were scandalized (and offences were sure to arise), he could not help it. When he has been remonstrated with for not making more concessions to the feelings of good people, he would retort by asking, What one point did these good people ever concede to him? He was temperate in his meals and diversions, but always kept a little on this side of abstemiousness. Only in the use of the Indian weed he might be thought a little excessive. He took it, he would say, as a solvent of speech. Marry — as the friendly vapor ascended, how his prattle would curl up sometimes with it! the ligaments, which tongue-tied him, were loosened, and the stammerer proceeded a statist!

I do not know whether I ought to bemoan or rejoice that my old friend is departed. His jests were beginning to grow obsolete, and his stories to be found out. He felt the approaches of age; and, while he pretended to cling to life, you saw how slender were the ties left to bind him. Discoursing with him latterly on this subject, he expressed himself with a pettishness which I thought unworthy of him. In our walks about his suburban retreat (as he called it) at Shacklewell, some children belonging to a school of industry had met us, and bowed and courtesied, as he thought, in an especial manner to *him*. "They take me for a visiting governor," he muttered earnestly. He had a horror, which he carried to a foible, of looking like any thing important and parochial. He thought that he approached nearer to that stamp daily. He had a general aversion from being treated like a grave or respectable character, and kept a wary eye upon the advances of age that should so entitle him. He herded always, while it was possible, with people younger than himself. He did not conform to the march of time, but was dragged along in the procession. His manners lagged behind his years. He was too much of the boy-man. The *toga virilis* never sat gracefully on his shoulders. The impressions of infancy had burnt into him, and he resented the impertinence of manhood. These were weaknesses; but, such as they were, they are a key to explicate some of his writings.

He left little property behind him. Of course, the little that is left (chiefly in India bonds) devolves upon his cousin Bridget. A few critical dissertations were found in his *escritoire*, which have been handed over to the editor of this magazine, in which it is to be hoped they will shortly appear, retaining his accustomed signature.

He has himself not obscurely hinted that his employment lay in a public office. The gentlemen in the export-department of the East-India House will forgive me if I acknowledge the readiness with which they assisted me in the retrieval of his few manuscripts. They pointed out in a most obliging manner the desk at which he had been planted for forty years; showed me ponderous tomes of figures, in his own remarkably neat hand, which, more properly than his few printed tracts, might be called his "Works." They seemed affectionate to his memory, and universally commended his expertness in book-keeping. It seems he was the inventor of some ledger which should combine the precision and certainty of the Italian double entry (I think they called it) with the brevity and facility of some newer German system; but I am not able to appreciate the worth of the discovery. I have often heard him express a warm regard for his associates in office, and how fortunate he considered himself in having his lot thrown in amongst them. There is more sense, more discourse, more shrewdness, and even talent, among these clerks (he would say), than in twice the number of authors by profession that I have conversed with. He would brighten up sometimes upon the "old days of the India House," when he consorted with Woodroffe and Wissett, and Peter Corbet (a descendant and worthy representative, bating the point of sanctity, of old facetious Bishop Corbet); and Hoole, who translated Tasso; and Bartlemy Brown, whose father (God assoil him therefore!) modernized Walton; and sly, warm-hearted old Jack Cole (King Cole they called him in those days) and Campe and Fombelle, and a world of choice spirits, more than I can remember to name, who associated in those days with Jack Burrell (the *bon vivant* of the South-Sea House); and little

Eyton (said to be a *fac-simile* of Pope, — he was a miniature of a gentleman), that was cashier under him; and Dan Voight of the custom-house, that left the famous library.

Well, Elia is gone, — for aught I know, to be re-united with them, — and these poor traces of his pen are all we have to show for it. How little survives of the wordiest authors! Of all they said or did in their lifetime, a few glittering words only! His Essays found some favorers, as they appeared separately. They shuffled their way in the crowd well enough singly: how they will *read*, now they are brought together, is a question for the publishers, who have thus ventured to draw out into one piece his "weaved-up follies."

PHIL-ELIA.

THE PAWNBROKER'S DAUGHTER.

A FARCE.

CHARACTERS.

FLINT, *a Pawnbroker.*
DAVENPORT, *in love with Marian.*
PENDULOUS, *a Reprieved Gentleman.*
CUTLET, *a Sentimental Butcher.*
GOLDING, *a Magistrate.*
WILLIAM, *Apprentice to Flint.*
BEN, *Cutlet's Boy.*
MISS FLYN.
BETTY, *her Maid.*
MARIAN, *Daughter to Flint.*
LUCY, *her Maid.*

THE PAWNBROKER'S DAUGHTER.*

A FARCE.

ACT I.

SCENE I.—*An Apartment at* FLINT'S *House.*

FLINT. WILLIAM.

Flint. CARRY those umbrellas, cottons, and wearing-apparel, up stairs. You may send that chest of tools to Robins's.

William. That which you lent six pounds upon to the journeyman carpenter that had the sick wife?

Flint. The same.

William. The man says, if you can give him till Thursday—

Flint. Not a minute longer. His time was out yesterday. These improvident fools!

* "For literary news, in my poor way," writes Lamb to Southey, in August, 1825, "I have a one-act farce, going to be acted at Haymarket; but when? is the question. 'Tis an extravaganza, and like enough to follow 'Mr. H.'"

Talfourd says that the farce thus referred to was founded upon Lamb's essay "On the Inconvenience of being Hanged;" and therefore it must be "The Pawnbroker's Daughter." But "The Pawnbroker's Daughter" is in two acts; and according to the letter to Mrs. Shelley, published in this volume, it was not finished in July, 1827; and, consequently, could not have been ready for the stage in the summer of 1825. The piece, however, was never performed, but was published, 1830, in "Blackwood's Magazine."—EDITOR.

William. The finical gentleman has been here about that seal that was his grandfather's.

Flint. He cannot have it. Truly, our trade would be brought to a fine pass if we were bound to humor the fancies of our customers. This man would be taking a liking to a snuff-box that he had inherited, and that gentlewoman might conceit a favorite chemise that had descended to her.

William. The lady in the carriage has been here crying about those jewels. She says, if you cannot let her have them at the advance she offers, her husband will come to know that she has pledged them.

Flint. I have use for those jewels. Send Marian to me. [*Exit* WILLIAM.] I know no other trade that is expected to depart from its fair advantages but ours. I do not see the baker, the butcher, the shoemaker, or, to go higher, the lawyer, the physician, the divine, give up any of their legitimate gains, even when the pretences of their art had failed; yet *we* are to be branded with an odious name, stigmatized, discountenanced even by the administrators of those laws which acknowledge us, — scowled at by lower sort of people, whose needs we serve!

Enter MARIAN.

Come hither, Marian. Come, kiss your father. The report runs that he is full of spotted crime. What is your belief, child?

Marian. That never good report went with our calling, father. I have heard you say, the poor look only to the advantages which we derive from them, and overlook the accommodations which they receive from us. But the poor *are* the poor, father, and have little leisure to make distinctions. I wish we could give up this business.

Flint. You have not seen that idle fellow, Davenport?

Marian. No, indeed, father, since your injunction.

Flint. I take but my lawful profit. The law is not over-favorable to us.

Marian. Marian is no judge of these things.

Flint. They call me oppressive, grinding—I know not what—

Marian. Alas!

Flint. Usurer, extortioner. Am I these things?

Marian. You are Marian's kind and careful father. That is enough for a child to know.

Flint. Here, girl, is a little box of jewels, which the necessities of a foolish woman of quality have transferred into our true and lawful possession. Go, place them with the trinkets that were your mother's. They are all yours, Marian, if you do not cross me in your marriage. No gentry shall match into this house to flout their wife hereafter with her parentage. I will hold this business with convulsive grasp to my dying day. I will plague these *poor*, whom you speak so tenderly of.

Marian. You frighten me, father. Do not frighten Marian.

Flint. I have heard them say, "There goes Flint!—Flint, the cruel pawnbroker!"

Marian. Stay at home with Marian. You shall hear no ugly words to vex you.

Flint. You shall ride in a gilded chariot upon the necks of these *poor*, Marian. Their tears shall drop pearls for my girl. Their sighs shall be good wind for us. They shall blow good for my girl. Put up the jewels, Marian. [*Exit.*

Enter LUCY.

Lucy. Miss, miss, your father has taken his hat, and stepped out; and Mr. Davenport is on the stairs: and I come to tell you—

Marian. Alas! who let him in?

Enter DAVENPORT.

Dav. My dearest girl—

Marian. My father will kill me if he finds you have been here!

Dav. There is no time for explanations. I have positive information that your father means, in less than a week, to dispose of you to that ugly Saunders. The wretch has bragged of it to his acquaintance, and already calls you *his.*

Marian. O Heavens!

Dav. Your resolution must be summary, as the time which calls for it. Mine or his you must be, without delay. There is no safety for you under this roof.

Marian. My father—

Dav. Is no father, if he would sacrifice you.

Marian. But he is unhappy. Do not speak hard words of my father.

Dav. Marian must exert her good sense.

Lucy (*as if watching at the window*). Oh, miss, your father has suddenly returned! I see him with Mr. Saunders coming down the street! Mr. Saunders, ma'am!

Marian. Begone, begone, if you love me, Davenport!

Dav. You must go with me, then, else here I am fixed.

Lucy. Ay, miss, you must go, as Mr. Davenport says. Here is your cloak, miss, and your hat, and your gloves. Your father, ma'am!—

Marian. Oh! where? where? Whither do you hurry me, Davenport?

Dav. Quickly, quickly, Marian! At the back-door.

[*Exit* MARIAN, *with* DAVENPORT, *reluctantly; in her flight still holding the jewels.*

Lucy. Away!—away! What a lucky thought of mine to say her father was coming! he would never have got her off else. Lord, Lord, I do love to help lovers!

[*Exit, following them.*

SCENE II.—*A Butcher's Shop.*

CUTLET. BEN.

Cutlet. Reach me down that book off the shelf where the shoulder of veal hangs.

Ben. Is this it?

Cutlet. No,—this is "Flowers of Sentiment:" the other,—ay, this is a good book. "An Argument against the Use of Animal Food. By J. R." *That* means Joseph Ritson. I will open it anywhere, and read, just as it happens. One cannot dip amiss in such books as these. The motto, I see, is from Pope; I dare say, very much to the purpose. (*Reads:*) —

"The lamb thy riot dooms to bleed to-day,
Had he thy reason, would he skip and play?
Pleased to the last, he crops the flowery food,
And licks the hand"—

Bless us! is that saddle of mutton gone home to Mrs. Simpson's? It should have gone an hour ago.

Ben. I was just going with it.

Cutlet. Well, go. Where was I? Oh! —

"And licks the hand just raised to shed its blood."

What an affecting picture! (*Turns over the leaves, and reads:*) —

"It is probable that the long lives which are recorded of the people before the Flood were owing to their being confined to vegetable diet."

Ben. The young gentleman in Pullen's Row, Islington, that has got the consumption, has sent to know if you can let him have a sweetbread.

Cutlet. Take two, — take all that are in the shop. What a disagreeable interruption! (*Reads again:*) —

"Those fierce and angry passions, which impel man to wage destructive war with man, may be traced to the ferment in the blood, produced by animal diet."

Ben. The two pounds of rump-steaks must go home to Mr. Molyneux's. He is in training to fight Cribb.

Cutlet. Well, take them: go along, and do not trouble me with your disgusting details.

Cutlet (*throwing down the book*). Why was I bred to this detestable business? Was it not plain that this trembling sensibility, which has marked my character from earliest infancy, must disqualify me for a profession which — what do ye want? — what do ye buy? Oh! it is only somebody going past. I thought it had been a customer — Why was not I bred a glover, like my cousin Langston? To see him poke his two little sticks into a delicate pair of real Woodstock, — "A very little stretching, ma'am, and they will fit exactly." — Or a haberdasher, like my next-door neighbor, — "Not a better bit of lace in all town, my lady: Mrs. Breakstock took the last of it last Friday; all but this bit, which I can afford to let your ladyship have at a bargain — reach down that drawer on your left hand, Miss Fisher."

Enter, in haste, DAVENPORT, MARIAN, *and* LUCY.

Lucy. This is the house I saw a bill up at, ma'am; and a droll creature the landlord is.

Dav. We have no time for nicety.

Cutlet. What do ye want? what do ye buy? Oh! it is only Mrs. Lucy.

LUCY *whispers* CUTLET.

Cutlet. I have a set of apartments at the end of my garden. They are quite detatched from the shop. A single lady at present occupies the ground-floor.

Marian. Ay, ay, anywhere.

Dav. In, in—

Cutlet. Pretty lamb! — she seems agitated.

DAVENPORT *and* MARIAN *go in with* CUTLET.

Lucy. I am mistaken if my young lady does not find an agreeable companion in these apartments. Almost a namesake. Only the difference of Flyn and Flint. I have some errands to do, or I would stop and have some fun with this droll butcher.

CUTLET *returns.*

Cutlet. Why, how odd this is! *Your* young lady knows *my* young lady. They are as thick as flies.

Lucy. You may thank me for your new lodger, Mr. Cutlet. But, bless me, you do not look well!

Cutlet. To tell you the truth, I am rather heavy about the eyes. Want of sleep, I believe.

Lucy. Late hours, perhaps. Raking last night?

Cutlet. No: that is not it, Mrs. Lucy. My repose

was disturbed by a very different cause from what you may imagine. It proceeded from too much thinking.

Lucy. The deuse it did! And what, if I may be so bold, might be the subject of your Night Thoughts?

Cutlet. The distress of my fellow-creatures. I never lay my head down on my pillow, but I fall a-thinking, How many at this very instant are perishing!—some with cold—

Lucy. What! in the midst of summer?

Cutlet. Ay. Not here; but in countries abroad, where the climate is different from ours. Our summers are their winters, and *vice versâ*, you know. Some with cold—

Lucy. What a canting rogue it is! I should like to trump up some fine story to plague him. [*Aside.*

Cutlet. Others with hunger; some a prey to the rage of wild beasts—

Lucy. He has got this by rote, out of some book.

Cutlet. Some drowning, crossing crazy bridges in the dark; some by the violence of the devouring flame—

Lucy. I have it. For that matter, you need not send your humanity a-travelling, Mr. Cutlet. For instance, last night—

Cutlet. Some by fevers, some by gunshot-wounds—

Lucy. Only two streets off—

Cutlet. Some in drunken quarrels—

Lucy (*aloud*). The butcher's shop at the corner.

Cutlet. What were you saying about poor Cleaver?

Lucy. He has found his ears at last. (*Aside.*) That he has had his house burnt down.

Cutlet. Bless me!

Lucy. I saw four small children taken in at the green-grocer's.

Cutlet. Do you know if he is insured?

Lucy. Some say he is, but not to the full amount.

Cutlet. Not to the full amount?—how shocking! He killed more meat than any of the trade between here and Carnaley Market; and the poor babes,—four of them, you say,—what a melting sight! He served some good customers about Marybone— I always think more of the children, in these cases, than of the fathers and mothers— Lady Lovebrown liked his veal better than any man's in the market— I wonder whether her ladyship is engaged— I must go and comfort poor Cleaver, however. [*Exit.*

Lucy. Now is this pretender to humanity gone to avail himself of a neighbor's supposed ruin to inveigle his customers from him. Fine feelings!—pshaw! [*Exit.*

Re-enter CUTLET.

Cutlet. What a deceitful young hussy! there is not a word of truth in her. There has been no fire. How can people play with one's feelings so? (*Sings:*)—

"For tenderness formed"—

No: I'll try the air I made upon myself. The words may compose me. (*Sings:*) —

A weeping Londoner I am:
A washer-woman was my dam;
She bred me up in a cock-loft,
And fed my mind with sorrows soft.

For when she wrung, with elbows stout,
From linen wet the water out,
The drops so like the tears did drip,
They gave my infant nerves the hyp.

Scarce three clean muckingers a week
Would dry the brine that dewed my cheek:
So, while I gave my sorrow scope,
I almost ruined her in soap.

My parish learning I did win
In ward of Farrington-Within;
Where, after school, I did pursue
My sports, as little boys will do.

Cockchafers — none like me was found
To set them spinning round and round.
Oh, how my tender heart would melt
To think what those poor varmin felt!

I never tied tin-kettle, clog,
Or salt-box, at the tail of dog,
Without a pang more keen at heart
Than he felt at his outward part.

And when the poor thing clattered off,
To all the unfeeling mob a scoff,
Thought I, "What that dumb creature feels,
With half the parish at his heels!"

Arrived, you see, to man's estate,
The butcher's calling is my fate;
Yet still I keep my feeling ways,
And leave the town on slaughtering-days.

At Kentish Town, or Highgate Hill,
I sit, retired, beside some rill;
And tears bedew my glistening eye,
To think my playful lambs must die.

But, when they're dead, I sell their meat
On shambles kept both clean and neat:
Sweetbreads also I guard full well,
And keep them from the blue-bottle.

Envy, with breath sharp as my steel,
Has ne'er yet blown upon my veal;
And mouths of dames, and daintiests fops,
Do water at my nice lamb-chops.

[*Exit, half laughing, half crying.*

SCENE. — *A Street.* DAVENPORT, *solus.*

Dav. Thus far have I secured my charming prize. I can appreciate, while I lament, the delicacy which makes her refuse the protection of my sister's roof. But who comes here?

Enter PENDULOUS, *agitated.*

It must be. That fretful animal-motion, — that face working up and down with uneasy sensibility, like new yeast, — Jack — Jack Pendulous!

Pen. It is your old friend, and very miserable.

Dav. Vapors, Jack. I have not known you fifteen years to have to guess at your complaint. Why, they troubled you at school. Do you remember when you had to speak the speech of Buckingham, when he is going to execution?

Pen. Execution!—he has certainly heard it. (*Aside.*)

Dav. What a pucker you were in over-night!

Pen. May be so, may be so, Mr. Davenport. That was an imaginary scene. I have had real troubles since.

Dav. Pshaw! so you call every common accident.

Pen. Do you call my case so common, then?

Dav. What case?

Pen. You have not heard, then?

Dav. Positively, not a word.

Pen. You must know I have been — (*whispers*) — tried for a felony since then.

Dav. Nonsense!

Pen. No subject for mirth, Mr. Davenport. A confounded short-sighted fellow swore that I stopped him and robbed him on the York race-ground, at nine on a fine moonlight evening, when I was two hundred miles off in Dorsetshire. These hands have been held up at a common bar.

Dav. Ridiculous!—it could not have gone so far.

Pen. A great deal farther, I assure you, Mr. Davenport. I am ashamed to say how far it went. You must know, that, in the first shock and surprise of the accusation, shame—you know I was always susceptible—shame put me upon disguising my *name*, that, at all events, it might bring no disgrace upon my family. I called myself *James Thompson*.

Dav. For Heaven's sake, compose yourself.

Pen. I will. An old family ours, Mr. Davenport,—never had a blot upon it till now,—a family famous for the jealousy of its honor for many generations,—think of that, Mr. Davenport,—that felt a stain like a wound—

Dav. Be calm, my dear friend.

Pen. This served the purpose of a temporary concealment well enough; but, when it came to the—*alibi*, I think they call it,—excuse these technical terms, they are hardly fit for the mouth of a gentleman,—the *witnesses*—that is another term—that I had sent for up from Melcombe Regis, and relied upon for clearing up my character, by disclosing my real name, *John Pendulous*, so discredited the cause which they came to serve, that it had quite a contrary effect to what was intended. In short, the usual forms passed, and you behold me here, the miserablest of mankind.

Dav. (*aside*). He must be light-headed.

Pen. Not at all, Mr. Davenport. I hear what you say; though you speak it all on one side, as they do at the play-house.

Dav. The sentence could never have been carried into—pshaw!—you are joking: the truth must have come out at last.

Pen. So it did, Mr. Davenport,—just two minutes and a second too late, by the sheriff's stop-watch. Time enough to save my life,—my wretched life,—but an age too late for my honor. Pray, change the subject: the detail must be as offensive to you.

Dav. With all my heart, to a more pleasing theme. The lively Maria Flyn—are you friends in that quarter still? Have the old folks relented?

Pen. They are dead, and have left her mistress of her inclinations. But it requires great strength of mind to—

Dav. To what?

Pen. To stand up against the sneers of the world. It is not every young lady that feels herself confident against the shafts of ridicule, though aimed by the hand of prejudice. Not but in her heart, I believe, she prefers me to all mankind. But think, what would the world say, if, in defiance of the opinions of all mankind, she should take to her arms a—reprieved man!

Dav. Whims! You might turn the laugh of the world upon itself in a fortnight. These things are but nine-days' wonders.

Pen. Do you think so, Mr. Davenport?

Dav. Where does she live?

Pen. She has lodgings in the next street, in a sort of garden-house, that belongs to one Cutlet. I have not seen her since the affair. I was going there at her request.

Dav. Ha, ha, ha!

Pen. Why do you laugh?

Dav. The oddest fellow! I will tell you— But here he comes.

Enter CUTLET.

Cutlet (*to Davenport*). Sir, the young lady at my house is desirous you should return immediately. She has heard something from home.

Pen. What do I hear?

Dav. 'Tis her fears, I dare say. My dear Pendulous, you will excuse me— I must not tell him our situation at present, though it cost him a fit of jealousy. We shall have fifty opportunities for explanation. [*Exit.*

Pen. Does that gentleman visit the lady at your lodgings?

Cutlet. He is quite familiar there, I assure you. He is all in all with her, as they say.

Pen. It is but too plain. Fool that I have been, not to suspect, that, while she pretended scruples, some rival was at the root of her infidelity!

Cutlet. You seem distressed, sir. Bless me!

Pen. I am, friend, above the reach of comfort.

Cutlet. Consolation, then, can be to no purpose?

Pen. None.

Cutlet. I am so happy to have met with him!

Pen. Wretch, wretch, wretch!

Cutlet. There he goes! How he walks about, biting his nails! I would not exchange this luxury of unavailing pity for worlds.

Pen. Stigmatized by the world—

Cutlet. My case exactly. Let us compare notes.

Pen. For an accident which—

Cutlet. For a profession which—

Pen. In the eye of reason, has nothing in it —

Cutlet. Absolutely nothing in it —

Pen. Brought up at a public bar —

Cutlet. Brought up to an odious trade —

Pen. With nerves like mine —

Cutlet. With nerves like mine—

Pen. Arraigned, condemned—

Cutlet. By a foolish world—

Pen. By a judge and jury—

Cutlet. By an invidious exclusion, disqualified for sitting upon a jury at all—

Pen. Tried, cast, and—

Cutlet. What?

Pen. HANGED, sir; HANGED by the neck, till I was—

Cutlet. Bless me!

Pen. Why should not I publish it to the whole world, since she, whose prejudice alone I wished to overcome, deserts me?

Cutlet. Lord have mercy upon us! Not so bad as that comes to, I hope?

Pen. When she joins in the judgment of an illiberal world against me—

Cutlet. You said HANGED, sir; that is, I mean — perhaps I mistook you. How ghostly he looks!

Pen. Fear me not, my friend: I am no ghost though I heartily wish I were one.

Cutlet. Why, then, ten to one you were—

Pen. *Cut down.* The odious words shall out, though it choke me.

Cutlet. Your case must have some things in it very curious. I dare say, you kept a journal of your sensations!

Pen. Sensations!

Cutlet. Ay: while you were being—you know what I mean. They say, persons in your situation have lights dancing before their eyes,—bluish. But, then, the worst of all is coming to one's self again.

Pen. Plagues, furies, tormentors! I shall go mad!

[*Exit.*

Cutlet. There, he says he shall go mad! Well, my head has not been very right of late: it goes with a whirl and a buzz, somehow. I believe I must not think so deeply. Common people, that don't reason, know nothing of these aberrations.

> "Great wits go mad, and small ones only dull;
> Distracting cares vex not the empty skull:
> They seize on heads that think, and hearts that feel,
> As flies attack the—better sort of veal."

ACT II.

SCENE *at* FLINT'S. FLINT. WILLIAM.

Flint. I have over-walked myself, and am quite exhausted. Tell Marian to come and play to me.

William. I shall, sir.

Flint. I have been troubled with an evil spirit of late; I think, an evil spirit. It goes and comes, as my daughter is with or from me. It cannot stand before her gentle look, when, to please her father, she takes down her music-book.

Enter WILLIAM.

William. Miss Marian went out soon after you, and is not returned.

Flint. That is a pity, — that is a pity! Where can the foolish girl be gadding?

William. The shopmen say she went out with Mr. Davenport.

Flint. Davenport? Impossible!

William. They say, they are sure it was he, by the same token that they saw her slip into his hand, when she was past the door, the casket which you gave her.

Flint. Gave her, William? I only intrusted it to her. She has robbed me! Marian is a thief! You must go to the justice, William, and get out a warrant against her immediately. Do you help them in the description. Put in "Marian Flint," in plain words, — no remonstrances, William, — "daughter of Reuben Flint," — no remonstrances; but do it —

William. Nay, sir —

Flint. I am rock, absolute rock, to all that you can say, — a piece of solid rock. What is it that makes my legs to fail, and my whole frame to totter, thus? It has been my over-walking. I am very faint: support me in, William. [*Exeunt.*

SCENE.—*The Apartment of* MISS FLYN.

MISS FLYN. BETTY.

Miss F. 'Tis past eleven. Every minute, I expect Mr. Pendulous here. What a meeting do I anticipate!

Betty. Anticipate, truly! what other than a joyful meeting can it be between two agreed lovers, who have been parted for these four months?

Miss F. But, in that cruel space, what accidents have happened! — (*aside*) — As yet, I perceive she is ignorant of this unfortunate affair.

Betty. Lord, madam! what accidents? He has not had a fall or a tumble, has he? He is not coming upon crutches?

Miss F. Not exactly a fall — (*aside*) — I wish I had courage to admit her to my confidence.

Betty. If his neck is whole, his heart is so too, I warrant it.

Miss F. His neck! — (*aside*) — She certainly mistrusts something. He writes me word that this must be his last interview.

Betty. Then I guess the whole business. The wretch is unfaithful. Some creature or other has got him into a noose.

Miss F. A noose!

Betty. And I shall never more see him hang —

Miss F. Hang! did you say, Betty?

Betty. About that dear, fond neck, I was going to add, madam; but you interrupted me.

Miss F. I can no longer labor with a secret which oppresses me thus. Can you be trusty?

Betty. Who? I, madam? — (*aside*) — Lord! I am so glad! Now I shall know all!

Miss F. This letter discloses the reasons of his unaccountable long absence from me. Peruse it, and say if we have not reason to be unhappy.

[BETTY *retires to the window to read the letter.* MR. PENDULOUS *enters.*

Miss F. My dear Pendulous!

Pen. Maria! — Nay, shun the embrace of a disgraced man, who comes but to tell you that you must renounce his society for ever.

Miss F. Nay, Pendulous, avoid me not.

Pen. (*aside*). That was tender. I may be mistaken. Whilst I stood on honorable terms, Maria might have met my caresses without a blush.

[BETTY, *who has not attended to the entrance of* PENDULOUS, *through her eagerness to read the letter, comes forward.*

Betty. Ha, ha, ha! What a funny story, madam! And is this all you make such a fuss about? I would not care if twenty of my lovers had been — (*seeing* PENDULOUS) — Lord! sir, I ask pardon.

Pen. Are we not alone, then?

Miss F. 'Tis only Betty, my old servant. You remember Betty?

Pen. What letter is that?

Miss F. Oh! something from her sweetheart, I suppose.

Betty. Yes, ma'am; that is all. I shall die of laughing.

Pen. You have not surely been showing her —

Miss F. I must be ingenuous. You must know, then, that I was just giving Betty a hint, as you came in.

Pen. A hint!

Miss F. Yes, of our unfortunate embarrassment.

Pen. My letter!

Miss F. I thought it as well that she should know it at first.

Pen. 'Tis mighty well, madam! — 'tis as it should be. I was ordained to be a wretched laughing-stock to all the world; and it is fit that our drabs and our servant wenches should have their share of the amusement.

Betty. Marry, come up! Drabs and servant wenches! and this from a person in his circumstances!

[BETTY *flings herself out of the room, muttering.*

Miss F. I understand not this language. I was prepared to give my Pendulous a tender meeting; to assure him, that, however in the eyes of the superficial and the censorious he may have incurred a partial degradation, in the esteem of one, at least, he stood as high as ever; that it was not in the power of a ridiculous *accident* — involving no guilt, no shadow of imputation — to separate two hearts cemented by holiest vows, as ours have been. This untimely repulse to my affections may awaken scruples in me, which hitherto, in tenderness to you, I have suppressed.

Pen. I very well understand what you call tenderness, madam; but, in some situations, pity — pity — is the greatest insult.

Miss F. I can endure no longer. When you are in a calmer mood, you will be sorry that you have wrung my heart so. [*Exit.*

Pen. Maria! She is gone — in tears; yet, it seems, she has had her scruples. She said she had tried to smother them. Her maid Betty intimated as much.

Re-enter BETTY.

Pen. Never mind Betty, sir: depend upon it, she will never peach.

Pen. Peach!

Betty. Lord, sir, these scruples will blow over. Go to her again when she is in a better humor. You know, we must stand off a little at first, to save appearances.

Pen. Appearances! *we!*

Betty. It will be decent to let some time elapse.

Pen. Time elapse! —

"Lost, wretched Pendulous! to scorn betrayed, —
The scoff alike of mistress and of maid!

What now remains for thee, forsaken man,
But to complete thy fate's abortive plan,
And finish what the feeble law began?" [*Exeunt.*

Re-enter Miss FLYN, *with* MARIAN.

Miss F. Now both our lovers are gone, I hope my friend will have less reserve. You must consider this apartment as yours while you stay here. 'Tis larger and more commodious than your own.

Marian. You are kind, Maria. My sad story I have troubled you with. I have some jewels here, which I unintentionally brought away. I have only to beg you will take the trouble to restore them to my father; and, without disclosing my present situation, to tell him that my next step — with or without the concurrence of Mr. Davenport — shall be to throw myself at his feet to be forgiven. I dare not see him till you have explored the way for me. I am convinced, I was tricked into this elopement.

Miss F. Your commands shall be obeyed implicitly.

Marian. You are good. (*Agitated.*)

Miss F. Moderate your apprehensions, my sweet friend. I, too, have known my sorrows — (*smiling*) — You have heard of the ridiculous affair?

Marian. Between Mr. Pendulous and you? Davenport informed me of it; and we both took the liberty of blaming the over-niceness of your scruples.

Miss F. You mistake me. The refinement is entirely on the part of my lover. He thinks me not nice enough. I am obliged to feign a little reluctance, that he may not take quite a distaste to me. Will you believe it, that he turns my very constancy into a reproach; and declares, that a woman must be devoid of all delicacy, that, after a thing of that sort, could endure the sight of her husband in —

Marian. In what?

Miss F. The sight of a man at all in —

Marian. I comprehend you not.

Miss F. In — in a — (*whispers*) — night-cap, my dear; and now the mischief is out.

Marian. Is there no way to cure him?

Miss F. None; unless I were to try the experiment, by placing myself in the hands of justice for a little while, how far an equality in misfortune might breed a sympathy in sentiment. Our reputations would be both upon a level then, you know. What think you of a little innocent shop-lifting, in sport?

Marian. And, by that contrivance, to be taken before a magistrate? The project sounds oddly.

Miss F. And yet I am more than half-persuaded it is feasible.

Enter BETTY.

Betty. Mr. Davenport is below, ma'am, and desires to speak with you.

Marian. You will excuse me. (*Going — turning back.*) You will remember the casket? [*Exit.*

Miss F. Depend on me.

Betty. And a strange man desires to see you, ma'am. I do not half like his looks.

Miss F. Show him in.

[*Exit* BETTY, *and returns with a police-officer.* BETTY *goes out.*

Officer. Your servant, ma'am. Your name is —

Miss F. Flyn, sir. Your business with me?

Officer (*alternately surveying the lady and his paper of instructions*). Marian Flint?

Miss F. Maria Flyn.

Officer. Ay, ay: Flyn or Flint. 'Tis all one. Some write plain Mary, and some put Ann after it. I come about a casket.

Miss F. I guess the whole business. He takes me for my friend. Something may come out of this. I will humor him.

Officer (*aside*). Answers to the description to a tittle. "Soft, gray eyes; pale complexion"—

Miss F. Yet I have been told by flatterers that my eyes were blue — (*takes out a pocket-glass*). I hope I look pretty tolerably to-day.

Officer. "Blue!" — they are a sort of bluish-gray, now I look better; and as for color, that comes and goes. Blushing is often a sign of a hardened offender. Do you know any thing of a casket?

Miss F. Here is one which a friend has just delivered to my keeping.

Officer. And which I must beg leave to secure, together with your ladyship's person. "Garnets, pearls, diamond-bracelet," — here they are, sure enough.

Miss F. Indeed I am innocent.

Officer. Every man is presumed so till he is found otherwise.

Miss F. Police wit! Have you a warrant?

Officer. Tolerably cool, that. Here it is, signed by Justice Golding, at the requisition of Reuben Flint, who deposes that you have robbed him.

Miss F. How lucky this turns out! — (*aside*) — Can I be indulged with a coach.

Officer. To Marlborough Street? certainly — an old offender — (*aside*) — The thing shall be conducted with as much delicacy as is consistent with security.

Miss F. Police manners! I will trust myself to your protection, then. [*Exeunt.*

SCENE. — *Police-office.*

JUSTICE, FLINT, OFFICERS, &c.

Justice. Before we proceed to extremities, Mr. Flint, let me entreat you to consider the consequences. What will the world say to your exposing your own child?

Flint. The world is not my friend. I belong to a profession which has long brought me acquainted with its injustice. I return scorn for scorn, and desire its censure above its plaudits.

Justice. But, in this case, delicacy must make you pause.

Flint. Delicacy! ha, ha! — pawnbroker! — fitly these words suit. Delicate pawnbroker! — delicate devil! — let the law take its course.

Justice. Consider, the jewels are found.

Flint. 'Tis not the silly bawbles I regard. Are you a man? are you a father? and think you I could stoop so low, vile as I stand here, as to make money — filthy money — of the stuff which a daughter's touch has desecrated? Deep in some pit first I would bury them.

Justice. Yet pause a little. Consider. An only child.

Flint. Only, only! — there, it is that stings me, — makes me mad. She was the only thing I had to love me, — to bear me up against the nipping injuries of the world. I prate when I should act. Bring in your prisoner.

[*The* JUSTICE *makes a sign to the* OFFICER, *who goes out, and returns with* Miss FLYN.

Flint. What a mockery of my sight is here! This is no daughter.

Officer. Daughter or no daughter, she has confessed to this casket.

Flint (*handling it*). The very same. Was it in the power of these pale splendors to dazzle the sight of honesty, — to put out the regardful eye of piety and daughter-love? Why, a poor glow-worm shows more brightly. Bear witness how I valued them! — (*tramples on them.*) — Fair lady, know you aught of my child?

Miss F. I shall here answer no questions.

Justice. You must explain how you came by these jewels, madam.

Miss F. (*aside*). Now, confidence, assist me! A gentleman in the neighborhood will answer for me.

Justice. His name?

Miss F. Pendulous.

Justice. That lives in the next street?

Miss F. The same. Now I have him, sure.

Justice. Let him be sent for: I believe the gentleman to be respectable, and will accept his security.

Flint. Why do I waste my time where I have no business? None,—I have none any more in the world, — none.

Enter PENDULOUS.

Pen. What is the meaning of this extraordinary summons? — Maria here!

Flint. Know you any thing of my daughter, sir?

Pen. Sir, I neither know her nor yourself, nor why I am brought hither; but for this lady, if you have any thing against her, I will answer with my life and fortune.

Justice. Make out the bail-bond.

Officer (*surveying Pendulous*). Please your worship,

before you take that gentleman's bond, may I have leave to put in a word?

Pen. (*agitated*). I guess what is coming.

Officer. I have seen that gentleman hold up his hand at a crimnal bar.

Justice. Ha!

Miss F. (*aside*). Better and better.

Officer. My eyes cannot deceive me. His lips quivered about, while he was being tried, just as they do now. His name is not Pendulous.

Miss F. Excellent!

Officer. He pleaded to the name of Thompson at York Assizes.

Jlustice. Can this be true?

Miss F. I could kiss the fellow!

Officer. He was had up for a foot-pad.

Miss F. A dainty fellow!

Pen. My iniquitous fate pursues me everywhere.

Justice. You confess, then?

Pen. I am steeped in infamy.

Miss F. I am as deep in the mire as yourself.

Pen. My reproach can never be washed out.

Miss F. Nor mine.

Pen. I am doomed to everlasting shame.

Miss F. We are both in a predicament.

Justice. I am in a maze where all this will end.

Enter MARIAN *and* DAVENPORT.

Marian (*kneeling*). My dear father!

Flint. Do I dream?

Marian. I am your Marian.

Justice. Wonders thicken.

Flint. The casket —

Miss F. Let me clear up the rest.

Flint. The casket —

Miss F. Was inadvertently in your daughter's hand, when, by an artifice of her maid Lucy, set on, as she confesses, by this gentleman here —

Dav. I plead guilty.

Miss F. She was persuaded that you were, in a hurry, going to marry her to an object of her dislike; nay, that he was actually in the house for the purpose. The speed of her flight admitted not of her depositing the jewels; but to me, who have been her inseparable companion since she quitted your roof, she intrusted the return of them, which the precipitate measures of this gentleman (*pointing to the officer*) alone prevented. Mr. Cutlet, whom I see coming, can witness this to be true.

Enter CUTLET, *in haste.*

Cutlet. Ay, poor lamb! poor lamb! I can witness. I have run in such a haste, hearing how affairs stood, that I have left my shambles without a protector. If your worship had seen how she cried (*pointing to Marian*) and trembled, and insisted upon being brought to her father! Mr. Davenport here could not stay her.

Flint. I can forbear no longer. Marian, will you play once again, to please your old father?

Marian. I have a good mind to make you buy me a new grand piano for your naughty suspicions of me.

Dav. What is to become of me?

Flint. I will do more than that: the poor lady shall have her jewels again.

Marian. Shall she?

Flint. Upon reasonable terms (*smiling*). And now, I suppose, the court may adjourn.

Dav. Marian!

Flint. I guess what is passing in your mind, Mr. Davenport: but you have behaved, upon the whole, so like a man of honor, that it will give me pleasure, if you will visit at my house for the future; but — (*smiling*) — not clandestinely, Marian.

Marian. Hush, father!

Flint. I own I had prejudices against gentry; but I have met with so much candor and kindness among my betters this day, — from this gentleman in particular (*turning to the* JUSTICE), — that I begin to think of leaving off business, and setting up for a gentleman myself.

Justice. You have the feelings of one.

Flint. Marian will not object to it.

Justice. But — (*turning to* Miss FLYN) — what motive could induce this lady to take so much disgrace upon herself, when a word's explanation might have relieved her?

Miss F. This gentleman — (*turning to* PENDULOUS) — can explain.

Pen. The devil!

Miss F. This gentleman, I repeat it, whose backwardness in concluding a long and honorable suit, from a mistaken delicacy —

Pen. How?

Miss F. Drove me upon the expedient of involving myself in the same disagreeable embarrassments with himself, in the hope that a more perfect sympathy might subsist between us for the future.

Pen. I see it, — I see it all!

Justice (*to* PENDULOUS). You were then tried at York?

Pen. I was — CAST —

Justice. Condemned.

Pen. EXECUTED.

Justice. How!

Pen. CUT DOWN, and CAME TO LIFE AGAIN! False delicacy, adieu! The true sort — which this lady has manifested, by an expedient, which, at first sight, might seem a little unpromising — has cured me of the other. We are now on even terms.

Miss F. And may —

Pen. Marry, — I know it was your word.

Miss F. And make a very quiet —

Pen. Exemplary —

Miss F. Agreeing pair of —

Pen. ACQUITTED FELONS.

Flint. And let the prejudiced against our profession acknowledge that a money-lender may have the heart of a father; and that, in the casket whose loss grieved him so sorely, he valued nothing so dear as — (*turning to* MARIAN) — one poor domestic jewel.

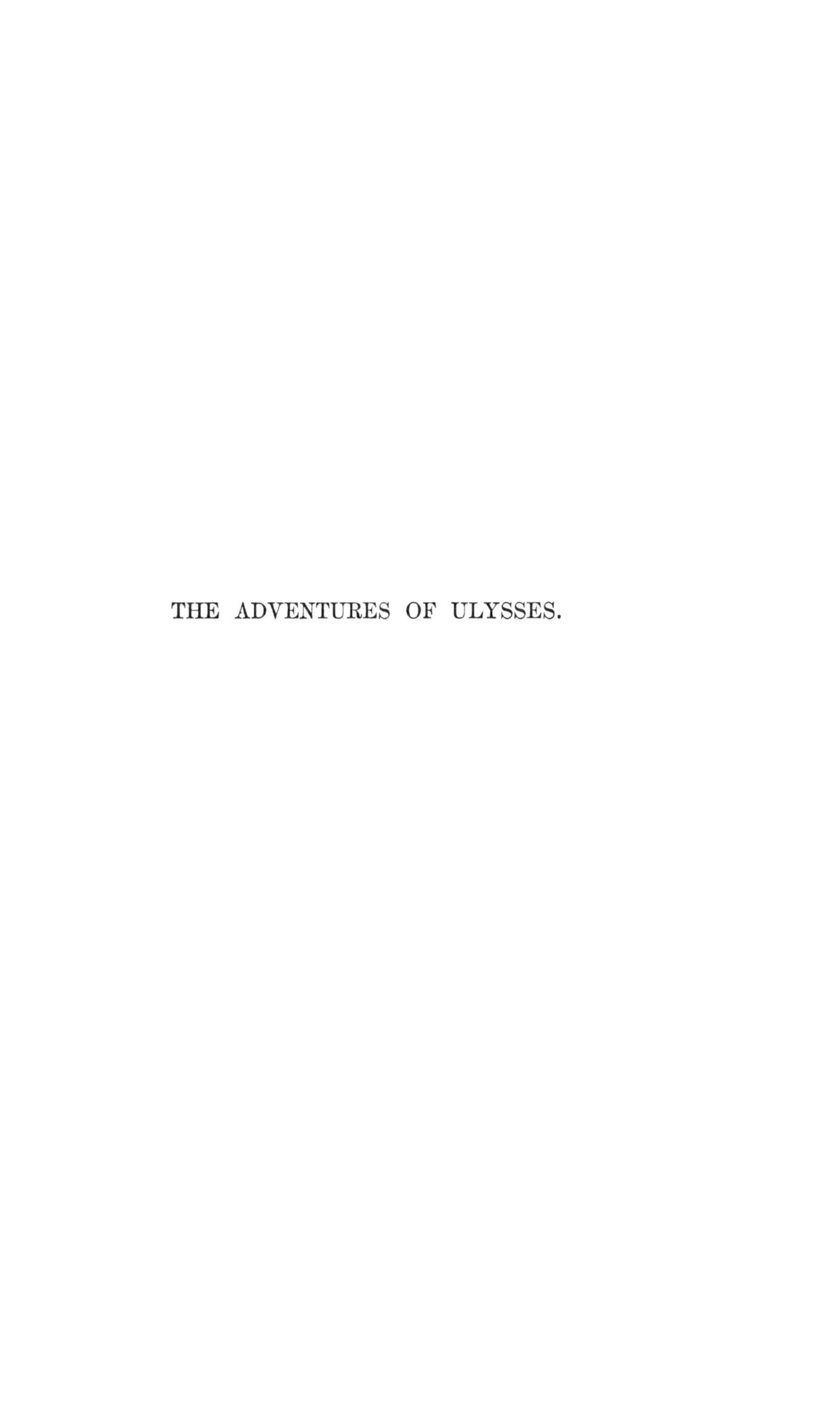

THE ADVENTURES OF ULYSSES.

"You like the 'Odyssey.' Did you ever read my 'Adventures of Ulysses,'—founded on Chapman's old translation,—for children or men? Chapman is divine; and my abridgment has not quite emptied him of his divinity."—LAMB, *in a letter to Bernard Barton.*

PREFACE

TO

THE ADVENTURES OF ULYSSES.

THIS work is designed as a supplement to the "Adventures of Telemachus." It treats of the conduct and sufferings of Ulysses, the father of Telemachus. The picture which it exhibits is that of a brave man struggling with adversity; by a wise use of events, and with an inimitable presence of mind under difficulties, forcing out a way for himself through the severest trials to which human life can be exposed; with enemies, natural and preternatural, surrounding him on all sides. The agents in this tale, besides men and women, are giants, enchanters, sirens, — things which denote external force or internal temptations; the twofold danger which a wise fortitude must expect to encounter in its course through this world. The fictions contained in it will be found to comprehend some of the most admired inventions of Grecian mythology.

The groundwork of the story is as old as the "Odyssey;" but the moral and the coloring are comparatively modern. By avoiding the prolixity which marks the speeches and the descriptions in Homer, I have gained a rapidity to the narration, which I hope will make it more attractive, and give it more the air of a romance, to young readers; though I am sensible, that, by the curtailment, I have sacrificed in many places the manners to the passion, the subordinate characteristics to the essential interest of the story. The attempt is not to be considered as seeking a comparison with any of the direct translations of the "Odyssey," either in prose or verse; though, if I were to state the obligations which I have had to one obsolete version,* I should run the hazard of depriving myself of the very slender degree of reputation which I could hope to acquire from a trifle like the present undertaking.

* The translation of Homer, by Chapman, in the reign of James I.

THE

ADVENTURES OF ULYSSES.

CHAPTER I.

THE CICONS.—THE FRUIT OF THE LOTOS-TREE.—POLYPHEMUS AND THE CYCLOPS.—THE KINGDOM OF THE WINDS, AND GOD ÆOLUS' FATAL PRESENT.—THE LÆSTRYGONIAN MAN-EATERS

THIS history tells of the wanderings of Ulysses and his followers in their return from Troy, after the destruction of that famous city of Asia by the Grecians. He was inflamed with a desire of seeing again, after a ten-years' absence, his wife and native country Ithaca. He was king of a barren spot, and a poor country in comparison of the fruitful plains of Asia, which he was leaving, or the wealthy kingdoms which he touched upon in his return; yet, wherever he came, he could never see a soil which appeared in his eyes half so sweet or desirable as his country earth. This made him refuse the offers of the goddess Calypso to stay with her, and partake of her immortality in the delightful island; and this gave him strength to break from the enchantments of Circe, the daughter of the Sun.

From Troy, ill winds cast Ulysses and his fleet upon the coast of the Cicons, a people hostile to the Grecians. Landing his forces, he laid siege to their chief city,

Ismarus, which he took, and with it much spoil, and slew many people. But success proved fatal to him; for his soldiers, elated with the spoil, and the good store of provisions which they found in that place, fell to eating and drinking, forgetful of their safety, till the Cicons, who inhabited the coast, had time to assemble their friends and allies from the interior; who, mustering in prodigious force, set upon the Grecians while they negligently revelled and feasted, and slew many of them, and recovered the spoil. They, dispirited and thinned in their numbers, with difficulty made their retreat good to the ships.

Thence they set sail, sad at heart, yet something cheered, that, with such fearful odds against them, they had not all been utterly destroyed. A dreadful tempest ensued, which for two nights and two days tossed them about; but, the third day, the weather cleared, and they had hopes of a favorable gale to carry them to Ithaca; but, as they doubled the Cape of Malea, suddenly a north wind arising drove them back as far as Cythera. After that, for the space of nine days, contrary winds continued to drive them in an opposite direction to the point to which they were bound; and the tenth day they put in at a shore where a race of men dwell that are sustained by the fruit of the lotos-tree. Here Ulysses sent some of his men to land for fresh water, who were met by certain of the inhabitants, that gave them some of their country food to eat, not with any ill intention towards them, though in the event it proved pernicious; for, having eaten of this fruit, so pleasant it proved to their appetite, that they in a minute quite forgot all thoughts of home or of their countrymen, or of ever returning back to the ships to give an account of what sort of inhabitants dwelt there, but they would needs stay and live there among them, and eat of that precious food for ever; and when Ulysses sent other of his men to look for them, and to bring them back by force, they strove and wept, and would not leave their food for heaven itself, so much the pleasure of that enchanting fruit had bewitched them. But Ulysses caused them to be bound hand and foot, and cast under the hatches; and set sail with all possible speed from that baneful coast, lest others after them might taste the lotos, which had such strange qualities to make men forget their native country and the thoughts of home.

Coasting on all that night by unknown and out-of-the-way shores, they came by daybreak to the land where the Cyclops dwell; a sort of giant shepherds, that neither sow nor plough, but the earth untilled produces for them rich wheat and barley and grapes: yet they have neither bread nor wine, nor know the arts of cultivation, nor care to know them; for they live each man to himself, without laws or government, or any thing like a state or kingdom; but their dwellings are in caves, on the steep heads of mountains, every man's household governed by his own caprice, or not governed at all, their wives and children as lawless as themselves; none caring for others, but each doing as he or she thinks good. Ships or boats they have none, nor artificers to make them; no trade or commerce, or wish to visit other shores: yet they have convenient places for harbors and for shipping. Here Ulysses, with a chosen party of twelve followers, landed, to explore what sort of men dwelt there, — whether hospitable and friendly to strangers, or altogether wild and savage; for, as yet, no dwellers appeared in sight.

The first sign of habitation which they came to was a giant's cave, rudely fashioned, but of a size which betokened the vast proportions of its owner; the pillars which supported it being the bodies of huge oaks or pines, in the natural state of the tree; and all about showed more marks of strength than skill in whoever built it. Ulysses, entering it, admired the savage contrivances and artless structure of the place, and longed to see the tenant of so outlandish a mansion; but well conjecturing that gifts would have more avail in extracting courtesy, than strength would succeed in forcing it, from such a one as he expected to find the inhabitant, he resolved to flatter his hospitality with a present of Greek wine, of which he had store in twelve great vessels, — so strong, that no one ever drank it without an infusion of twenty parts of water to one of wine, yet the fragrance of it even then so delicious, that it would have vexed a man who smelled it to abstain from tasting it; but whoever tasted it, it was able to raise his courage to the height of heroic deeds. Taking with them a goat-skin flagon full of this precious liquor, they ventured into the recesses of the cave. Here they pleased themselves a whole day with beholding the giant's kitchen, where the flesh of sheep and goats lay strewed; his dairy, where goat-milk stood ranged in troughs and pails; his pens, where he kept his live animals; but those he had driven forth to pasture with him when he went out in the morning. While they were feasting their eyes with a sight of these curiosities, their ears were suddenly deafened with a noise like the falling of a house. It was the owner of the cave, who had been abroad all day, feeding his flock, as his custom was, in the mountains, and now drove them home in the evening from pasture. He threw down a pile of firewood, which he had been gathering against supper-time, before the mouth of the cave, which occasioned the crash they heard. The Grecians hid themselves in the remote parts of the cave at sight of the uncouth monster. It was Polyphemus, the largest and savagest of the Cyclops, who boasted himself to be the son of Neptune. He looked more like a mountain crag than a man; and to his brutal body he had a brutish mind answerable. He drove his flock, all that gave milk, to the interior of the cave, but left the rams and the he-goats without. Then, taking up a stone so massy that twenty oxen could not have drawn it, he placed it at the mouth of the cave to defend the entrance, and sat him down to milk his ewes and his goats; which done, he lastly kindled a fire, and, throwing his great eye round the cave (for the Cyclops have no more than one eye, and that placed in the midst of their forehead), by the glimmering light he discerned some of Ulysses' men.

"Ho, guests! what are you? — merchants or wandering thieves?" he bellowed out in a voice which took from them all power of reply, it was so astounding.

Only Ulysses summoned resolution to answer, that they came neither for plunder nor traffic, but were Grecians, who had lost their way, returning from Troy; which famous city, under the conduct of Agamemnon, the renowned son of Atreus, they had sacked, and laid level with the ground. Yet now they prostrated themselves humbly before his feet, whom they acknowledged to be mightier than they, and besought him that he would bestow the rites of hospitality upon them; for that Jove was the avenger of wrongs done to strangers, and would fiercely resent any injury which they might suffer.

"Fool!" said the Cyclop, "to come so far to preach to me the fear of the gods. We Cyclops care not for your Jove, whom you fable to be nursed by a goat, nor any of your blessed ones. We are stronger than they, and dare bid open battle to Jove himself, though you and all your fellows of the earth join with him!" And he bade them tell him where their ship was in which they came, and whether they had any companions. But Ulysses, with a wise caution, made answer, that they had no ship or companions, but were unfortunate men, whom the sea, splitting their ship in pieces, had dashed upon his coast, and they alone had escaped. He replied nothing, but, griping two of the nearest of them as if they had been no more than children, he dashed their brains out against the earth, and, shocking to relate, tore in pieces their limbs, and devoured them, yet warm and trembling, making a lion's meal of them, lapping the blood: for the Cyclops are *man-eaters*, and esteem human flesh to be a delicacy far above goat's or kid's; though, by reason of their abhorred customs, few men approach their coast, except some stragglers, or now and then a shipwrecked mariner. At a sight so horrid, Ulysses and his men were like distracted people. He, when he had made an end of his wicked supper, drained a draught of goat's milk down his prodigious throat, and lay down and slept among his goats. Then Ulysses drew his sword, and half resolved to thrust it with all his might in at the bosom of the sleeping monster: but wiser thoughts restrained him, else they had there without help all perished; for none but Polyphemus himself could have removed that mass of stone which he had placed to guard the entrance. So they were constrained to abide all that night in fear.

When day came, the Cyclop awoke, and, kindling a fire, made his breakfast of two other of his unfortunate prisoners; then milked his goats, as he was accustomed; and pushing aside the vast stone, and shutting it again, when he had done, upon the prisoners, with as much ease as a man opens and shuts a quiver's lid, he let out his flock, and drove them before him with whistlings (as sharp as winds in storms) to the mountains.

Then Ulysses, of whose strength or cunning the Cyclop seems to have had as little heed as of an infant's, being left alone with the remnant of his men which the Cyclop had not devoured, gave manifest proof how far manly wisdom excels brutish force. He chose a stake from among the wood which the Cyclop had piled up for firing, in length and thickness like a mast, which he sharpened, and hardened in the fire; and selected four men, and instructed them what they should do with this stake, and made them perfect in their parts.

When the evening was come, the Cyclop drove home his sheep; and as fortune directed it, either of purpose, or that his memory was overruled by the gods to his hurt (as in the issue it proved), he drove the males of his flock, contrary to his custom, along with the dams into the pens. Then shutting to the stone of the cave, he fell to his horrible supper. When he had despatched two more of the Grecians, Ulysses waxed bold with the contemplation of his project, and took a bowl of Greek wine, and merrily dared the Cyclop to drink.

"Cyclop," he said, "take a bowl of wine from the hand of your guest: it may serve to digest the man's flesh that you have eaten, and show what drink our ship held before it went down. All I ask in recompense, if you find it good, is to be dismissed in a whole skin. Truly you must look to have few visitors, if you observe this new custom of eating your guests."

The brute took and drank, and vehemently enjoyed the taste of wine, which was new to him, and swilled again at the flagon, and entreated for more; and prayed Ulysses to tell him his name, that he might bestow a gift upon the man who had given him such brave liquor. The Cyclops, he said, had grapes; but this rich juice, he swore, was simply divine. Again Ulysses plied him with the wine, and the fool drank it as fast as he poured out; and again he asked the name of his benefactor, which Ulysses, cunningly dissembling, said, "My name is Noman: my kindred and friends in my own country call me Noman."—"Then," said the Cyclop, "this is the kindness I will show thee, Noman: I will eat thee last of all thy friends." He had scarce expressed his savage kindness, when the fumes of the strong wine overcame him, and he reeled down upon the floor, and sank into a dead sleep.

Ulysses watched his time while the monster lay insensible; and, heartening up his men, they placed the sharp end of the stake in the fire till it was heated red-hot; and some god gave them a courage beyond that which they were used to have, and the four men with difficulty bored the sharp end of the huge stake, which they had heated red-hot, right into the eye of the drunken cannibal; and Ulysses helped to thrust it in with all his might still further and further, with effort, as men bore with an auger, till the scalded blood gushed out, and the eyeball smoked, and the strings of the eye cracked as the burning rafter broke in it, and the eye hissed as hot iron hisses when it is plunged into water.

He, waking, roared with the pain, so loud that all the cavern broke into claps like thunder. They fled, and dispersed into corners. He plucked the burning stake from his eye, and hurled the wood madly about the cave. Then he cried out with a mighty voice for his brethren the Cyclops, that dwelt hard by in caverns upon hills. They, hearing the terrible shout, came flocking from all parts to inquire what ailed Polyphemus, and what cause he had for making such horrid clamors in the night-time to break their sleeps; if his fright proceeded from any mortal; if strength or craft had given him his death's blow. He made answer from within, that Noman had hurt him, Noman had killed him, Noman was with him in the cave. They replied, "If no man has hurt thee, and no man is with thee, then thou art alone; and the evil that afflicts thee is from the hand of Heaven, which none can resist or help." So they left him, and went their way, thinking that some disease troubled him. He, blind, and ready to split with the anguish of th pain, went groaning up and down in the dark to find the doorway; which when he found, he removed the stone, and sat in the threshold, feeling if he could lay hold on any man going out with the sheep, which (the day now breaking) were beginning to issue forth to their accustomed pastures. But Ulysses, whose first artifice in giving himself that ambiguous name had succeeded so well with the Cyclop, was not of a wit so gross to be caught by that palpable device; but, casting about in his mind all the ways which he could contrive for escape (no less than all their lives depending on the success), at last he thought of this expedient. He made knots of the osier twigs upon which the Cyclop commonly slept, with which he tied the fattest and fleeciest of the rams together, three in a rank; and under the belly of the middle ram he tied a man, and himself last; wrapping himself fast with both his hands in the rich wool of one, the fairest of the flock.

And now the sheep began to issue forth very fast: the males went first; the females, unmilked, stood by, bleating, and requiring the hand of their shepherd in vain to milk them, their full bags sore with being unemptied, but he much sorer with the loss of sight. Still, as the males passed, he felt the backs of those fleecy fools, never dreaming that they carried his enemies under their bellies. So they passed on till the last ram came loaded with his wool and Ulysses together. He stopped that ram, and felt him, and had his hand once in the hair of Ulysses, yet knew it not; and he chid the ram for being last, and spoke to it as if it understood him, and asked it whether it did not wish that its master had his eye again, which that abominable Noman with his execrable rout had put out, when they had got him down with wine; and he willed the ram to tell him whereabouts in the cave his enemy lurked, that he might dash his brains, and strew them about, to ease his heart of that tormenting revenge which rankled in it. After a deal of such foolish talk to the beast, he let it go.

When Ulysses found himself free, he let go his hold, and assisted in disengaging his friends. The rams which had befriended them they carried off with them to the ships, where their companions, with tears in their eyes, received them as men escaped from death. They plied their oars, and set their sails; and, when they were got as far off from shore as a voice could reach, Ulysses cried out to the Cyclop, "Cyclop, thou shouldst not have so much abused thy monstrous strength as to devour thy guests. Jove by my hand sends thee requital to pay thy savage inhumanity." The Cyclop heard, and came forth enraged; and in his anger he plucked a fragment of a rock, and threw it with blind fury at the ships. It narrowly escaped lighting upon the bark in which Ulysses sat; but with the fall it raised so fierce an ebb as bore back the ship till it almost touched the shore. "Cyclop," said Ulysses, "if any ask thee who imposed on thee that unsightly blemish in thine eye, say it was Ulysses, son of Laertes: the King of Ithaca am I called, the waster of cities." Then they crowded sail, and beat the old sea, and forth they went with a forward gale,—sad for fore-past losses, yet glad to have escaped at any rate, — till they came to the isle where Æolus reigned, who is god of the winds.

Here Ulysses and his men were courteously received by the monarch, who showed him his twelve children which have rule over the twelve winds. A month they staid and feasted with him; and at the end of the month he dismissed them with many presents, and gave to Ulysses at parting an ox's hide, in which were enclosed *all the winds:* only he left abroad the western wind, to play upon their sails, and waft them gently home to

Ithaca. This bag, bound in a glittering silver band so close that no breath could escape, Ulysses hung up at the mast. His companions did not know its contents, but guessed that the monarch had given to him some treasures of gold or silver.

Nine days they sailed smoothly, favored by the western wind; and by the tenth they approached so nigh as to discern lights kindled on the shores of their country earth: when, by ill fortune, Ulysses, overcome with fatigue of watching the helm, fell asleep. The mariners seized the opportunity, and one of them said to the rest, "A fine time has this leader of ours: wherever he goes, he is sure of presents, when we come away empty-handed. And see what King Æolus has given him! — store, no doubt, of gold and silver." A word was enough to those covetous wretches, who, quick as thought, untied the bag; and, instead of gold, out rushed with mighty noise *all the winds*. Ulysses with the noise awoke, and saw their mistake, but too late: for the ship was driving with all the winds back far from Ithaca, far as to the Island of Æolus from which they had parted; in one hour measuring back what in nine days they had scarcely tracked, and in sight of home too! Up he flew amazed, and, raving, doubted whether he should not fling himself into the sea for grief of his bitter disappointment. At last, he hid himself under the hatches for shame. And scarce could he be prevailed upon, when he was told he was arrived again in the harbor of King Æolus, to go himself or send to that monarch for a second succor; so much the disgrace of having misused his royal bounty (though it was the crime of his followers, and not his own) weighed upon him: and when at last he went, and took a herald with him, and came where the god sat on his throne, feasting with his children, he would not thrust in among them at their meat, but set himself down, like one unworthy, in the threshold.

Indignation seized Æolus to behold him in that manner returned; and he said, "Ulysses, what has brought you back? Are you so soon tired of your country? or did not our present please you? We thought we had given you a kingly passport." Ulysses made answer: "My men have done this ill mischief to me: they did it while I slept."—"Wretch!" said Æolus, "avaunt, and quit our shores! it fits not us to convoy men whom the gods hate, and will have perish."

Forth they sailed, but with far different hopes than when they left the same harbor the first time with all the winds confined, only the west wind suffered to play upon their sails to waft them in gentle murmurs to Ithaca. They were now the sport of every gale that blew, and despaired of ever seeing home more. Now those covetous mariners were cured of their surfeit for gold, and would not have touched it if it had lain in untold heaps before them.

Six days and nights they drove along; and on the seventh day they put into Lamos, a port of the Læstrygonians. So spacious this harbor was, that it held with ease all their fleet, which rode at anchor, safe from any storms, all but the ship in which Ulysses was embarked. He, as if prophetic of the mischance which followed, kept still without the harbor, making fast his bark to a rock at the land's point, which he climbed with purpose to survey the country. He saw a city with smoke ascending from the roofs, but neither ploughs going, nor oxen yoked, nor any sign of agricultural works. Making choice of two men, he sent them to the city to explore what sort of inhabitants dwelt there. His messengers had not gone far before they met a damsel, of stature surpassing human, who was coming to draw water from a spring. They asked her who dwelt in that land. She made no reply, but led them in silence to her father's palace. He was a monarch, and named Antiphas. He and all his people were giants. When they entered the palace, a woman, the mother of the damsel, but far taller than she, rushed abroad, and called for Antiphas. He came, and, snatching up one of the two men, made as if he would devour him. The other fled. Antiphas raised a mighty shout; and instantly, this way and that, multitudes of gigantic people issued out at the gates, and, making for the harbor, tore up huge pieces of the rocks, and flung them at the ships which lay there, — all which they utterly overwhelmed and sank; and the unfortunate bodies of men which floated, and which the sea did not devour, these cannibals thrust through with harpoons, like fishes, and bore them off to their dire feast. Ulysses, with his single bark that had never entered the harbor, escaped; that bark which was now the only vessel left of all the gallant navy that had set sail with him from Troy. He pushed off from the shore, cheering the sad remnant of his men, whom horror at the sight of their countrymen's fate had almost turned to marble.

CHAPTER II.

THE HOUSE OF CIRCE.—MEN CHANGED INTO BEASTS.—THE VOYAGE TO HELL.—THE BANQUET OF THE DEAD.

On went the single ship till it came to the Island of Ææa, where Circe, the dreadful daughter of the Sun, dwelt. She was deeply skilled in magic, a haughty beauty, and had hair like the Sun. The Sun was her parent, and begot her and her brother Ææetes (such another as herself) upon Perse, daughter to Oceanus.

Here a dispute arose among Ulysses' men, which of them should go ashore, and explore the country; for there was a necessity that some should go to procure water and provisions, their stock of both being nigh spent: but their hearts failed them when they called to mind the shocking fate of their fellows whom the Læstrygonians had eaten, and those which the foul Cyclop Polyphemus had crushed between his jaws; which moved them so tenderly in the recollection, that they wept. But tears never yet supplied any man's wants: this Ulysses knew full well; and dividing his men (all that were left) into two companies, at the head of one of which was himself, and at the head of the other Eurylochus, a man of tried courage, he cast lots which of them should go up into the country; and the lot fell upon Eurylochus and his company, two and twenty in number, who took their leave, with tears, of Ulysses and his men that staid, whose eyes wore the same wet badges of weak humanity; for they surely thought never to see these their companions again, but that, on every coast where they should come, they should find nothing but savages and cannibals.

Eurylochus and his party proceeded up the country, till in a dale they descried the house of Circe, built of bright stone, by the road's side. Before her gate lay many beasts, — as wolves, lions, leopards, — which, by her art, of wild she had rendered tame. These arose when they saw strangers, and ramped upon their hinder paws, and fawned upon Eurylochus and his men, who dreaded the effects of such monstrous kindness; and, staying at the gate, they heard the enchantress within, sitting at her loom, singing such strains as suspended all mortal faculties, while she wove a web, subtile and glorious, and of texture inimitable on earth, as all the housewiferies of the deities are. Strains so ravishingly sweet provoked even the sagest and prudentist heads among the party to knock and call at the gate. The shining gate the enchantress opened, and bade them come in and feast. They unwise followed, all but Eurylochus, who staid without the gate, suspicious that some train was laid for them. Being entered, she placed them in chairs of state, and set before them meal and honey and Smyrna wine, but mixed with baneful drugs of powerful enchantment. When they had eaten of these, and drunk of her cup, she touched them with her charming-rod, and straight they were transformed into swine, — having the bodies of swine, the bristles and snout and grunting noise of that animal; only they still retained the minds of men, which made them the more to lament their brutish transformation. Having changed them, she shut them up in her sty with many more whom her wicked sorceries had formerly changed, and gave them swine's food — mast and acorns and chestnuts — to eat.

Eurylochus, who beheld nothing of these sad changes from where he was stationed without the gate, only, instead of his companions that entered (who he thought had all vanished by witchcraft), beheld a herd of swine, hurried back to the ship to give an account of what he had seen; but so frighted and perplexed, that he could give no distinct report of any thing: only he remembered a palace, and a woman singing at her work, and gates guarded by lions. But his companions, he said, were all vanished.

Then Ulysses — suspecting some foul witchcraft — snatched his sword and his bow, and commanded Eurylochus instantly to lead him to the place; but Eurylochus fell down, and, embracing his knees, besought him, by the name of a man whom the gods had in their protection, not to expose his safety, and the safety of them all, to certain destruction.

"Do thou then stay, Eurylochus," answered Ulysses; "eat thou and drink in the ship in safety, while I go alone upon this adventure: necessity, from whose law is no appeal, compels me."

So saying, he quitted the ship, and went on shore, accompanied by none: none had the hardihood to offer to partake that perilous adventure with him, so much they dreaded the enchantments of the witch. Singly he pursued his journey till he came to the shining gates which stood before her mansion; but, when he essayed to put his foot over her threshold, he was suddenly stopped by the apparition of a young man bearing a golden rod in his hand, who was the god Mercury. He held Ulysses by the wrist, to stay his entrance; and "Whither wouldest thou go," he said, "O thou most erring of the sons of men? Knowest thou not that this is the house of great Circe, where she keeps thy friends in a loathsome sty, changed from the fair forms of men into the detestable and ugly shapes of swine? Art thou prepared to share their fate, from which nothing can ransom thee?" But neither his words, nor his coming from heaven, could stop the daring foot of Ulysses, whom compassion for the misfortune of his friends had rendered careless of danger; which when the god perceived, he had pity to see valor so misplaced, and gave him the flower of the herb *moly*, which is sovereign against enchantments. The moly is a small unsightly root, its virtues but little known, and in low estimation; the dull shepherd treads on it every day with his clouted shoes: but it bears a small white flower, which is medicinal against charms, blights, mildews, and damps. "Take this in thy hand," said Mercury, "and with it boldly enter her gates: when she shall strike thee with her rod, thinking to change thee, as she has changed thy friends, boldly rush in upon her with thy sword, and extort from her the dreadful oath of the gods, that she will use no enchantments against thee; then force her to restore thy abused companions." He gave Ulysses the little white flower; and, instructing him how to use it, vanished.

When the god was departed, Ulysses with loud knockings beat at the gate of the palace. The shining gates were opened as before, and great Circe with hospitable cheer invited in her guest. She placed him on a throne with more distinction than she had used to his fellows; she mingled wine in a costly bowl, and he drank of it, mixed with those poisonous drugs. When he had drunk, she struck him with her charming-rod, and "To your sty!" she cried. "Out, swine! mingle with your companions." But those powerful words were not proof against the preservative which Mercury had given to Ulysses: he remained unchanged, and, as the god had directed him, boldly charged the witch with his sword, as if he meant to take her life; which when she saw, and perceived that her charms were weak against the antidote which Ulysses bore about him, she cried out, and bent her knees beneath his sword, embracing his, and said, "Who or what manner of man art thou? Never drank any man before thee of this cup, but he repented it in some brute's form. Thy shape remains unaltered as thy mind. Thou canst be none other than Ulysses, renowned above all the world for wisdom, whom the Fates have long since decreed that I must love. This haughty bosom bends to thee. O Ithacan! a goddess wooes thee to her bed."

"O Circe!" he replied, "how canst thou treat of love or marriage with one whose friends thou hast turned into beasts? and now offerest him thy hand in wedlock, only that thou mightest have him in thy power, to live the life of a beast with thee, — naked, effeminate, subject to thy will, perhaps to be advanced in time to the honor of a place in thy sty. What pleasure canst thou promise which may tempt the soul of a reasonable man, — thy meats, spiced with poison; or thy wines, drugged with death? Thou must swear to me, that thou wilt never attempt against me the treasons which thou hast practised upon my friends." The enchantress, won by the terror of his threats, or by the violence of that new love which she felt kindling in her veins for him, swore by Styx, the great oath of the gods, that she meditated no injury to him. Then Ulysses made show of gentler treatment, which gave her hopes of inspiring him with a passion equal to that which she felt. She called her handmaids, four that served her in chief, — who were daughters to her silver fountains, to her sacred rivers, and to her consecrated woods, — to deck her apartments, to spread rich carpets, and set out her silver tables with dishes of the purest gold, and meat as precious as that which the gods eat, to entertain her guest. One brought water to wash his feet; and one brought wine to chase away, with a refreshing sweetness, the sorrows that had come of late so thick upon him, and hurt his noble mind. They strewed perfumes on his head; and, after he had bathed in a bath of the choicest aromatics, they brought him rich and costly apparel to put on. Then he was conducted to a throne of massy silver; and a regale, fit for Jove when he banquets, was placed before him. But the feast which Ulysses desired was to see his friends (the partners of his voyage) once more in the shapes of men; and the food which could give him nourishment must be taken in at his eyes. Because he missed this sight, he sat melancholy and thoughtful, and would taste of none of the rich delicacies placed before him; which when Circe noted, she easily divined the cause of his sadness, and, leaving the seat in which she sat throned, went to her sty, and let abroad his men, who came in like swine, and filled the ample hall, where Ulysses sat, with gruntings. Hardly had he time to let his sad eye run over their altered forms and brutal metamorphosis, when, with an ointment which she smeared over them, suddenly their bristles fell off, and they started up in their own shapes, men as before. They knew their leader again, and clung about him, with joy of their late restoration, and some shame for their late change; and wept so loud, blubbering out their joy in broken accents, that the palace was filled with a sound of pleasing mourning; and the witch herself, great Circe, was not unmoved at the sight. To make her atonement complete, she sent for the remnant of Ulysses' men who staid behind at the ship, giving up their great commander for lost; who when they came, and saw him again alive, circled with their fellows, no expression can tell what joy they felt: they even cried out with rapture; and, to have seen their frantic expressions of mirth, a man might have supposed that they were just in sight of their country earth, the cliffs of rocky Ithaca. Only Eurylochus would hardly be persuaded to enter that palace of wonders; for he remembered with a kind of horror how his companions had vanished from his sight.

Then great Circe spake, and gave order that there should be no more sadness among them, nor remembering of past sufferings. For as yet they fared like men that are exiles from their country; and, if a gleam of mirth shot among them, it was suddenly quenched with the thought of their helpless and homeless condition. Her kind persuasions wrought upon Ulysses and the rest, that they spent twelve months in all manner of delight with her in her palace. For Circe was a powerful magician, and could command the moon from her sphere, or unroot the solid oak from its place to make it dance for their diversion; and by the help of her illusions she could vary the taste of pleasures, and contrive delights, recreations, and jolly pastimes, — to "fetch the day about from sun to sun, and rock the tedious year as in a delightful dream."

At length, Ulysses awoke from the trance of the faculties into which her charms had thrown him; and the thought of home returned with tenfold vigor to goad and sting him, — that home where he had left his virtuous wife Penelope, and his young son Telemachus. One day, when Circe had been lavish of her caresses, and was in her kindest humor, he moved to her subtly, and as it were afar off, the question of his home-return; to which she answered firmly, "O Ulysses! it is not in my power to detain one whom the gods have destined to further trials. But leaving me, before you pursue your journey home, you must visit the house of Ades, or Death, to consult the shade of Tiresias, the Theban prophet; to whom alone, of all the dead, Proserpine, queen of hell, has committed the secret of future events: it is he that must inform you whether you shall ever see again your wife and country." — "O Circe!" he cried; "that is impossible: who shall steer my course to Pluto's kingdom? Never ship had strength to make that voyage." — "Seek no guide," she replied; "but raise you your mast, and hoist your white sails, and sit in your ship in peace: the north wind shall waft you through the seas, till you shall cross the expanse of the ocean, and come to where grow the poplar groves, and willows pale, of Proserpine; where Pyriphlegethon and Cocytus and Acheron mingle their waves. Cocytus is an arm of Styx, the forgetful river. Here dig a pit, and make it a cubit broad and a cubit long; and pour in milk and honey and wine, and the blood of a ram, and the blood of a black ewe; and turn away thy face while thou pourest in, and the dead shall come flocking to taste the milk and the blood: but suffer none to approach thy offering till thou hast inquired of Tiresias all which thou wishest to know."

He did as great Circe had appointed. He raised his mast, and hoisted his white sails, and sat in his ship in peace. The north wind wafted him through the seas, till he crossed the ocean, and came to the sacred woods of Proserpine. He stood at the confluence of the three floods, and digged a pit, as she had given directions, and poured in his offering,—the blood of a ram and the blood of a black ewe, milk and honey and wine; and the dead came to his banquet,—aged men and women and youths, and children who died in infancy. But none of them would he suffer to approach, and dip their thin lips in the offering, till Tiresias was served,—not though his own mother was among the number, whom now for the first time he knew to be dead; for he had left her living when he went to Troy; and she had died since his departure, and the tidings never reached him: though it irked his soul to use constraint upon her, yet, in compliance with the injunction of great Circe, he forced her to retire along with the other ghosts. Then Tiresias, who bore a golden sceptre, came and lapped of the offering; and immediately he knew Ulysses, and began to prophesy: *he denounced woe to Ulysses, woe, woe, and many sufferings, through the anger of Neptune for the putting-out of the eye of the sea-god's son.*

Yet there was safety after suffering, if they could abstain from slaughtering the oxen of the Sun after they landed in the Triangular Island. For Ulysses, the gods had destined him from a king to become a beggar, and to perish by his own guests, unless he slew those who knew him not.

This prophecy, ambiguously delivered, was all that Tiresias was empowered to unfold, or else there was no longer place for him; for now the souls of the other dead came flocking in such numbers, tumultuously demanding the blood, that freezing horror seized the limbs of the living Ulysses, to see so many, and all dead, and he the only one alive in that region. Now his mother came and lapped the blood, without restraint from her son: and now she knew him to be her son, and inquired of him why he had come alive to their comfortless habitations; and she said, that affliction for Ulysses' long absence had preyed upon her spirits, and brought her to the grave.

Ulysses' soul melted at her moving narration; and forgetting the state of the dead, and that the airy texture of disembodied spirits does not admit of the embraces of flesh and blood, he threw his arms about her to clasp her: the poor ghost melted from his embrace, and, looking mournfully upon him, vanished away.

Then saw he other females, — Tyro, who, when she lived, was the paramour of Neptune, and by him had Pelias and Neleus; Antiope, who bore two like sons to Jove, — Amphion and Zethus, founders of Thebes; Alcmena, the mother of Hercules, with her fair daughter, afterwards her daughter-in-law, Megara. There also Ulysses saw Jocasta, the unfortunate mother and wife of Œdipus; who, ignorant of kin, wedded with her son, and, when she had discovered the unnatural alliance, for shame and grief hanged herself. He continued to drag a wretched life above the earth, haunted by the dreadful Furies. There was Leda, the wife of Tyndarus, the mother of the beautiful Helen, and of the two brave brothers, Castor and Pollux, who obtained this grace from Jove, — that, being dead, they should enjoy life alternately, living in pleasant places under the earth. For Pollux had prayed that his brother Castor, who was subject to death, as the son of Tyndarus, should partake of his own immortality, which he derived from an immortal sire: this the Fates denied; therefore Pollux was permitted to divide his immortality with his brother Castor, dying and living alternately. There was Iphimedeia, who bore two sons to Neptune, that were giants, — Otus and Ephialtes: Earth in her prodigality never nourished bodies to such portentous size and beauty as these two children were of, except Orion. At nine years old they had imaginations of climbing to heaven to see what the gods were doing: they thought to make stairs of mountains, and were for piling Ossa upon Olympus, and setting Pelion upon that; and had perhaps performed it, if they had lived till they were striplings; but they were cut off by death in the infancy of their ambitious project. Phædra was there, and Procris and Ariadne, mournful for Theseus' desertion; and Mæra and Clymene and Eryphile, who preferred gold before wedlock faith.

But now came a mournful ghost, that late was Agamemnon, son of Atreus, the mighty leader of all the host of Greece and their confederate kings that warred against Troy. He came with the rest to sip a little of the blood at that uncomfortable banquet. Ulysses was moved with compassion to see him among them, and asked him what untimely fate had brought him there; if storms had overwhelmed him coming from Troy, or if he had perished in some mutiny by his own soldiers at a division of the prey.

"By none of these," he replied, "did I come to my death; but slain at a banquet to which I was invited by Ægisthus after my return home. He conspiring with my adulterous wife, they laid a scheme for my destruction, training me forth to a banquet as an ox goes to the slaughter; and, there surrounding me, they slew me with all my friends about me.

"Clytemnestra, my wicked wife, forgetting the vows which she swore to me in wedlock, would not lend a hand to close my eyes in death. But nothing is so heaped with impieties as such a woman, who would kill her spouse that married her a maid. When I brought her home to my house a bride, I hoped in my heart that she would be loving to me and to my children. Now her black treacheries have cast a foul aspersion on her whole sex. Blest husbands will have their loving wives in suspicion for her bad deeds."

"Alas!" said Ulysses, "there seems to be a fatality in your royal house of Atreus, and that they are hated of Jove for their wives. For Helen's sake, your brother Menelaus' wife, what multitudes fell in the wars of Troy!"

Agamemnon replied, "For this cause, be not thou more kind than wise to any woman. Let not thy words express to her at any time all that is in thy mind:

keep still some secrets to thyself. But thou by any bloody contrivances of thy wife never needst fear to fall. Exceeding wise she is, and to her wisdom she has a goodness as eminent; Icarius' daughter, Penelope the chaste: we left her a young bride when we parted from our wives to go to the wars, her first child suckling at her breast,—the young Telemachus, whom you shall see grown up to manhood on your return; and he shall greet his father with befitting welcomes. My Orestes, my dear son, I shall never see again. His mother has deprived his father of the sight of him, and perhaps will slay him as she slew his sire. It is now no world to trust a woman in.—But what says fame? is my son yet alive? lives he in Orchomen, or in Pylus? or is he resident in Sparta, in his uncle's court? As yet, I see, divine Orestes is not here with me."

To this Ulysses replied, that he had received no certain tidings where Orestes abode; only some uncertain rumors, which he could not report for truth.

While they held this sad conference, with kind tears striving to render unkind fortunes more palatable, the soul of great Achilles joined them. "What desperate adventure has brought Ulysses to these regions?" said Achilles: "to see the end of dead men, and their foolish shades?"

Ulysses answered him, that he had come to consult Tiresias respecting his voyage home. "But thou, O son of Thetis!" said he, "why dost thou disparage the state of the dead? Seeing that, as alive, thou didst surpass all men in glory, thou must needs retain thy pre eminence here below: so great Achilles triumphs over death."

But Achilles made reply, that he had much rather be a peasant-slave upon the earth, than reign over all the dead, — so much did the inactivity and slothful condition of that state displease his unquenchable and restless spirit. Only he inquired of Ulysses if his father Peleus were living, and how his son Neoptolemus conducted himself.

Of Peleus, Ulysses could tell him nothing; but of Neoptolemus he thus bore witness: "From Scyros I convoyed your son by sea to the Greeks; where I can speak of him; for I knew him. He was chief in council and in the field. When any question was proposed, so quick was his conceit in the forward apprehension of any case, that he ever spoke first, and was heard with more attention than the older heads. Only myself and aged Nestor could compare with him in giving advice. In battle I cannot speak his praise, unless I could count all that fell by his sword. I will only mention one instance of his manhood. When we sat hid in the belly of the wooden horse, in the ambush which deceived the Trojans to their destruction, I, who had the management of that stratagem, still shifted my place from side to side to note the behavior of our men. In some I marked their hearts trembling, through all the pains which they took to appear valiant; and, in others, tears, that, in spite of manly courage, would gush forth. And, to say truth, it was an adventure of high enterprise, and as perilous a stake as was ever played in war's game. But in him I could not observe the least sign of weakness; no tears nor tremblings, but his hand still on his good sword, and ever urging me to set open the machine, and let us out before the time was come for doing it: and, when we sallied out, he was still first in that fierce destruction and bloody midnight desolation of King Priam's city."

This made the soul of Achilles to tread a swifter pace, with high-raised feet, as he vanished away, for the joy which he took in his son being applauded by Ulysses.

A sad shade stalked by, which Ulysses knew to be the ghost of Ajax, his opponent, when living, in that famous dispute about the right of succeeding to the arms of the deceased Achilles. They being adjudged by the Greeks to Ulysses, as the prize of wisdom above bodily strength, the noble Ajax in despite went mad, and slew himself. The sight of his rival, turned to a shade by his dispute, so subdued the passion of emulation in Ulysses, that, for his sake, he wished that judgment in that controversy had been given against himself, rather than so illustrious a chief should have perished for the desire of those arms which his prowess (second only to Achilles in fight) so eminently had deserved. "Ajax!" he cried, "all the Greeks mourn for thee as much as they lamented for Achilles. Let not thy wrath burn for ever, great son of Telamon. Ulysses seeks peace with thee, and will make any atonement to thee that can appease thy hurt spirit." But the shade stalked on, and would not exchange a word with Ulysses, though he prayed it with many tears and many earnest entreaties. "He might have spoken to me," said Ulysses, "since I spoke to him; but I see the resentments of the dead are eternal."

Then Ulysses saw a throne, on which was placed a judge distributing sentence. He that sat on the throne was Minos, and he was dealing out just judgments to the dead. He it is that assigns them their place in bliss or woe.

Then came by a thundering ghost, — the large-limbed Orion, the mighty hunter, who was hunting there the ghosts of the beasts which he had slaughtered in desert hills upon the earth; for the dead delight in the occupations which pleased them in the time of their living upon the earth.

There was Tityus, suffering eternal pains because he had sought to violate the honor of Latona as she passed from Pytho into Panopeus. Two vultures sat perpetually preying upon his liver with their crooked beaks; which, as fast as they devoured, is for ever renewed: nor can he fray them away with his great hands.

There was Tantalus, plagued for his great sins, standing up to his chin in water, which he can never taste; but still, as he bows his head, thinking to quench his burning thirst, instead of water he licks up unsavory dust. All fruits pleasant to the sight, and of delicious flavor, hang in ripe clusters about his head, seeming as though they offered themselves to be plucked by him; but, when he reaches out his hand, some wind carries them far out of his sight into the clouds: so he is starved in the midst of plenty by the righteous doom of Jove, in memory of that inhuman banquet at which the sun turned pale, when the unnatural father served up the limbs of his little son in a dish, as meat for his divine guests.

There was Sisyphus, that sees no end to his labors. His punishment is, to be for ever rolling up a vast stone to the top of a mountain; which, when it gets to the top, falls down with a crushing weight, and all his work is to be begun again. He was bathed all over in sweat, that reeked out a smoke which covered his head like a mist. His crime had been the revealing of state secrets.

There Ulysses saw Hercules: not that Hercules who enjoys immortal life in heaven among the gods, and is married to Hebe, or Youth; but his shadow, which remains below. About him the dead flocked as thick as bats, hovering around, and cuffing at his head: he stands with his dreadful bow, ever in the act to shoot.

There also might Ulysses have seen and spoken with the shades of Theseus and Pirithous and the old heroes; but he had conversed enough with horrors: therefore, covering his face with his hands that he might see no more spectres, he resumed his seat in his ship, and pushed off. The bark moved of itself, without the help of any oar, and soon brought him out of the regions of death into the cheerful quarters of the living, and to the Island of Ææa, whence he had set forth.

CHAPTER III.

THE SONG OF THE SIRENS. — SCYLLA AND CHARYBDIS. — THE OXEN OF THE SUN. — THE JUDGMENT. — THE CREW KILLED BY LIGHTNING.

"UNHAPPY man, who at thy birth wast appointed twice to die! Others shall die once; but thou, besides that death that remains for thee, common to all men, hast in thy lifetime visited the shades of death. Thee Scylla, thee Charybdis, expect. Thee the deathful Sirens lie in wait for, that taint the minds of whoever listen to them with their sweet singing. Whosoever shall but hear the call of any Siren, he will so despise both wife and children, through their sorceries, that the stream of his affection never again shall set homewards; nor shall he take joy in wife or children thereafter, or they in him."

With these prophetic greetings great Circe met Ulysses on his return. He besought her to instruct him in the nature of the Sirens, and by what method their baneful allurements were to be resisted.

"They are sisters three," she replied, "that sit in a mead (by which your ship must needs pass) circled with dead men's bones. These are the bones of men whom they have slain, after with fawning invitements they have enticed them into their fen. Yet such is the celestial harmony of their voice accompanying the persuasive magic of their words, that, knowing this, you shall not be able to withstand their enticements. Therefore, when you are to sail by them, you shall stop the ears of your companions with wax, that they may hear no note of that dangerous music; but for yourself, that you may hear, and yet live, give them strict command to bind you hand and foot to the mast, and in no case to set you free till you are out of the danger of the temptation, though you should entreat it, and implore it ever so much, but to bind you rather the more for your requesting to be loosed. So shall you escape that snare."

Ulysses then prayed her that she would inform him what Scylla and Charybdis were, which she had taught him by name to fear. She replied, "Sailing from Ææa to Trinacria, you must pass at an equal distance between two fatal rocks. Incline never so little either to the one side or the other, and your ship must meet with certain destruction. No vessel ever yet tried that pass without being lost, but the 'Argo,' which owed her safety to the sacred freight she bore, — the fleece of the golden-backed ram, which could not perish. The biggest of these rocks which you shall come to, Scylla hath in charge. There, in a deep whirlpool at the foot of the rock, the abhorred monster shrouds her face; who if she were to show her full form, no eye of man or god could endure the sight: thence she stretches out all her six long necks, peering and diving to suck up fish, dolphins, dog-fish, and whales, whole ships and their men, — whatever comes within her raging gulf. The other rock is lesser, and of less ominous aspect; but there dreadful Charybdis sits, supping the black deeps. Thrice a day she drinks her pits dry, and thrice a day again she belches them all up: but, when she is drinking, come not nigh; for, being once caught, the force of Neptune cannot redeem you from her swallow. Better trust to Scylla; for she will but have for her six necks six men: Charybdis, in her insatiate draught, will ask all."

Then Ulysses inquired, in case he should escape Charybdis, whether he might not assail that other monster with his sword: to which she replied, that he must not think that he had an enemy subject to death or wounds to contend with; for Scylla could never die. Therefore his best safety was in flight, and to invoke none of the gods but Cratis, who is Scylla's mother, and might perhaps forbid her daughter to devour them. For his conduct after he arrived at Trinacria, she referred him to the admonitions which had been given him by Tiresias.

Ulysses having communicated her instructions, as far as related to the Sirens, to his companions, who had not been present at that interview,—but concealing from them the rest, as he had done the terrible predictions of Tiresias, that they might not be deterred by fear from pursuing their voyage, — the time for departure being come, they set their sails, and took a final leave of great Circe; who by her art calmed the heavens, and gave them smooth seas, and a right fore-wind (the seaman's friend) to bear them on their way to Ithaca.

They had not sailed past a hundred leagues, before the breeze which Circe had lent them suddenly stopped. It was stricken dead. All the sea lay in prostrate slumber. Not a gasp of air could be felt. The ship stood still. Ulysses guessed that the island of the Sirens was not far off, and that they had charmed the air so with their devilish singing. Therefore he made him cakes of wax, as Circe had instructed him, and stopped the ears of his men with them: then, causing himself to be bound hand and foot, he commanded the rowers to ply their oars, and row as fast as speed could carry them past that fatal shore. They soon came within sight of the Sirens, who sang in Ulysses' hearing, —

"Come here, thou, worthy of a world of praise,
That dost so high the Grecian glory raise, —
Ulysses! Stay thy ship, and that song hear
That none passed ever, but it bent his ear,
But left him ravished, and instructed more
By us than any ever heard before.
For we know all things, — whatsoever were
In wide Troy labored; whatsoever there

The Grecians and the Trojans both sustained
By those high issues that the gods ordained:
And whatsoever all the earth can show,
To inform a knowledge of desert, we know."

These were the words; but the celestial harmony of the voices which sang them no tongue can describe: it took the ear of Ulysses with ravishment. He would have broken his bonds to rush after them; and threatened, wept, sued, entreated, commanded, crying out with tears and passionate imprecations, conjuring his men by all the ties of perils past which they had endured in common, by fellowship and love, and the authority which he retained among them, to let him loose; but at no rate would they obey him. And still the Sirens sang. Ulysses made signs, motions, gestures, promising mountains of gold if they would set him free; but their oars only moved faster. And still the Sirens sang. And still, the more he adjured them to set him free, the faster with cords and ropes they bound him; till they were quite out of hearing of the Sirens' notes, whose effect great Circe had so truly predicted. And well she might speak of them; for often she had joined her own enchanting voice to theirs, while she has sat in the flowery meads, mingled with the Sirens and the Water Nymphs, gathering their potent herbs and drugs of magic quality. Their singing altogether has made the gods stoop, and "heaven drowsy with the harmony."

Escaped that peril, they had not sailed yet a hundred leagues further, when they heard a roar afar off, which Ulysses knew to be the barking of Scylla's dogs, which surround her waist, and bark incessantly. Coming nearer, they beheld a smoke ascend, with a horrid mur-

mur, which arose from that other whirlpool, to which they made nigher approaches than to Scylla. Through the furious eddy which is in that place, the ship stood still as a stone: for there was no man to lend his hand to an oar; the dismal roar of Scylla's dogs at a distance, and the nearer clamors of Charybdis, where every thing made an echo, quite taking from them the power of exertion. Ulysses went up and down, encouraging his men, one by one; giving them good words; telling them that they were in greater perils when they were blocked up in the Cyclop's cave; yet, Heaven assisting his counsels, he had delivered them out of that extremity. That he could not believe but they remembered it; and wished them to give the same trust to the same care which he had now for their welfare. That they must exert all the strength and wit which they had, and try if Jove would not grant them an escape, even out of this peril. In particular, he cheered up the pilot who sat at the helm, and told him that he must show more firmness than other men, as he had more trust committed to him; and had the sole management, by his skill, of the vessel in which all their safeties were embarked. That a rock lay hid within those boiling whirlpools which he saw, on the outside of which he must steer, if he would avoid his own destruction, and the destruction of them all.

They heard him, and, like men, took to the oars; but little knew what opposite danger, in shunning that rock, they must be thrown upon. For Ulysses had concealed from them the wounds, never to be healed, which Scylla was to open: their terror would else have robbed them all of all care to steer, or move an oar, and have made them hide under the hatches, for fear of seeing her, where he and they must have died an idle death. But, even then, he forgot the precautions which Circe had given him to prevent harm to his person; who had willed him not to arm, or show himself once to Scylla: but, disdaining not to venture life for his brave companions, he could not contain, but armed in all points, and taking a lance in either hand, he went up to the fore-deck, and looked when Scylla would appear.

She did not show herself as yet; and still the vessel steered closer by her rock, as it sought to shun that other more dreaded: for they saw how horribly Charybdis' black throat drew into her all the whirling deep, which she disgorged again; that all about her boiled like a kettle, and the rock roared with troubled waters; which when she supped in again, all the bottom turned up, and disclosed far under shore the swart sands naked, whose whole stern sight frayed the startled blood from their faces, and made Ulysses turn his to view the wonder of whirlpools. Which when Scylla saw from out her black den, she darted out her six long necks, and swooped up as many of his friends; whose cries Ulysses heard, and saw them too late, with their heels turned up, and their hands thrown to him for succor, who had been their help in all extremities, but could not deliver them now; and he heard them shriek out as she tore them; and, to the last, they continued to throw their hands out to him for sweet life. In all his sufferings, he never had beheld a sight so full of miseries.

Escaped from Scylla and Charybdis, but with a diminished crew, Ulysses and the sad remains of his followers reached the Trinacrian shore. Here, landing, he beheld oxen grazing, of such surpassing size and beauty, that, both from them and from the shape of the island (having three promontories jutting into the sea), he judged rightly that he was come to the Triangular Island, and the oxen of the Sun, of which Tiresias had forewarned him.

So great was his terror, lest through his own fault, or that of his men, any violence or profanation should be offered to the holy oxen, that even then, tired as they were with the perils and fatigues of the day past, and unable to stir an oar or use any exertion, and though night was fast coming on, he would have had them re-embark immediately, and make the best of their way from that dangerous station: but his men, with one voice, resolutely opposed it; and even the too-cautious Eurylochus himself withstood the proposal; so much did the temptation of a little ease and refreshment (ease tenfold sweet after such labors) prevail over the sagest counsels, and the apprehension of certain evil outweigh the prospect of contingent danger. They expostulated, that the nerves of Ulysses seemed to be made of steel, and his limbs not liable to lassitude like other men's; that waking or sleeping seemed indifferent to him; but that they were men, not gods, and felt the common appetites for food and sleep; that, in the night-time, all the winds most destructive to ships are generated; that black night still required to be served with meat and sleep, and quiet havens and ease; that the best sacrifice to the sea was in the morning. With such sailor-like sayings and mutinous arguments, which the majority have always ready to justify disobedience to their betters, they forced Ulysses to comply with their requisition, and, against his will, to take up his night-quarters on shore. But he first exacted from them an oath, that they would neither maim nor kill any of the cattle which they saw grazing, but content themselves with such food as Circe had stowed their vessel with when they parted from Ææa. This they, man by man, severally promised, imprecating the heaviest curses on whoever should break it; and, mooring their bark within a creek, they went to supper, contenting themselves that night with such food as Circe had given them, not without many sad thoughts of their friends whom Scylla had devoured, the grief of which kept them, great part of the night, waking.

In the morning, Ulysses urged them again to a religious observance of the oath that they had sworn; not in any case to attempt the blood of those fair herds which they saw grazing, but to content themselves with the ship's food; for the god who owned those cattle sees and hears all.

They faithfully obeyed, and remained in that good mind for a month; during which they were confined to that station by contrary winds, till all the wine and the bread were gone which they had brought with them. When their victuals were gone, necessity compelled them to stray in quest of whatever fish or fowl they could snare, which that coast did not yield in any great abundance. Then Ulysses prayed to all the gods that dwelt in bountiful heaven, that they would be pleased to yield them some means to stay their hunger, without having recourse to profane and forbidden violations: but the ears of heaven seemed to be shut, or some god incensed plotted his ruin; for at mid-day, when he should chiefly have been vigilant and watchful to prevent mischief, a deep sleep fell upon the eyes of Ulysses, during which he lay totally insensible of all that passed in the world, and what his friends or what his enemies might do for his welfare or destruction. Then Eurylochus took his advantage. He was the man of most authority with them after Ulysses. He represented to them all the misery of their condition: how that every death is hateful and grievous to mortality; but that, of all deaths, famine is attended with the most painful, loathsome, and humiliating circumstances; that the subsistence which they could hope to draw from fowling or fishing was too precarious to be depended upon; that there did not seem to be any chance of the winds changing to favor their escape; but that they must inevitably stay there and perish, if they let an irrational superstition deter them from the means which Nature offered to their hands; that Ulysses might be deceived in his belief that these oxen had any sacred qualities above other oxen; and even admitting that they were the property of the god of the Sun, as he said they were, the Sun did neither eat nor drink; and the gods were best served, not by a scrupulous conscience, but by a thankful heart, which took freely what they as freely offered. With these and such like persuasions, he prevailed on his half-famished and half-mutinous companions to begin the impious violation of their oath by the slaughter of seven of the fairest of these oxen which were grazing. Part they roasted and ate, and part they offered in sacrifice to the gods; particularly to Apollo, god of the Sun, vowing to build a temple to his godhead when they should arrive in Ithaca, and deck it with magnificent and numerous gifts. Vain men, and superstition worse than that which they so lately derided, to imagine that prospective penitence can excuse a present violation of duty, and that the pure natures of the heavenly powers will admit of compromise or dispensation for sin!

But to their feast they fell; dividing the roasted portions of the flesh, savory and pleasant meat to them, but a sad sight to the eyes, and a savor of death in the nostrils, of the waking Ulysses, who just woke in time to witness, but not soon enough to prevent, their rash and sacrilegious banquet. He had scarce time to ask what great mischief was this which they had done unto him, when, behold, a prodigy! The ox-hides which they had stripped began to creep as if they had life; and the roasted flesh bellowed, as the ox used to do when he was living. The hair of Ulysses stood up an end with affright at these omens; but his companions, like men whom the gods had infatuated to their destruction, persisted in their horrible banquet.

The Sun, from his burning chariot, saw how Ulysses' men had slain his oxen; and he cried to his father Jove, "Revenge me upon these impious men, who have slain my oxen, which it did me good to look upon when I walked my heavenly round. In all my daily course, I never saw such bright and beautiful creatures as those my oxen were." The father promised that ample retribution should be taken of those accursed men; which was fulfilled shortly after, when they took their leaves of the fatal island.

Six days they feasted, in spite of the signs of heaven; and on the seventh, the wind changing, they set their sails, and left the island: and their hearts were cheerful with the banquets they had held; all but the heart of

Ulysses, which sank within him, as with wet eyes he beheld his friends, and gave them for lost, as men devoted to divine vengeance. Which soon overtook them; for they had not gone many leagues before a dreadful tempest arose which burst their cables. Down came their mast, crushing the skull of the pilot in its fall: off he fell from the stern into the water; and the bark, wanting his management, drove along at the wind's mercy. Thunders roared, and terrible lightnings of Jove came down: first a bolt struck Eurylochus, then another, and then another, till all the crew were killed, and their bodies swam about like sea-mews; and the ship was split in pieces. Only Ulysses survived; and he had no hope of safety but in tying himself to the mast, where he sat riding upon the waves, like one that in no extremity would yield to fortune. Nine days was he floating about with all the motions of the sea, with no other support than the slender mast under him, till the tenth night cast him, all spent and weary with toil, upon the friendly shores of the Island Ogygia.

CHAPTER IV.

THE ISLAND OF CALYPSO. — IMMORTALITY REFUSED.

HENCEFORTH the adventures of the single Ulysses must be pursued. Of all those faithful partakers of his toil, who with him left Asia, laden with the spoils of Troy, now not one remains, but all a prey to the remorseless waves, and food for some great fish; their gallant navy reduced to one ship, and that finally swallowed up and lost. Where now are all their anxious thoughts of home? that perseverance with which they went through the severest sufferings and the hardest labors to which poor seafarers were ever exposed, that their toils at last might be crowned with the sight of their native shores and wives at Ithaca? Ulysses is now in the Isle Ogygia, called the Delightful Island. The poor shipwrecked chief, the slave of all the elements, is once again raised by the caprice of fortune into a shadow of prosperity. He that was cast naked upon the shore, bereft of all his companions, has now a goddess to attend upon him; and his companions are the nymphs which never die. Who has not heard of Calypso,—her grove crowned with alders and poplars; her grotto, against which the luxuriant vine laid forth his purple grapes; her ever-new delights, crystal fountains, running brooks, meadows flowering with sweet balm-gentle and with violet,—blue violets, which, like veins, enamelled the smooth breasts of each fragrant mead? It were useless to describe over again what has been so well told already, or to relate those soft arts of courtship which the goddess used to detain Ulysses,—the same in kind which she afterwards practised upon his less wary son, whom Minerva, in the shape of Mentor, hardly preserved from her snares, when they came to the Delightful Island together in search of the scarce departed Ulysses.

A memorable example of married love, and a worthy instance how dear to every good man his country is, was exhibited by Ulysses. If Circe loved him sincerely, Calypso loves him with tenfold more warmth and passion. She can deny him nothing but his departure.

She offers him every thing, even to a participation of her immortality: if he will stay and share in her pleasures, he shall never die. But death with glory has greater charms for a mind heroic than a life that shall never die, with shame; and, when he pledged his vows to his Penelope, he reserved no stipulation that he would forsake her whenever a goddess should think him worthy of her bed, but they had sworn to live and grow old together: and he would not survive her if he could; nor meanly share in immortality itself, from which she was excluded.

These thoughts kept him pensive and melancholy in the midst of pleasure. His heart was on the seas, making voyages to Ithaca. Twelve months had worn away, when Minerva from heaven saw her favorite; how he sat still pining on the sea-shores (his daily custom), wishing for a ship to carry him home. She (who is Wisdom herself) was indignant that so wise and brave a man as Ulysses should be held in effeminate bondage by an unworthy goddess; and, at her request, her father Jove ordered Mercury to go down to the earth to command Calypso to dismiss her guest. The divine messenger tied fast to his feet his winged shoes, which bear him over land and seas; and took in his hand his golden rod, the ensign of his authority. Then, wheeling in many an airy round, he staid not till he alighted on the firm top of the Mountain Pieria: thence he fetched a second circuit over the seas, kissing the waves in his flight with his feet, as light as any sea-mew fishing dips her wings, till he touched the Isle Ogygia, and soared up from the blue sea to the grotto of the goddess, to whom his errand was ordained.

His message struck a horror, checked by love, through all the faculties of Calypso. She replied to it, incensed, "You gods are insatiate, past all that live, in all things which you affect; which makes you so envious and grudging. It afflicts you to the heart when any goddess seeks the love of a mortal man in marriage, though you yourselves without scruple link yourselves to women of the earth. So it fared with you when the delicious-fingered Morning shared Orion's bed: you could never satisfy your hate and your jealousy till you had incensed the chastity-loving dame, Diana, *who leads the precise life*, to come upon him by stealth in Ortygia, and pierce him through with her arrows. And when rich-haired Ceres gave the reins to her affections, and took Iasion (well worthy) to her arms, the secret was not so cunningly kept but Jove had soon notice of it; and the poor mortal paid for his felicity with death, struck through with lightnings. And now you envy me the possession of a wretched man, whom tempests have cast upon my shores, making him lawfully mine; whose ship Jove rent in pieces with his hot thunderbolts, killing all his friends. Him I have preserved, loved, nourished; made him mine by protection; my creature, — by every tie of gratitude, mine; have vowed to make him deathless like myself: him you will take from me. But I know your power, and that it is vain for me to resist. Tell your king that I obey his mandates."

With an ill grace, Calypso promised to fulfil the commands of Jove; and, Mercury departing, she went to find Ulysses, where he sat outside the grotto, not knowing of the heavenly message, drowned in discontent, not seeing any human probability of his ever returning home.

She said to him, "Unhappy man, no longer afflict yourself with pining after your country, but build you a ship, with which you may return home; since it is the will of the gods; who doubtless, as they are greater in power than I, are greater in skill, and best can tell what is fittest for man. But I call the gods, and my inward conscience, to witness, that I had no thought but what stood with thy safety, nor would have done or counselled any thing against thy good. I persuaded thee to nothing which I should not have followed myself in thy extremity; for my mind is innocent and simple. Oh! if thou knewest what dreadful sufferings thou must yet endure, before ever thou reachest thy native land, thou wouldest not esteem so hardly of a goddess's offer to share her immortality with thee; nor, for a few years' enjoyment of a perishing Penelope, refuse an imperishable and never-dying life with Calypso."

He replied, "Ever-honored, great Calypso, let it not displease thee, that I, a mortal man, desire to see and converse again with a wife that is mortal: human objects are best fitted to human infirmities. I well know how far in wisdom, in feature, in stature, proportion, beauty, in all the gifts of the mind, thou exceedest my Penelope: she is a mortal, and subject to decay; thou immortal, ever growing, yet never old: yet in her sight all my desires terminate, all my wishes; in the sight of her, and of my country earth. If any god, envious of my return, shall lay his dreadful hand upon me as I pass the seas, I submit; for the same powers have given me a mind not to sink under oppression. In wars and waves, my sufferings have not been small."

She heard his pleaded reasons, and of force she must assent: so to her nymphs she gave in charge from her sacred woods to cut down timber, to make Ulysses a ship. They obeyed, though in a work unsuitable to their soft fingers; yet to obedience no sacrifice is hard: and Ulysses busily bestirred himself, laboring far more hard than they, as was fitting, till twenty tall trees, driest and fittest for timber, were felled. Then, like a skilful shipwright, he fell to joining the planks; using the plane, the axe, and the auger, with such expedition, that in four days' time a ship was made, complete with all her decks, hatches, side-boards, yards. Calypso added linen for the sails, and tackling; and, when she was finished, she was a goodly vessel for a man to sail in, alone or in company, over the wide seas. By the fifth morning, she was launched; and Ulysses, furnished with store of provisions, rich garments, and gold and silver, given him by Calypso, took a last leave of her and of her nymphs, and of the Isle Ogygia which had so befriended him.

CHAPTER V.

THE TEMPEST.—THE SEA-BIRD'S GIFT.—THE ESCAPE BY SWIMMING.—THE SLEEP IN THE WOODS.

AT the stern of his solitary ship, Ulysses sat, and steered right artfully. No sleep could seize his eyelids. He beheld the Pleiads, the Bear, which is by some called the Wain, that moves round about Orion, and keeps still above the ocean; and the slow-setting sign Bootes, which some name the Wagoner. Seventeen days he held his course; and, on the eighteenth, the coast of Phæacia was in sight. The figure of the land, as seen from the sea, was pretty and circular, and looked something like a shield.

Neptune, returning from visiting his favorite Æthiopians, from the mountains of the Solymi descried Ulysses ploughing the waves, his domain. The sight of the man he so much hated for Polyphemus' sake, his son, whose eye Ulysses had put out, set the god's heart on fire; and snatching into his hand his horrid sea-sceptre, the trident of his power, he smote the air and the sea, and conjured up all his black storms, calling down night from the cope of heaven, and taking the earth into the sea, as it seemed, with clouds, through the darkness and indistinctness which prevailed; the billows rolling up before the fury of all the winds, that contended together in their mighty sport.

Then the knees of Ulysses bent with fear, and then all his spirit was spent; and he wished that he had been among the number of his countrymen who fell before Troy, and had their funerals celebrated by all the Greeks, rather than to perish thus, where no man could mourn him or know him.

As he thought these melancholy thoughts, a huge wave took him, and washed him overboard: ship and all upset amidst the billows; he struggling afar off, clinging to her stern broken off, which he yet held; her mast cracking in two with the fury of that gust of mixed winds that struck it; sails and sail-yards fell into the deep; and he himself was long drowned under water, nor could get his head above, wave so met with wave, as if they strove which should depress him most; and the gorgeous garments given him by Calypso clung about him, and hindered his swimming. Yet neither for this, nor for the overthrow of his ship, nor his own perilous condition, would he give up his drenched vessel; but, wrestling with Neptune, got at length hold of her again, and then sat in her hull, insulting over death, which he had escaped, and the salt waves, which he gave the seas again to give to other men. His ship, striving to live, floated at random, cuffed from wave to wave, hurled to and fro by all the winds: now Boreas tossed it to Notus, Notus passed it to Eurus, and Eurus to the West Wind, who kept up the horrid tennis.

Them in their mad sport Ino Leucothea beheld,—Ino Leucothea, now a sea-goddess, but once a mortal, and the daughter of Cadmus. She with pity beheld Ulysses the mark of their fierce contention; and, rising from the waves, alighted on the ship, in shape like to the sea-bird which is called a cormorant; and in her beak she held a wonderful girdle made of sea-weeds, which grow at the bottom of the ocean, which she dropped at his feet; and the bird spake to Ulysses, and counselled him not to trust any more to that fatal vessel against which God Neptune had levelled his furious wrath, nor to those ill-befriending garments which Calypso had given him, but to quit both it and them, and trust for his safety to swimming. "And here," said the seeming bird: "take this girdle, and tie about your middle, which has virtue to protect the wearer at sea, and you shall safely reach the shore; but, when you have landed, cast it far from you back into the sea." He did as the sea-bird instructed him: he stripped himself naked, and, fastening the wondrous girdle about his middle, cast himself into the seas to swim. The bird dived past his sight into the fathomless abyss of the ocean.

Two days and two nights he spent in struggling with the waves, though sore buffeted, and almost spent, never giving up himself for lost; such confidence he had in that charm which he wore about his middle, and in the words of that divine bird. But, the third morning, the winds grew calm, and all the heavens were clear. Then he saw himself nigh land, which he knew to be the coast of the Phæacians, a people good to strangers, and abounding in ships; by whose favor he doubted not that he should soon obtain a passage to his own country. And such joy he conceived in his heart as good sons have, that esteem their father's life dear, when long sickness has held him down to his bed, and wasted his body, and they see at length health return to the old man, with restored strength and spirits, in reward of their many prayers to the gods for his safety: so precious was the prospect of home-return to Ulysses, that he might restore health to his country (his better parent), that had long languished as full of distempers in his absence. And then for his own safety's sake he had joy to see the shores, the woods, so nigh and within his grasp as they seemed; and he labored with all the might of hands and feet to reach with swimming that nigh-seeming land.

But, when he approached near, a horrid sound of a huge sea beating against rocks informed him that here was no place for landing, nor any harbor for man's resort: but, through the weeds and the foam which the sea belched up against the land, he could dimly discover the rugged shore all bristled with flints, and all that part of the coast one impending rock, that seemed impossible to climb; and the water all about so deep, that not a sand was there for any tired foot to rest upon; and every moment he feared lest some wave more cruel than the rest should crush him against a cliff, rendering worse than vain all his landing: and, should he swim to seek a more commodious haven farther on, he was fearful, lest, weak and spent as he was, the winds would force him back a long way off into the main, where the terrible god Neptune, for wrath that he had so nearly escaped his power, having gotten him again into his domain, would send out some great whale (of which those seas breed a horrid number) to swallow him up alive; with such malignity he still pursued him.

While these thoughts distracted him with diversity of dangers, one bigger wave drove against a sharp rock his naked body, which it gashed and tore, and wanted little of breaking all his bones, so rude was the shock. But, in this extremity, she prompted him that never failed him at need. Minerva (who is Wisdom itself) put it into his thoughts no longer to keep swimming off and on, as one dallying with danger, but boldly to force the shore that threatened him, and to hug the rock that had torn him so rudely; which with both hands he clasped, wrestling with extremity, till the rage of that billow which had driven him upon it was passed: but then again the rock drove back that wave so furiously, that it reft him of his hold, sucking him with it in its return;

and the sharp rock, his cruel friend, to which he clinged for succor, rent the flesh so sore from his hands in parting, that he fell off, and could sustain no longer. Quite under water he fell; and, past the help of fate, there had the hapless Ulysses lost all portion that he had in this life, if Minerva had not prompted his wisdom in that peril to essay another course, and to explore some other shelter, ceasing to attempt that landing-place.

She guided his wearied and nigh-exhausted limbs to the mouth of the fair river Callicoe, which, not far from thence, disbursed its watery tribute to the ocean. Here the shores were easy and accessible, and the rocks (which rather adorned than defended its banks) so smooth, that they seemed polished of purpose to invite the landing of our sea-wanderer, and to atone for the uncourteous treatment which those less hospitable cliffs had afforded him. And the god of the river, as if in pity, stayed his current, and smoothed his waters, to make his landing more easy: for sacred to the ever-living deities of the fresh waters, be they mountain-stream, river, or lake, is the cry of erring mortals that seek their aid; by reason, that, being inland-bred, they partake more of the gentle humanities of our nature than those marine deities whom Neptune trains up in tempests in the unpitying recesses of his salt abyss.

So, by the favor of the river's god, Ulysses crept to land, half-drowned. Both his knees faltering, his strong hands falling down through weakness from the excessive toils he had endured, his cheeks and nostrils flowing with froth of the sea-brine, much of which he had swallowed in that conflict, voice and breath spent, down he sank as in death. Dead weary he was. It seemed that the sea had soaked through his heart, and the pains he felt in all his veins were little less than those which one feels that has endured the torture of the rack. But when his spirits came a little to themselves, and his recollection by degrees began to return, he rose up, and unloosing from his waist the girdle or charm which that divine bird had given him, and remembering the charge which he had received with it, he flung it far from him into the river. Back it swam with the course of the ebbing stream till it reached the sea, where the fair hands of Ino Leucothea received it, to keep it as a pledge of safety to any future shipwrecked mariner, that, like Ulysses, should wander in those perilous waves.

Then he kissed the humble earth in token of safety; and on he went by the side of that pleasant river, till he came where a thicker shade of rushes that grew on its banks seemed to point out the place where he might rest his sea-wearied limbs. And here a fresh perplexity divided his mind, — whether he should pass the night, which was coming on, in that place, where, though he feared no other enemies, the damps and frosts of the chill sea-air in that exposed situation might be death to him in his weak state; or whether he had better climb the next hill, and pierce the depth of some shady wood, in which he might find a warm and sheltered though insecure repose, subject to the approach of any wild beast that roamed that way. Best did this last course appear to him, though with some danger, as that which was more honorable, and savored more of strife and self-exertion, than to perish without a struggle, the passive victim of cold and the elements.

So he bent his course to the nearest woods; where, entering in, he found a thicket, mostly of wild olives and such low trees, yet growing so intertwined and knit together, that the moist wind had not leave to play through their branches, nor the sun's scorching beams to pierce their recesses, nor any shower to beat through, they grew so thick, and, as it were, folded each in the other. Here, creeping in, he made his bed of the leaves which were beginning to fall, of which was such abundance, that two or three men might have spread them ample coverings, such as might shield them from the winter's rage, though the air breathed steel, and blew as it would burst. Here, creeping in, he heaped up store of leaves all about him, as a man would billets upon a winter fire, and lay down in the midst. Rich seed of virtue lying hid in poor leaves! Here Minerva soon gave him sound sleep; and here all his long toils past seemed to be concluded, and shut up within the little sphere of his refreshed and closed eyelids.

CHAPTER VI.

THE PRINCESS NAUSICAA. — THE WASHING. — THE GAME WITH THE BALL. — THE COURT OF PHÆACIA AND KING ALCINOUS.

MEANTIME Minerva, designing an interview between the king's daughter of that country and Ulysses when he should awake, went by night to the palace of King Alcinous, and stood at the bedside of the Princess Nausicaa in the shape of one of her favorite attendants, and thus addressed the sleeping princess: —

"Nausicaa, why do you lie sleeping here, and never bestow a thought upon your bridal ornaments? of which you have many and beautiful, laid up in your wardrobe against the day of your marriage, which cannot be far distant; when you shall have need of all, not only to deck your own person, but to give away in presents to the virgins, that, honoring you, shall attend you to the temple. Your reputation stands much upon the timely care of these things: these things are they which fill father and reverend mother with delight. Let us arise betimes to wash your fair vestments of linen and silks in the river: and request your sire to lend you mules and a coach; for your wardrobe is heavy, and the place where we must wash is distant; and, besides, it fits not a great princess like you to go so far on foot."

So saying, she went away, and Nausicaa awoke full of pleasing thoughts of her marriage, which the dream had told her was not far distant; and, as soon as it was dawn, she arose and dressed herself, and went to find her parent.

The queen, her mother, was already up, and seated among her maids, spinning at her wheel, as the fashion was in those primitive times, when great ladies did not disdain housewifery; and the king, her father, was preparing to go abroad at that early hour to council with his grave senate.

"My father," she said, "will you not order mules and a coach to be got ready, that I may go and wash, I and my maids, at the cisterns that stand without the city?"

"What washing does my daughter speak of?" said Alcinous.

"Mine and my brothers' garments," she replied, "that

have contracted soil by this time with lying by so long in the wardrobe. Five sons have you, that are my brothers: two of them are married, and three are bachelors. These last it concerns to have their garments neat and unsoiled: it may advance their fortunes in marriage. And who but I, their sister, should have a care of these things? You yourself, my father, have need of the whitest apparel, when you go, as now, to the council."

She used this plea, modestly dissembling her care of her own nuptials to her father; who was not displeased at this instance of his daughter's discretion: for a seasonable care about marriage may be permitted to a young maiden, provided it be accompanied with modesty, and dutiful submission to her parents in the choice of her future husband. And there was no fear of Nausicaa choosing wrongly or improperly; for she was as wise as she was beautiful, and the best in all Phæacia were suitors to her for her love. So Alcinous readily gave consent that she should go, ordering mules and a coach to be prepared. And Nausicaa brought from her chamber all her vestments, and laid them up in the coach; and her mother placed bread and wine in the coach, and oil in a golden cruse, to soften the bright skins of Nausicaa and her maids when they came out of the river.

Nausicaa, making her maids get up into the coach with her, lashed the mules, till they brought her to the cisterns which stood a little on the outside of the town, and were supplied with water from the river Callicoe.

There her attendants unyoked the mules, took out the clothes, and steeped them in the cisterns, washing them in several waters, and afterwards treading them clean with their feet; venturing wagers who should have done soonest and cleanest, and using many pretty pastimes to beguile their labors as young maids use, while the princess looked on. When they had laid their clothes to dry, they fell to playing again; and Nausicaa joined them in a game with the ball, which is used in that country; which is performed by tossing the ball from hand to hand with great expedition, she who begins the pastime singing a song. It chanced that the princess, whose turn it became to toss the ball, sent it so far from its mark, that it fell beyond into one of the cisterns of the river; at which the whole company, in merry consternation, set up a shriek so loud as waked the sleeping Ulysses, who was taking his rest, after his long toils, in the woods, not far distant from the place where these young maids had come to wash.

At the sound of female voices, Ulysses crept forth from his retirement; making himself a covering with boughs and leaves as well as he could to shroud his nakedness. The sudden appearance of his weather-beaten and almost naked form so frighted the maidens, that they scudded away into the woods and all about to hide themselves: only Minerva (who had brought about this interview, to admirable purposes, by seemingly accidental means) put courage into the breast of Nausicaa, and she staid where she was, and resolved to know what manner of man he was, and what was the occasion of his strange coming to them.

He, not venturing (for delicacy) to approach and clasp her knees, as suppliants should, but standing far off, addressed this speech to the young princess:—

"Before I presume rudely to press my petitions, I

should first ask whether I am addressing a mortal woman, or one of the goddesses. If a goddess, you seem to me to be likest to Diana, the chaste huntress, the daughter of Jove. Like hers are your lineaments, your stature, your features, and air divine."

She making answer that she was no goddess, but a mortal maid, he continued: —

"If a woman, thrice blessed are both the authors of your birth; thrice blessed are your brothers, who even to rapture must have joy in your perfections, to see you grown so like a young tree, and so graceful. But most blessed of all that breathe is he that has the gift to engage your young neck in the yoke of marriage. I never saw that man that was worthy of you. I never saw man or woman that at all parts equalled you. Lately at Delos (where I touched) I saw a young palm which grew beside Apollo's temple; it exceeded all the trees which ever I beheld for straightness and beauty: I can compare you only to that. A stupor past admiration strikes me, joined with fear, which keeps me back from approaching you to embrace your knees. Nor is it strange; for one of freshest and firmest spirit would falter, approaching near to so bright an object: but I am one whom a cruel habit of calamity has prepared to receive strong impressions. Twenty days the unrelenting seas have tossed me up and down, coming from Ogygia; and at length cast me shipwrecked last night upon your coast. I have seen no man or woman since I landed but yourself. All that I crave is clothes, which you may spare me; and to be shown the way to some neighboring town. The gods, who have care of strangers, will requite you for these courtesies."

She, admiring to hear such complimentary words proceed out of the mouth of one whose outside looked so rough and unpromising, made answer: "Stranger, I discern neither sloth nor folly in you; and yet I see that you are poor and wretched: from which I gather that neither wisdom nor industry can secure felicity; only Jove bestows it upon whomsoever he pleases. He, perhaps, has reduced you to this plight. However, since your wanderings have brought you so near to our city, it lies in our duty to supply your wants. Clothes, and what else a human hand should give to one so suppliant, and so tamed with calamity, you shall not want. We will show you our city, and tell you the name of our people. This is the land of the Phæacians, of which my father, Alcinous, is king."

Then calling her attendants, who had dispersed on the first sight of Ulysses, she rebuked them for their fear, and said, "This man is no Cyclop, nor monster of sea or land, that you should fear him; but he seems manly, staid, and discreet, and though decayed in his outward appearance, yet he has the mind's riches, wit and fortitude, in abundance. Show him the cisterns where he may wash him from the seaweeds and foam that hang about him, and let him have garments that fit him out of those which we have brought with us to the cisterns."

Ulysses, retiring a little out of sight, cleansed him in the cisterns from the soil and impurities with which the rocks and waves had covered all his body; and, clothing himself with befitting raiment which the princess's attendants had given him, he presented himself in more worthy shape to Nausicaa. She admired to see what a comely personage he was, now he was dressed in all parts: she thought him some king or hero, and secretly wished that the gods would be pleased to give her such a husband.

Then causing her attendants to yoke her mules, and lay up the vestments, which the sun's heat had sufficiently dried, in the coach, she ascended with her maids, and drove off to the palace: bidding Ulysses, as she departed, keep an eye upon the coach, and to follow it on foot at some distance; which she did, because, if she had suffered him to have ridden in the coach with her, it might have subjected her to some misconstructions of the common people, who are always ready to vilify and censure their betters, and to suspect that charity is not always pure charity, but that love or some sinister intention lies hid under its disguise. So discreet and attentive to appearance in all her actions was this admirable princess.

Ulysses, as he entered the city, wondered to see its magnificence; its markets, buildings, temples; its walls and rampires; its trade, and resort of men; its harbors for shipping, which is the strength of the Phæacian state. But when he approached the palace, and beheld its riches, the proportion of its architecture, its avenues, gardens, statues, fountains, he stood rapt in admiration, and almost forgot his own condition in surveying the flourishing estate of others: but, recollecting himself, he passed on boldly into the inner apartment, where the king and queen were sitting at dinner with their peers; Nausicaa having prepared them for his approach.

To them humbly kneeling, he made it his request, that, since fortune had cast him naked upon their shores, they would take him into their protection, and grant him a conveyance by one of the ships, of which their great Phæacian state had such good store, to carry him to his own country. Having delivered his request, to grace it with more humility, he went and sat himself down upon the hearth among the ashes, as the custom was in those days when any would make a petition to the throne.

He seemed a petitioner of so great state, and of so superior a deportment, that Alcinous himself arose to do him honor, and, causing him to leave that abject station which he had assumed, placed him next to his throne upon a chair of state; and thus he spake to his peers: —

"Lords and councillors of Phæacia, ye see this man, who he is we know not, that is come to us in the guise of a petitioner. He seems no mean one: but, whoever he is, it is fit, since the gods have cast him upon our protection, that we grant him the rights of hospitality while he stays with us; and, at his departure, a ship well manned, to convey so worthy a personage as he seems to be, in a manner suitable to his rank, to his own country."

This counsel the peers with one consent approved; and, wine and meat being set before Ulysses, he ate and drank, and gave the gods thanks who had stirred up the royal bounty of Alcinous to aid him in that extremity. But not as yet did he reveal to the king and queen who he was, or whence he had come: only in brief terms he related his being cast upon their shores, his sleep in the woods, and his meeting with the Princess Nausicaa; whose generosity, mingled with discretion, filled her parents with delight, as Ulysses in eloquent phrases adorned and commended her virtues. But Alcinous, humanely considering that the troubles which his guest had undergone required rest, as well as refreshment by food, dismissed him early in the evening to his chamber; where, in a magnificent apartment, Ulysses found a smoother bed, but not a sounder repose, than he had enjoyed the night before, sleeping upon leaves which he had scraped together in his necessity.

CHAPTER VII.

THE SONGS OF DEMODOCUS. — THE CONVOY HOME. — THE MARINERS TRANSFORMED TO STONE. — THE YOUNG SHEPHERD.

When it was daylight, Alcinous caused it to be proclaimed by the heralds about the town, that there was come to the palace a stranger, shipwrecked on their coast, that in mien and person resembled a god; and inviting all the chief people of the city to come and do honor to the stranger.

The palace was quickly filled with guests, old and young; for whose cheer, and to grace Ulysses more, Alcinous made a kingly feast, with banquetings and music. Then Ulysses being seated at a table next the king and queen, in all men's view, after they had feasted, Alcinous ordered Demodocus, the court-singer, to be called to sing some song of the deeds of heroes, to charm the ear of his guest. Demodocus came, and reached his harp, where it hung between two pillars of silver; and then the blind singer, to whom, in recompense of his lost sight, the Muses had given an inward discernment, a soul and a voice to excite the hearts of men and gods to delight, began in grave and solemn strains to sing the glories of men highliest famed. He chose a poem, whose subject was, The stern Strife stirred up between Ulysses and great Achilles, as, at a banquet sacred to the gods, in dreadful language they expressed their difference; while Agamemnon sat rejoiced in soul to hear those Grecians jar: for the oracle in Pytho had told him, that the period of their wars in Troy should then be, when the kings of Greece, anxious to arrive at the wished conclusion, should fall to strife, and contend which must end the war, force or stratagem.

This brave contention he expressed so to the life, in the very words which they both used in the quarrel, as brought tears into the eyes of Ulysses at the remembrance of past passages of his life; and he held his large purple weed before his face to conceal it. Then, craving a cup of wine, he poured it out in secret libation to the gods, who had put into the mind of Demodocus unknowingly to do him so much honor. But, when the moving poet began to tell of other occurrences where Ulysses had been present, the memory of his brave followers who had been with him in all difficulties, now swallowed up and lost in the ocean, and of those kings that had fought with him at Troy, some of whom were dead, some exiles like himself, forced itself so strongly upon his mind, that, forgetful where he was, he sobbed outright with passion; which yet he restrained, but not so cunningly but Alcinous perceived it, and, without taking notice of it to Ulysses, privately gave signs that Demodocus should cease from his singing.

Next followed dancing in the Phæacian fashion, when they would show respect to their guests; which was succeeded by trials of skill, games of strength, running, racing, hurling of the quoit, mock fights, hurling of the javelin, shooting with the bow; in some of which, Ulysses, modestly challenging his entertainers, performed such feats of strength and prowess, as gave the admiring Phæacians fresh reason to imagine that he was either some god, or hero of the race of the gods.

These solemn shows and pageants in honor of his guest, King Alcinous continued for the space of many days, as if he could never be weary of showing courtesies to so worthy a stranger. In all this time he never asked him his name, nor sought to know more of him than he of his own accord disclosed; till on a day as they were seated feasting, after the feast was ended, Demodocus, being called, as was the custom, to sing some grave matter, sang how Ulysses, on that night when Troy was fired, made dreadful proof of his valor, maintaining singly a combat against the whole household of Deiphobus; to which the divine expresser gave both act and passion, and breathed such a fire into Ulysses' deeds, that it inspired old death with life in the lively expressing of slaughters, and rendered life so sweet and passionate in the hearers, that all who heard felt it fleet from them in the narration: which made Ulysses even pity his own slaughterous deeds, and feel touches of remorse, to see how song can revive a dead man from the grave, yet no way can it defend a living man from death; and in imagination he underwent some part of death's horrors, and felt in his living body a taste of those dying pangs which he had dealt to others, that, with the strong conceit, tears (the true interpreters of unutterable emotion) stood in his eyes.

Which King Alcinous noting, and that this was now the second time that he had perceived him to be moved at the mention of events touching the Trojan wars, he took occasion to ask whether his guest had lost any friend or kinsman at Troy, that Demodocus' singing had brought into his mind. Then Ulysses, drying the tears with his cloak, and observing that the eyes of all the company were upon him, desirous to give them satisfaction in what he could, and thinking this a fit time to reveal his true name and destination, spake as follows:—

"The courtesies which ye all have shown me, and in particular yourself and princely daughter, O King Alcinous! demand from me that I should no longer keep you in ignorance of what or who I am; for to reserve any secret from you, who have with such openness of friendship embraced my love, would argue either a pusillanimous or an ungrateful mind in me. Know, then, that I am that *Ulysses*, of whom I perceive ye have heard something; who heretofore have filled the world with the renown of my policies. I am he, by whose counsels, if Fame is to be believed at all, more than by the united valor of all the Grecians, Troy fell. I am that unhappy man whom the heavens and angry gods have conspired to keep an exile on the seas, wandering to seek my home, which still flies from me. The land which I am in quest of is Ithaca; in whose ports some ship belonging to your navigation-famed Phæacian state may haply at some time have found a refuge from tempests. If ever you have experienced such kindness, requite it now, by granting to me, who am the king of that land, a passport to that land."

Admiration seized all the court of Alcinous to behold in their presence one of the number of those heroes who fought at Troy; whose divine story had been made known to them by songs and poems, but of the truth they had little known, or rather they had hitherto accounted those heroic exploits as fictions and exaggerations of poets: but, having seen and made proof of the real Ulysses, they began to take those supposed inventions to be real verities, and the tale of Troy to be as true as it was delightful.

Then King Alcinous made answer: "Thrice fortunate ought we to esteem our lot in having seen and conversed with a man of whom report hath spoken so loudly, but, as it seems, nothing beyond the truth. Though we could desire no felicity greater than to have you always among us, renowned Ulysses, yet, your desire having been expressed so often and so deeply to return home, we can deny you nothing, though to our own loss. Our kingdom of Phæacia, as you know, is chiefly rich in shipping. In all parts of the world, where there are navigable seas, or ships can pass, our vessels will be found. You cannot name a coast to which they do not resort. Every rock and every quicksand is known to them, that lurks in the vast deep. They pass a bird in flight; and with such unerring certainty they make to their destination, that some have said that they have no need of pilot or rudder, but that they move instinctively, self-directed, and know the minds of their voyagers. Thus much, that you may not fear to trust yourself in one of our Phæacian ships. To-morrow, if you please, you shall launch forth. To-day spend with us in feasting, who never can do enough when the gods send such visitors."

Ulysses acknowledged King Alcinous' bounty; and, while these two royal personages stood interchanging courteous expressions, the heart of the Princess Nausicaa was overcome. She had been gazing attentively upon her father's guest, as he delivered his speech: but, when he came to that part where he declared himself to be Ulysses, she blessed herself, and her fortune, that in relieving a poor shipwrecked mariner, as he seemed no better, she had conferred a kindness on so divine a hero as he proved; and, scarce waiting till her father had done speaking, with a cheerful countenance she addressed Ulysses, bidding him be cheerful, and when he returned home, as by her father's means she trusted he would shortly, sometimes to remember to whom he owed his life, and who met him in the woods by the river Callicoe.

"Fair flower of Phæacia," he replied, "so may all the gods bless me with the strife of joys in that desired day, whenever I shall see it, as I shall always acknowledge to be indebted to your fair hand for the gift of life which I enjoy, and all the blessings which shall follow upon my home-return. The gods give thee, Nausicaa, a princely husband; and from you two spring blessings to this state." So prayed Ulysses, his heart overflowing with admiration and grateful recollections of King Alcinous' daughter.

Then, at the king's request, he gave them a brief relation of all the adventures that had befallen him since he launched forth from Troy: during which the

Princess Nausicaa took great delight (as ladies are commonly taken with these kind of travellers' stories) to hear of the monster Polyphemus, of the men that devour each other in Læstrygonia, of the enchantress Circe, of Scylla, and the rest; to which she listened with a breathless attention, letting fall a shower of tears from her fair eyes, every now and then, when Ulysses told of some more than usual distressful passage in his travels: and all the rest of his auditors, if they had before entertained a high respect for their guest, now felt their veneration increased tenfold, when they learned from his own mouth what perils, what sufferance, what endurance, of evils beyond man's strength to support, this much-sustaining, almost heavenly man, by the greatness of his mind and by his invincible courage, had struggled through.

The night was far spent before Ulysses had ended his narrative: and with wishful glances he cast his eyes towards the eastern parts, which the sun had begun to flecker with his first red; for, on the morrow, Alcinous had promised that a bark should be in readiness to convoy him to Ithaca.

In the morning, a vessel well manned and appointed was waiting for him; into which the king and queen heaped presents of gold and silver, massy plate, apparel, armor, and whatsoever things of cost or rarity they judged would be most acceptable to their guest: and, the sails being set, Ulysses, embarking with expressions of regret, took his leave of his royal entertainers, of the fair princess (who had been his first friend), and of the peers of Phæacia; who, crowding down to the beach to have the last sight of their illustrious visitant, beheld the gallant ship with all her canvas spread, bounding and curvetting over the waves like a horse proud of his rider, or as if she knew that in her capacious womb's rich freightage she bore Ulysses.

He whose life past had been a series of disquiets, in seas among rude waves, in battles amongst ruder foes, now slept securely, forgetting all; his eyelids bound in such deep sleep as only yielded to death: and, when they reached the nearest Ithacan port by the next morning, he was still asleep. The mariners, not willing to awake him, landed him softly, and laid him in a cave at the foot of an olive-tree, which made a shady recess in that narrow harbor, the haunt of almost none but the sea-nymphs, which are called Naiads; few ships before this Phæacian vessel having put into that haven, by reason of the difficulty and narrowness of the entrance. Here leaving him asleep, and disposing in safe places near him the presents with which King Alcinous had dismissed him, they departed for Phæacia, where these wretched mariners never again set foot: but just as they arrived, and thought to salute their country earth,—in sight of their city's turrets, and in open view of their friends, who from the harbor with shouts greeted their return,—their vessel and all the mariners which were in her were turned to stone, and stood transformed and fixed in sight of the whole Phæacian city; where it yet stands, by Neptune's vindictive wrath, who resented thus highly the contempt which those Phæacians had shown in convoying home a man whom the god had destined to destruction. Whence it comes to pass, that the Phæacians at this day will at no price be induced to lend their ships to strangers, or to become the carriers for other nations, so highly do they still dread the displeasure of their sea-god, while they see that terrible monument ever in sight.

When Ulysses awoke (which was not till some time after the mariners had departed), he did not at first know his country again; either that long absence had made it strange, or that Minerva (which was more likely) had cast a cloud about his eyes, that he should have greater pleasure hereafter in discovering his mistake: but like a man suddenly awaking in some desert isle, to which his sea-mates have transported him in his sleep, he looked around, and, discerning no known objects, he cast his hands to heaven for pity, and complained on those ruthless men who had beguiled him with a promise of conveying him home to his country, and perfidiously left him to perish in an unknown land. But then the rich presents of gold and silver given him by Alcinous, which he saw carefully laid up in secure places near him, staggered him; which seemed not like the act of wrongful or unjust men, such as turn pirates for gain, or land helpless passengers in remote coasts to possess themselves of their goods.

While he remained in this suspense, there came up to him a young shepherd, clad in the finer sort of apparel, such as kings' sons wore in those days when princes did not disdain to tend sheep; who, accosting him, was saluted again by Ulysses, who asked him what country that was on which he had been just landed, and whether it were part of a continent or an island. The young shepherd made show of wonder to hear any one ask the name of that land; as country people are apt to esteem those for mainly ignorant and barbarous who do not know the names of places which are familiar to *them*, though perhaps they who ask have had no opportunities of knowing, and may have come from far countries.

"I had thought," said he, "that all people knew our land. It is rocky and barren, to be sure; but well enough: it feeds a goat or an ox well; it is not wanting either in wine or in wheat; it has good springs of water, some fair rivers, and wood enough, as you may see. It is called Ithaca."

Ulysses was joyed enough to find himself in his own country: but so prudently he carried his joy, that, dissembling his true name and quality, he pretended to the shepherd that he was only some foreigner who by stress of weather had put into that port; and framed on the sudden a story to make it plausible how he had come from Crete in a ship of Phæacia: when the young shepherd, laughing, and taking Ulysses' hand in both his, said to him, "He must be cunning, I find, who thinks to overreach you. What! cannot you quit your wiles and your subtleties, now that you are in a state of security? must the first word with which you salute your native earth be an untruth? and think you that you are unknown?"

Ulysses looked again; and he saw, not a shepherd, but a beautiful woman, whom he immediately knew to be the goddess Minerva, that in the wars of Troy had frequently vouchsafed her sight to him; and had been with him since in perils, saving him unseen.

"Let not my ignorance offend thee, great Minerva," he cried, "or move thy displeasure, that in that shape I knew thee not; since the skill of discerning of deities is not attainable by wit or study, but hard to be hit by the wisest of mortals. To know thee truly, through all thy changes, is only given to those whom thou art pleased to grace. To all men thou takest all likenesses. All men in their wits think that they know thee, and that they have thee. Thou art Wisdom itself. But a semblance of thee, which is false wisdom, often is taken for thee; so thy counterfeit view appears to many, but thy true presence to few: those are they, which, loving thee above all, are inspired with light from thee to know thee. But this I surely know, that, all the time the sons of Greece waged war against Troy, I was sundry times graced with thy appearance; but, since, I have never been able to set eyes upon thee till now, but have wandered at my own discretion, to myself a blind guide, erring up and down the world, wanting thee."

Then Minerva cleared his eyes, and he knew the ground on which he stood to be Ithaca, and that cave to be the same which the people of Ithaca had in former times made sacred to the sea-nymphs, and where he himself had done sacrifices to them a thousand times; and full in his view stood Mount Nerytus, with all his woods: so that now he knew for a certainty that he was arrived in his own country; and, with the delight which he felt, he could not forbear stooping down, and kissing the soil.

CHAPTER VIII.

THE CHANGE FROM A KING TO A BEGGAR. — EUMÆUS AND THE HERDSMEN TELEMACHUS.

NOT long did Minerva suffer him to indulge vain transports; but, briefly recounting to him the events which had taken place in Ithaca during his absence, she showed him that his way to his wife and throne did not lie so open, but that, before he were re-instated in the secure possession of them, he must encounter many difficulties. His palace, wanting its king, was become the resort of insolent and imperious men, the chief nobility of Ithaca and of the neighboring isles, who, in the confidence of Ulysses being dead, came as suitors to Penelope. The queen (it was true) continued single, but was little better than a state-prisoner in the power of these men, who, under a pretence of waiting her decision, occupied the king's house, rather as owners than guests, lording and domineering at their pleasure, profaning the palace, and wasting the royal substance, with their feasts and mad riots. Moreover, the goddess told him, how, fearing the attempts of these lawless men upon the person of his young son Telemachus, she herself had put it into the heart of the prince to go and seek his father in far countries; how, in the shape of Mentor, she had borne him company in his long search; which though failing, as she meant it should fail, in its first object, had yet had this effect, — that through hardships he had learned endurance; through experience he had gathered wisdom; and, wherever his footsteps had been, he had left such memorials of his worth, as the fame of Ulysses' son was already blown throughout the world. That it was now not many days since Telemachus had arrived in the island, to the great joy of the queen, his mother, who had thought him dead, by reason of his long absence, and had begun to mourn for him with a grief equal to that which she endured for Ulysses; the goddess herself having so ordered the course of his adventures, that the time of his return should correspond with the return of Ulysses, that they might together concert measures how to repress the power and insolence of those wicked suitors. This the goddess told him; but of the particulars of his son's adventures, of his having been detained in the Delightful Island, which his father had so lately left, of Calypso and her nymphs, and the many strange occurrences which may be read with profit and delight in the history of the prince's adventures, she forbore to tell him as yet, as judging that he would hear them with greater pleasure from the lips of his son, when he should have him in an hour of stillness and safety, when their work should be done, and none of their enemies left alive to trouble them.

Then they sat down, the goddess and Ulysses, at the foot of a wild olive-tree, consulting how they might with safety bring about his restoration. And when Ulysses revolved in his mind how that his enemies were a multitude, and he single, he began to despond; and he said, "I shall die an ill death, like Agamemnon: in the threshold of my own house I shall perish, like that unfortunate monarch, slain by some one of my wife's suitors." But then, again, calling to mind his ancient courage, he secretly wished that Minerva would but breathe such a spirit into his bosom as she inflamed him with in the hour of Troy's destruction, that he might encounter with three hundred of those impudent suitors at once, and strew the pavements of his beautiful palace with their bloods and brains.

And Minerva knew his thoughts; and she said, "I will be strongly with thee, if thou fail not to do thy part. And for a sign between us that I will perform my promise, and for a token on thy part of obedience, I must change thee, that thy person may not be known of men."

Then Ulysses bowed his head to receive the divine impression; and Minerva, by her great power, changed his person so that it might not be known. She changed him to appearance into a very old man, yet such a one as by his limbs and gait seemed to have been some considerable person in his time, and to retain yet some remains of his once prodigious strength. Also, instead of those rich robes in which King Alcinous had clothed him, she threw over his limbs such old and tattered rags as wandering beggars usually wear. A staff supported his steps, and a scrip hung to his back, such as travel ling mendicants use to hold the scraps which are given to them at rich men's doors. So from a king he became a beggar, as wise Tiresias had predicted to him in the shades.

To complete his humiliation, and to prove his obedience by suffering, she next directed him in this beggarly attire to go and present himself to his old herdsman, Eumæus, who had the care of his swine and his cattle, and had been a faithful steward to him all the time of his absence. Then, strictly charging Ulysses that he should reveal himself to no man but to his own son, whom she would send to him when she saw occasion, the goddess went her way.

The transformed Ulysses bent his course to the cottage of the herdsman; and, entering in at the front court, the dogs, of which Eumæus kept many fierce ones for the protection of the cattle, flew with open mouths upon him, as those ignoble animals have oftentimes an antipathy to the sight of any thing like a beggar; and would have rent him in pieces with their teeth, if Ulysses had not had the prudence to let fall his staff, which had chiefly provoked their fury, and sat himself down in a careless fashion upon the ground. But, for all that, some serious hurt had certainly been done to him, so raging the dogs were, had not the herdsman, whom the barking of the dogs had fetched out of the house, with shouting and with throwing of stones repressed them.

He said, when he saw Ulysses, "Old father, how near you were to being torn in pieces by these rude dogs! I should never have forgiven myself, if, through neglect of mine, any hurt had happened to you. But Heaven has given me so many cares to my portion, that I might well be excused for not attending to every thing; while here I lie grieving and mourning for the absence of that majesty which once ruled here, and am forced to fatten his swine and his cattle for food to evil men, who hate him, and who wish his death; when he perhaps strays up and down the world, and has not wherewith to appease hunger, if indeed he yet lives (which is a question), and enjoys the cheerful light of the sun." This he said, little thinking that he of whom he spoke now stood before him, and that in that uncouth disguise and beggarly obscurity was present the hidden majesty of Ulysses.

Then he had his guest into the house, and set meat and drink before him; and Ulysses said, "May Jove and all the other gods requite you for the kind speeches and hospitable usage which you have shown me!"

Eumæus made answer, "My poor guest, if one in much worse plight than yourself had arrived here, it were a shame to such scanty means as I have, if I had let him depart without entertaining him to the best of my ability. Poor men, and such as have no houses of their own, are by Jove himself recommended to our care. But the cheer which we that are servants to other men have to bestow is but sorry at most; yet freely and lovingly I give it you. Indeed, there once ruled here a man, whose return the gods have set their faces against, who, if he had been suffered to reign in peace and grow old among us, would have been kind to me and mine. But he is gone; and, for his sake, would to God that the whole posterity of Helen might perish with her, since in her quarrel so many worthies have perished! But such as your fare is, eat it, and be welcome; such lean beasts as are food for poor herdsmen. The fattest go to feed the voracious stomachs of the queen's suitors. Shame on their unworthiness! There is no day in which two or three of the noblest of the herd are not slain to support their feasts and their surfeits."

Ulysses gave good ear to his words; and, as he ate his meat, he even tore it and rent it with his teeth, for mere vexation that his fat cattle should be slain to glut the appetites of those godless suitors. And he said, "What chief or what ruler is this that thou commendest so highly, and sayest that he perished at Troy? I am but a stranger in these parts. It may be I have heard of some such in my long travels."

Eumæus answered, "Old father, never any one, of all the strangers that have come to our coast with news of Ulysses being alive, could gain credit with the queen or her son yet. These travellers, to get raiment or a meal, will not stick to invent any lie. Truth is not the commodity they deal in. Never did the queen get any thing of them but lies. She receives all that come, graciously; hears their stories, inquires all she can; but all ends in tears and dissatisfaction. But in God's name, old father, if you have got a tale, make the most on't; it may gain you a cloak or a coat from somebody to keep you warm: but, for him who is the subject of it, dogs and vultures long since have torn him limb from limb, or some great fish at sea has devoured him, or he lieth with no better monument upon his bones than the sea-sand. But for me past all the race of men were tears created; for I never shall find so kind a royal master more: not if my father or my mother could come again, and visit me from the tomb, would my eyes be so blessed as they should be with the sight of him again, coming as from the dead. In his last rest my soul shall love him. He is not here, nor do I name him as a flatterer, but because I am thankful for his love and care which he had to me, a poor man; and, if I knew surely that he were past all shores that the sun shines upon, I would invoke him as a deified thing."

For this saying of Eumæus the waters stood in Ulysses' eyes; and he said, "My friend, to say and to affirm positively that he cannot be alive is to give too much license to incredulity. For, not to speak at random, but with as much solemnity as an oath comes to, I say to you, that Ulysses shall return; and whenever that day shall be, then shall you give to me a cloak and a coat; but till then I will not receive so much as a thread of a garment, but rather go naked: for no less than the gates of hell do I hate that man whom poverty can force to tell an untruth. Be Jove, then, witness to my words, that this very year, nay, ere this month be fully ended, your eyes shall behold Ulysses dealing vengeance in his own palace upon the wrongers of his wife and his son."

To give the better credence to his words, he amused Eumæus with a forged story of his life; feigning of himself that he was a Cretan born, and one that went with Idomeneus to the wars of Troy. Also he said that he knew Ulysses, and related various passages which he alleged to have happened betwixt Ulysses and himself; which were either true in the main, as having really happened between Ulysses and some other person, or were so like to truth, as corresponding with the known character and actions of Ulysses, that Eumæus' incredulity was not a little shaken. Among other things, he asserted that he had lately been entertained in the court of Thesprotia, where the king's son of the country had told him that Ulysses had been there but just before him, and was gone upon a voyage to the oracle of Jove in Dodona, whence he should shortly return, and a ship would be ready by the bounty of the Thesprotians to convoy him straight to Ithaca. "And, in token that what I tell you is true," said Ulysses, "if your king come not within the period which I have named, you shall have leave to give your servants commandment to take my old carcass, and throw it headlong from some steep rock into the sea, that poor men, taking example by me, may fear to lie." But Eumæus made answer, that that should be small satisfaction or pleasure to him.

So, while they sat discoursing in this manner, supper was served in; and the servants of the herdsman, who had been out all day in the fields, came in to supper, and took their seats at the fire; for the night was bitter and frosty. After supper, Ulysses, who had well eaten and drunken, and was refreshed with the herdsman's good cheer, was resolved to try whether his host's hospitality would extend to the lending him a good warm mantle or rug to cover him in the night season; and, framing an artful tale for the purpose, in a merry mood, filling a cup of Greek wine, he thus began: —

"I will tell you a story of your king Ulysses and myself. If there is ever a time when a man may have leave to tell his own stories, it is when he has drunken a little too much. Strong liquor driveth the fool, and moves even the heart of the wise, — moves and impels him to sing and to dance, and break forth in pleasant laughters, and perchance to prefer a speech too, which were better kept in. When the heart is open, the tongue will be stirring. But you shall hear. We led our powers to ambush once under the walls of Troy."

The herdsmen crowded about him, eager to hear any thing which related to their king Ulysses and the wars of Troy; and thus he went on: —

"I remember Ulysses and Menelaus had the direction of that enterprise; and they were pleased to join me with them in the command. I was at that time in some repute among men; though fortune has played me a trick since, as you may perceive. But I was somebody in those times, and could do something. Be that as it may, a bitter freezing night it was, — such a night as this: the air cut like steel, and the sleet gathered on our shields like crystal. There were some twenty of us, that lay close couched down among the reeds and bulrushes that grew in the moat that goes round the city. The rest of us made tolerable shift; for every man had been careful to bring with him a good cloak or mantle to wrap over his armor and keep himself warm: but I, as it chanced, had left my cloak behind me, as not expecting that the night would prove so cool; or rather, I believe, because I had at that time a brave suit of new armor on, which, being a soldier, and having some of the soldier's vice about me, — *vanity*, — I was not willing should be hidden under a cloak. But I paid for my indiscretion with my sufferings; for with the inclement night, and the wet of the ditch in which we lay, I was well-nigh frozen to death: and, when I could endure no longer, I jogged Ulysses, who was next to me, and had a nimble ear, and made known my case to him, assuring him that I must inevitably perish. He answered, in a low whisper, 'Hush! lest any Greek should hear you, and take notice of your softness.' Not a word more he said, but showed as if he had no pity for the plight I was in. But he was as considerate as he was brave; and even then, as he lay with his head reposing upon his hand, he was meditating how to relieve me, without exposing my weakness to the soldiers. At last, raising up his head, he made as if he had been asleep, and said, 'Friends, I have been warned in a dream to send to the fleet to King Agamemnon for a supply, to recruit our numbers; for we are not sufficient for this enterprise:' and, they believing him, one Thoas was despatched on that errand, who departing, for more speed, as Ulysses had foreseen, left his upper garment behind him, a good warm mantle, to which I succeeded, and, by the help of it, got through the night with credit. This shift Ulysses made for one in need; and would to Heaven that I had now that strength in my limbs which made me in those days to be accounted fit to be a leader under Ulysses! I should not then want the loan of a cloak or a mantle to wrap about me, and shield my old limbs from the night-air."

The tale pleased the herdsmen; and Eumæus, who more than all the rest was gratified to hear tales of Ulysses, true or false, said, that for his story he deserved a mantle and a night's lodging, which he should have; and he spread for him a bed of goat and sheep skins by the fire: and the seeming beggar, who was indeed the true Ulysses, lay down and slept under that poor roof, in that abject disguise to which the will of Minerva had subjected him.

When morning was come, Ulysses made offer to depart, as if he were not willing to burthen his host's hospitality any longer, but said that he would go and try the humanity of the town's folk, if any there would bestow upon him a bit of bread or a cup of drink. Perhaps the queen's suitors (he said) out of their full feasts would bestow a scrap on him: for he could wait at table, if need were, and play the nimble serving-man; he could fetch wood (he said) or build a fire, prepare roast meat or boiled, mix the wine with water, or do any of those offices which recommended poor men like him to services in great men's houses.

"Alas! poor guest," said Eumæus, "you know not what you speak. What should so poor and old man as you do at the suitors' tables? Their light minds are not given to such grave servitors. They must have youths, richly tricked out in flowing vests, with curled hair, like so many of Jove's cup-bearers, to fill out the wine to them as they sit at table, and to shift their trenchers. Their gorged insolence would but despise and make a mock at thy age. Stay here. Perhaps the queen or Telemachus, hearing of thy arrival, may send to thee of their bounty."

As he spake these words, the steps of one crossing the front court were heard, and a noise of the dogs fawning and leaping about as for joy: by which token Eumæus guesed that it was the prince, who, hearing of a traveller being arrived at Eumæus' cottage that brought tidings of his father, was come to search the truth; and Eumæus said, "It is the tread of Telemachus, the son of King Ulysses." Before he could well speak the words, the prince was at the door; whom Ulysses rising to receive, Telemachus would not suffer that so aged a man as he appeared should rise to do respect to him; but he courteously and reverently took him by the hand, and inclined his head to him, as if he had surely known that it was his father indeed: but Ulysses covered his eyes with his hands, that he might not show the waters which stood in them. And Telemachus said, "Is this the man who can tell us tidings of the king, my father?"

"He brags himself to be a Cretan born," said Eumæus, "and that he has been a soldier and a traveller; but whether he speak the truth or not, he alone can tell. But, whatsoever he has been, what he is now is apparent. Such as he appears, I give him to you; do what you will with him: his boast at present is that he is at the very best a supplicant."

"Be he what he may," said Telemachus, "I accept him at your hands. But where I should bestow him I know not, seeing that, in the palace, his age would not exempt him from the scorn and contempt which my mother's suitors in their light minds would be sure to fling upon him: a mercy if he escaped without blows; for they are a company of evil men, whose profession is wrongs and violence."

Ulysses answered, "Since it is free for any man to speak in presence of your greatness, I must say that my heart puts on a wolfish inclination to tear and to devour, hearing your speech, that these suitors should with such injustice rage, where you should have the rule solely. What should the cause be? Do you wilfully give way to their ill manners? or has your government been such as has procured ill-will towards you from your people? or do you mistrust your kinsfolk and friends in such sort, as, without trial, to decline their aid? A man's kindred are they that he might trust to when extremities run high."

Telemachus replied, "The kindred of Ulysses are few. I have no brothers to assist me in the strife. But the suitors are powerful in kindred and friends. The house of old Arcesius has had this fate from the heavens, that from old it still has been supplied with single heirs. To Arcesius, Laertes only was born; from Laertes decended only Ulysses; from Ulysses, I alone have sprung, whom he left so young, that from me never comfort arose to him. But the end of all rests in the hands of the gods."

Then, Eumæus departing to see to some necessary business of his herds, Minerva took a woman's shape, and stood in the entry of the door, and was seen to Ulysses: but by his son she was not seen; for the presences of the gods are invisible save to those to whom they will to reveal themselves. Nevertheless, the dogs which were about the door saw the goddess, and durst not bark, but went crouching and licking of the dust for fear. And, giving signs to Ulysses that the time was now come in which he should make himself known to his son, by her great power she changed back his shape into the same which it was before she transformed him; and Telemachus, who saw the change, but nothing of the manner by which it was effected, only he saw the appearance of a king in the vigor of his age where but just now he had seen a worn and decrepit beggar, was struck with fear, and said, "Some god has done this house this honor;" and he turned away his eyes, and would have worshipped. But his father permitted not, but said, "Look better at me. I am no deity: why put you upon me the reputation of godhead? I am no more but thy father: I am even he. I am that Ulysses, by reason of whose absence thy youth has been exposed to such wrongs from injurious men." Then kissed he his son, nor could any longer refrain those tears which he had held under such mighty restraint before, though they would ever be forcing themselves out in spite of him; but now, as if their sluices had burst, they came out like rivers, pouring upon the warm cheeks of his son. Nor yet by all these violent arguments could Telemachus be persuaded to believe that it was his father, but he said some deity had taken that shape to mock him; for he affirmed, that it was not in the power of any man, who is sustained by mortal food, to change his shape so in a moment from age to youth: for "but now," said he, "you were all wrinkles, and were old; and now you look as the gods are pictured."

His father replied, "Admire, but fear not, and know me to be at all parts substantially thy father, who in the inner powers of his mind, and the unseen workings of a father's love to thee, answers to his outward shape and pretence. There shall no more Ulysseses come here. I am he, that after twenty years' absence, and suffering a world of ill, have recovered at last the sight of my country earth. It was the will of Minerva that I should be changed as you saw me. She put me thus together: she puts together or takes to pieces whom she pleases. It is in the law of her free power to do it, — sometimes to show her favorites under a cloud, and poor, and again to restore to them their ornaments. The gods raise and throw down men with ease."

Then Telemachus could hold out no longer: but he gave way now to a full belief and persuasion of that which for joy at first he could not credit, — that it was indeed his true and very father that stood before him; and they embraced, and mingled their tears.

Then said Ulysses, "Tell me who these suitors are,

what are their numbers, and how stands the queen thy mother affected to them."

"She bears them still in expectation," said Telemachus, "which she never means to fulfil, that she will accept the hand of some one of them in second nuptials; for she fears to displease them by an absolute refusal. So from day to day she lingers them on with hope, which they are content to bear the deferring of, while they have entertainment at free cost in our palace."

Then said Ulysses, "Reckon up their numbers, that we may know their strength and ours, if we, having none but ourselves, may hope to prevail against them."

"O father!" he replied, "I have ofttimes heard of your fame for wisdom, and of the great strength of your arm; but the venturous mind which your speeches now indicate moves me even to amazement: for in no wise can it consist with wisdom or a sound mind, that two should try their strengths against a host. Nor five, or ten, or twice ten strong, are these suitors, but many more by much: from Dulichium came there fifty and two, they and their servants; twice twelve crossed the seas hither from Samos; from Zacynthus, twice ten; of our native Ithacans, men of chief note, are twelve who aspire to the bed and crown of Penelope; and all these under one strong roof, — a fearful odds against two! My father, there is need of caution, lest the cup which your great mind so thirsts to taste of vengeance prove bitter to yourself in the drinking; and therefore it were well that we should bethink us of some one who might assist us in this undertaking."

"Thinkest thou," said his father, "if we had Minerva and the king of skies to be our friends, would their sufficiencies make strong our part? or must we look out for some further aid yet?"

"They you speak of are above the clouds," said Telemachus, "and are sound aids indeed, as powers that not only exceed human, but bear the chiefest sway among the gods themselves."

Then Ulysses gave directions to his son to go and mingle with the suitors, and in no wise to impart his secret to any,— not even to the queen, his mother; but to hold himself in readiness, and to have his weapons and his good armor in preparation. And he charged him, that when he himself should come to the palace, as he meant to follow shortly after, and present himself in his beggar's likeness to the suitors, that whatever he should see which might grieve his heart, with what foul usage and contumelious language soever the suitors should receive his father, coming in that shape, though they should strike and drag him by the heels along the floors, that he should not stir nor make offer to oppose them, further than by mild words to expostulate with them, until Minerva from heaven should give the sign which should be the prelude to their destruction. And Telemachus, promising to obey his instructions, departed: and the shape of Ulysses fell to what it had been before; and he became to all outward appearance a beggar, in base and beggarly attire.

CHAPTER IX.

THE QUEEN'S SUITORS. — THE BATTLE OF THE BEGGARS. — THE ARMOR TAKEN DOWN. — THE MEETING WITH PENELOPE.

FROM the house of Eumæus the seeming beggar took his way, leaning on his staff, till he reached the palace; entering in at the hall where the suitors sat at meat. They, in the pride of their feasting, began to break their jests in mirthful manner when they saw one looking so poor and so aged approach. He, who expected no better entertainment, was nothing moved at their behavior; but, as became the character which he had assumed, in a suppliant posture crept by turns to every suitor, and held out his hands for some charity, with such a natural and beggar-resembling grace, that he might seem to have practised begging all his life: yet there was a sort of dignity in his most abject stoopings, that whoever had seen him would have said, "If it had pleased Heaven that this poor man had been born a king, he would gracefully have filled a throne." And some pitied him, and some gave him alms, as their present humors inclined them; but the greater part reviled him, and bade him begone, as one that spoiled their feast: for the presence of misery has this power with it, — that, while it stays, it can dash and overturn the mirth even of those who feel no pity, or wish to relieve it; Nature bearing this witness of herself in the hearts of the most obdurate.

Now, Telemachus sat at meat with the suitors, and knew that it was the king, his father, who in that shape begged an alms; and when his father came and presented himself before him in turn, as he had done to the suitors one by one, he gave him of his own meat which he had in his dish, and of his own cup to drink: and the suitors were past measure offended to see a pitiful beggar, as they esteemed him, to be so choicely regarded by the prince.

Then Antinous, who was a great lord, and of chief note among the suitors, said, "Prince Telemachus does ill to encourage these wandering beggars, who go from place to place, affirming that they have been some considerable persons in their time; filling the ears of such as hearken to them with lies, and pressing with their bold feet into kings' palaces. This is some saucy vagabond, some travelling Egyptian."

"I see," said Ulysses, "that a poor man should get but little at your board: scarce should he get salt from your hands, if he brought his own meat."

Lord Antinous, indignant to be answered with such sharpness by a supposed beggar, snatched up a stool, with which he smote Ulysses where the neck and shoulders join. This usage moved not Ulysses: but in his great heart he meditated deep evils to come upon them all, which for a time must be kept close; and he went and sat himself down in the doorway to eat of that which was given him; and he said, "For life or possessions a man will fight; but for his belly this man smites. If a poor man has any god to take his part, my Lord Antinous shall not live to be the queen's husband."

Then Antinous raged highly, and threatened to drag him by the heels, and to rend his rags about his ears, if he spoke another word.

But the other suitors did in no wise approve of the harsh language, nor of the blow which Antinous had dealt; and some of them said, "Who knows but one of the deities goes about, hid under that poor disguise? for, in the likeness of poor pilgrims, the gods have many times descended to try the dispositions of men, whether they be humane or impious." While these things passed, Telemachus sat and observed all, but held his peace, remembering the instructions of his father. But secretly he waited for the sign which Minerva was to send from heaven.

That day, there followed Ulysses to the court one of the common sort of beggars, Irus by name, — one that had received alms before-time of the suitors, and was their ordinary sport, when they were inclined (as that day) to give way to mirth, to see him eat and drink; for he had the appetite of six men, and was of huge stature and proportions of body, yet had in him no spirit nor courage of a man. This man, thinking to curry favor with the suitors, and recommend himself especially to such a great lord as Antinous was, began to revile and scorn Ulysses, putting foul language upon him, and fairly challenging him to fight with the fist. But Ulysses, deeming his railings to be nothing more than jealousy, and that envious disposition which beggars commonly manifest to brothers in their trade, mildly besought him not to trouble him, but to enjoy that portion which the liberality of their entertainers gave him, as he did, quietly; seeing that, of their bounty, there was sufficient for all.

But Irus, thinking that this forbearance in Ulysses was nothing more than a sign of fear, so much the more highly stormed and bellowed, and provoked him to fight: and by this time the quarrel had attracted the notice of the suitors, who with loud laughters and shouting egged on the dispute; and Lord Antinous swore by all the gods it should be a battle, and that in that hall the strife should be determined. To this the rest of the suitors, with violent clamors, acceded; and a circle was made for the combatants, and a fat goat was proposed as the victor's prize, as at the Olympic or the Pythian games. Then Ulysses, seeing no remedy, or being not unwilling that the suitors should behold some proof of that strength which ere long in their own persons they were to taste of, stripped himself, and prepared for the combat. But first he demanded that he should have fair play shown him; that none in that assembly should aid his opponent, or take part against him: for, being an old man, they might easily crush him with their strengths. And Telemachus passed his word that no foul play should be shown him, but that each party should be left to their own unassisted strengths; and to this he made Antinous and the rest of the suitors swear.

But when Ulysses had laid aside his garments, and was bare to the waist, all the beholders admired at the goodly sight of his large shoulders being of such exquisite shape and whiteness, and at his great and brawny bosom, and the youthful strength which seemed to remain in a man thought so old; and they said, "What limbs and what sinews he has!" and coward fear seized on the mind of that great vast beggar, and he dropped his threats and his big words, and would have fled: but Lord Antinous stayed him, and threatened him, that, if he declined the combat, he would put him in a ship, and land him on the shores where King Echetus reigned, — the roughest tyrant which at that time the world contained, and who had that antipathy to rascal beggars such as he, that, when any landed on his coast, he would crop their ears and noses, and give them to the dogs to tear. So Irus, in whom fear of King Echétus prevailed above the fear of Ulysses, addressed himself to fight. But Ulysses, provoked to be engaged in so odious a strife with a fellow of his base conditions, and loathing longer to be made a spectacle to entertain the eyes of his foes, with one blow, which he struck him beneath the ear, so shattered the teeth and jaw-bone of this soon-baffled coward, that he laid him sprawling in the dust, with small stomach or ability to renew the contest. Then, raising him on his feet, he led him bleeding and sputtering to the door, and put his staff into his hand, and bade him go use his command upon dogs and swine, but not presume himself to be lord of the guests another time, nor of the beggary!

The suitors applauded in their vain minds the issue of the contest, and rioted in mirth at the expense of poor Irus, who they vowed should be forthwith embarked, and sent to King Echetus; and they bestowed thanks on Ulysses for ridding the court of that unsavory morsel, as they called him: but in their inward souls they would not have cared if Irus had been victor, and Ulysses had taken the foil; but it was mirth to them to see the beggars fight. In such pastimes and light entertainments the day wore away.

When evening was come, the suitors betook themselves to music and dancing; and Ulysses leaned his back against a pillar from which certain lamps hung which gave light to the dancers, and he made show of watching the dancers; but very different thoughts were in his head. And, as he stood near the lamps, the light fell upon his head, which was thin of hair, and bald, as an old man's. And Eurymachus, a suitor, taking occasion from some words which were spoken before, scoffed, and said, "Now I know for a certainty that some god lurks under the poor and beggarly appearance of this man; for, as he stands by the lamps, his sleek head throws beams around it, like as it were a glory." And another said, "He passes his time, too, not much unlike the gods; lazily living exempt from labor, taking offerings of men." — "I warrant," said Eurymachus again, "he could not raise a fence or dig a ditch for his livelihood, if a man would hire him to work in a garden."

"I wish," said Ulysses, "that you who speak this, and myself, were to be tried at any task-work; that I had a good crooked scythe put in my hand, that was sharp and strong, and you such another, where the grass grew longest, to be up by daybreak, mowing the meadows till the sun went down, not tasting of food till we had finished; or that we were set to plough four acres in one day of good glebe land, to see whose furrows were evenest and cleanest; or that we might have one wrestling-bout together; or that in our right hands a good steel-headed lance were placed, to try whose blows fell heaviest and thickest upon the adversary's head-piece. I would cause you such work, as you should have small reason to reproach me with being slack at work. But you would do well to spare me this reproach, and to save your strength till the owner of this house shall return, — till the day when Ulysses shall return; when, returning, he shall enter upon his birthright."

This was a galling speech to those suitors, to whom Ulysses' return was indeed the thing which they most dreaded; and a sudden fear fell upon their souls, as if they were sensible of the real presence of that man who did indeed stand amongst them, but not in that form as they might know him; and Eurymachus, incensed, snatched a massy cup which stood on a table near, and hurled it at the head of the supposed beggar, and but narrowly missed the hitting of him; and all the suitors rose, as at once, to thrust him out of the hall, which they said his beggarly presence and his rude speeches had profaned. But Telemachus cried to them to forbear, and not to presume to lay hands upon a wretched man to whom he had promised protection. He asked if they were mad, to mix such abhorred uproar with his feasts. He bade them take their food and their wine; to sit up or to go to bed at their free pleasures, so long as he should give license to that freedom: but why should they abuse his banquet, or let the words which a poor beggar spake have power to move their spleens so fiercely?

They bit their lips, and frowned for anger, to be checked so by a youth: nevertheless, for that time they had the grace to abstain, either for shame, or that Minerva had infused into them a terror of Ulysses' son.

So that day's feast was concluded without bloodshed; and the suitors, tired with their sports, departed severally each man to his apartment. Only Ulysses and Telemachus remained. And now Telemachus, by his father's direction, went and brought down into the hall armor and lances from the armory; for Ulysses said, "On the morrow we shall have need of them." And moreover he said, "If any one shall ask why you have taken them down, say it is to clean them, and scour them from the rust which they have gathered since the owner of this house went for Troy." And, as Telemachus stood by the armor, the lights were all gone out, and it was pitch dark, and the armor gave out glistering beams as of fire; and he said to his father, "The pillars of the house are on fire." And his father said, "It is the gods who sit above the stars, and have power to make the night as light as the day;" and he took it for a good omen. And Telemachus fell to cleaning and sharpening of the lances.

Now, Ulysses had not seen his wife Penelope in all the time since his return; for the queen did not care to mingle with the suitors at their banquets, but, as became one that had been Ulysses' wife, kept much in private, spinning, and doing her excellent housewiferies among her maids in the remote apartments of the palace. Only upon solemn days she would come down and show herself to the suitors. And Ulysses was filled with a longing desire to see his wife again, whom for twenty years he had not beheld; and he softly stole through the known passages of his beautiful house, till he came where the maids were lighting the queen through a stately gallery that led to the chamber where she slept. And, when the maids saw Ulysses, they said, "It is the beggar who came to the court to-day, about whom all that uproar was stirred up in the hall: what does he here?" But Penelope gave commandment that he should be brought before her; for she said, "It may be that he has travelled, and has heard something concerning Ulysses."

Then was Ulysses right glad to hear himself named by his queen; to find himself in no wise forgotten, nor her great love towards him decayed in all that time that he had been away. And he stood before his queen; and she knew him not to be Ulysses, but supposed that he had been some poor traveller. And she asked him of what country he was.

He told her (as he had before told to Eumæus) that he was a Cretan born, and, however poor and cast down he now seemed, no less a man than brother to Idomeneus, who was grandson to King Minos; and, though he now wanted bread, he had once had it in his power to feast Ulysses. Then he feigned how Ulysses, sailing for Troy, was forced by stress of weather to put his fleet in at a port of Crete, where for twelve days he was his guest, and entertained by him with all befitting guest-rites; and he described the very garments which Ulysses had on, by which Penelope knew he had seen her lord.

In this manner, Ulysses told his wife many tales of himself, at most but painting, but painting so near to the life, that the feeling of that which she took in at her ears became so strong, that the kindly tears ran down her fair cheeks, while she thought upon her lord, dead as she thought him, and heavily mourned the loss of him whom she missed, whom she could not find, though in very deed he stood so near her.

Ulysses was moved to see her weep: but he kept his own eyes as dry as iron or horn in their lids; putting a bridle upon his strong passion, that it should not issue to sight.

Then told he how he had lately been at the court of Thresprotia, and what he had learned concerning Ulysses there, in order as he had delivered to Eumæus: and Penelope was wont to believe that there might be a possibility of Ulysses being alive; and she said, "I dreamed a dream this morning. Methought I had twenty household fowl which did eat wheat steeped in water from my hand; and there came suddenly from the clouds a crook-beaked hawk, who soused on them, and killed them all, trussing their necks; then took his flight back up to the clouds. And, in my dream, methought that I wept and made great moan for my fowls, and for the destruction which the hawk had made; and my maids came about me to comfort me. And, in the height of my griefs, the hawk came back; and, lighting upon the beam of my chamber, he said to me in a man's voice, which sounded strangely, even in my dream, to hear a hawk to speak: 'Be of good cheer,' he said, 'O daughter of Icarius! for this is no dream which thou hast seen, but that which shall happen to thee indeed. Those household fowl which thou lamentest so without reason are the suitors who devour thy substance, even as thou sawest the fowl eat from thy hand; and the hawk is thy husband, who is coming to give death to the suitors.' And I awoke, and went to see to my fowls, if they were alive, whom I found eating wheat from their troughs, all well and safe as before my dream."

Then said Ulysses, "This dream can endure no other interpretation than that which the hawk gave to it, who is your lord, and who is coming quickly to effect all that his words told you."

"Your words," she said, "my old guest, are so sweet, that, would you sit and please me with your speech, my ears would never let my eyes close their spheres for very joy of your discourse: but none that is merely mortal can live without the death of sleep, so the gods who are without death themselves have ordained it, to keep the memory of our mortality in our minds, while we experience, that, as much as we live, we die every day; in which consideration I will ascend my bed, which I have nightly watered with my tears since he that was the joy of it departed for that bad city:" she so speaking, because she could not bring her lips to name the name of Troy, so much hated. So for that night they parted, — Penelope to her bed, and Ulysses to his son, and to the armor and the lances in the hall; where they sat up all night cleaning and watching by the armor.

CHAPTER X.

THE MADNESS FROM ABOVE. — THE BOW OF ULYSSES. — THE SLAUGHTER. — THE CONCLUSION.

When daylight appeared, a tumultuous concourse of the suitors again filled the hall; and some wondered, and some inquired, what meant that glittering store of armor and lances which lay on heaps by the entry of the door: and all that asked, Telemachus made reply, that he had caused them to be taken down to cleanse them of the rust and of the stain which they had contracted by lying so long unused, even ever since his father went for Troy; and with that answer their minds were easily satisfied. So to their feasting and vain rioting again they fell. Ulysses, by Telemachus' order, had a seat and a mess assigned him in the doorway; and he had his eye ever on the lances. And it moved gall in some of the great ones there present to have their feast still dulled with the society of that wretched beggar, as they deemed him; and they reviled and spurned at him with their feet. Only there was one Philætius, who had something of a better nature than the rest, that spake kindly to him, and had his age in respect. He, coming up to Ulysses, took him by the hand with a kind of fear, as if touched exceedingly with imagination of his great worth, and said thus to him: "Hail, father stranger! My brows have sweat to see the injuries which you have received; and my eyes have broken forth in tears when I have only thought, that, such being oftentimes the lot of worthiest men, to this plight Ulysses may be reduced, and that he now may wander from place to place as you do: for such, who are compelled by need to range here and there, and have no firm home to fix their feet upon, God keeps them in this earth, as under water; so are they kept down and depressed. And a dark thread is sometimes spun in the fates of kings."

At this bare likening of the beggar to Ulysses, Minerva from heaven made the suitors for foolish joy to go mad, and roused them to such a laughter as would never stop: they laughed without power of ceasing; their eyes stood full of tears for violent joys. But fears and horrible misgivings succeeded; and one among them stood up and prophesied: "Ah, wretches!" he said, "what madness from heaven has seized you, that you can laugh? See you not that your meat drops blood? A night, like the night of death, wraps you about; you shriek without knowing it; your eyes thrust forth tears; the fixed walls, and the beam that bears the whole house up, fall blood; ghosts choke up the entry; full is the hall with apparitions of murdered men; under your feet is hell; the sun falls from heaven, and it is midnight at noon." But, like men whom the gods had infatuated to their destruction, they mocked at his fears; and Eurymachus said, "This man is surely mad: conduct him forth into the market-place; set him in the light; for he dreams that 'tis night within the house."

But Theoclymenus (for that was the prophet's name), whom Minerva had graced with a prophetic spirit, that he, foreseeing, might avoid the destruction which awaited them, answered, and said, "Eurymachus, I will not require a guide of thee: for I have eyes and ears, the use of both my feet, and a sane mind within me; and with these I will go forth of the doors, because I know the imminent evils which await all you that stay, by reason of this poor guest, who is a favorite with all the gods." So saying, he turned his back upon those inhospitable men, and went away home, and never returned to the palace.

These words which he spoke were not unheard by Telemachus, who kept still his eye upon his father, expecting fervently when he would give the sign which was to precede the slaughter of the suitors.

They, dreaming of no such thing, fell sweetly to their

dinner, as joying in the great store of banquet which was heaped in full tables about them; but there reigned not a bitterer banquet planet in all heaven than that which hung over them this day, by secret destination of Minerva.

There was a bow which Ulysses left when he went for Troy. It had lain by since that time, out of use, and unstrung; for no man had strength to draw that bow save Ulysses. So it had remained as a monument of the great strength of its master. This bow, with the quiver of arrows belonging thereto, Telemachus had brought down from the armory on the last night, along with the lances: and now Minerva, intending to do Ulysses an honor, put it into the mind of Telemachus to propose to the suitors to try who was strongest to draw that bow; and he promised, that, to the man who should be able to draw that bow, his mother should be given in marriage, — Ulysses' wife the prize to him who should bend the bow of Ulysses.

There was great strife and emulation stirred up among the suitors at those words of the Prince Telemachus. And to grace her son's words, and to confirm the promise which he had made, Penelope came and showed herself that day to the suitors; and Minerva made her that she appeared never so comely in their sight as that day: and they were inflamed with the beholding of so much beauty, proposed as the price of so great manhood; and they cried out, that if all those heroes who sailed to Colchis for the rich purchase of the golden-fleeced ram had seen earth's richer prize, Penelope, they would not have made their voyage, but would have vowed their valors and their lives to her; for she was at all parts faultless.

And she said, "The gods have taken my beauty from me since my lord went for Troy." But Telemachus willed his mother to depart, and not be present at that contest; for he said, "It may be, some rougher strife shall chance of this than may be expedient for a woman to witness." And she retired, she and her maids, and left the hall.

Then the bow was brought into the midst, and a mark was set up by Prince Telemachus; and Lord Antinous, as the chief among the suitors, had the first offer; and he took the bow, and, fitting an arrow to the string, he strove to bend it. But not with all his might and main could he once draw together the ends of that tough bow; and, when he found how vain a thing it was to endeavor to draw Ulysses' bow, he desisted, blushing for shame and for mere anger. Then Eurymachus adventured, but with no better suceess: but as it had torn the hands of Antinous, so did the bow tear and strain his hands, and marred his delicate fingers; yet could he not once stir the string. Then called he to the attendants to bring fat and unctuous matter; which melting at the fire, he dipped the bow therein, thinking to supple it, and make it more pliable: but not with all the helps of art could he succeed in making it to move. After him Liodes and Amphinomus and Polybus and Eurynomus and Polyctorides essayed their strength; but not any one of them, or of the rest of those aspiring suitors, had any better luck: yet not the meanest of them there but thought himself well worthy of Ulysses' wife; though, to shoot with Ulysses' bow, the completest champion among them was by proof found too feeble.

Then Ulysses prayed that he might have leave to try:

and immediately a clamor was raised among the suitors, because of his petition; and they scorned and swelled with rage at his presumption, and that a beggar should seek to contend in a game of such noble mastery. But Telemachus ordered that the bow should be given him, and that he should have leave to try, since they had failed; "for," he said, "the bow is mine, to give or to withhold:" and none durst gainsay the prince.

Then Ulysses gave a sign to his son, and he commanded the doors of the hall to be made fast; and all wondered at his words, but none could divine the cause. And Ulysses took the bow into his hands; and, before he essayed to bend it, he surveyed it at all parts, to see whether, by long lying by, it had contracted any stiffness which hindered the drawing: and, as he was busied in the curious surveying of his bow, some of the suitors mocked him, and said, "Past doubt, this man is a right cunning archer, and knows his craft well. See how he turns it over and over, and looks into it, as if he could see through the wood!" And others said, "We wish some one would tell out gold into our laps but for so long a time as he shall be in drawing of that string." But when he had spent some little time in making proof of the bow, and had found it to be in good plight, like as an harper in tuning of his harp draws out a string, with such ease or much more did Ulysses draw to the head the string of his own tough bow; and, in letting of it go, it twanged with such a shrill noise as a swallow makes when it sings through the air: which so much amazed the suitors, that their colors came and went, and the skies gave out a noise of thunder, which at heart cheered Ulysses; for he knew that now his long labors, by the disposal of the Fates, drew to an end. Then fitted he an arrow to the bow; and, drawing it to the head, he sent it right to the mark which the prince had set up. Which done, he said to Telemachus, "You have got no disgrace yet by your guest; for I have struck the mark I shot at, and gave myself no such trouble in teasing the bow with fat and fire as these men did, but have made proof that my strength is not impaired, nor my age so weak and contemptible as these were pleased to think it. But come: the day going down calls us to supper; after which succeed poem and harp, and all delights which used to crown princely banquetings."

So saying, he beckoned to his son, who straight girt his sword to his side, and took one of the lances (of which there lay great store from the armory) in his hand, and, armed at all points, advanced towards his father.

The upper rags which Ulysses wore fell from his shoulder, and his own kingly likeness returned; when he rushed to the great hall-door with bow and quiver full of shafts, which down at his feet he poured, and in bitter words presignified his deadly intent to the suitors. "Thus far," he said, "this contest has been decided harmless: now for us there rests another mark, harder to hit, but which my hands shall essay notwithstanding, if Phœbus, god of archers, be pleased to give me the mastery." With that he let fly a deadly arrow at Antinous, which pierced him in the throat, as he was in the act of lifting a cup of wine to his mouth. Amazement seized the suitors as their great champion fell dead; and they raged highly against Ulysses, and said that it should prove the dearest shaft which he ever let fly; for he had slain a man whose like breathed not in any part of the kingdom: and they flew to their arms, and would have seized the lances; but Minerva struck them with dimness of sight, that they went erring up and down the hall, not knowing where to find them. Yet so infatuated were they by the displeasure of Heaven, that they did not see the imminent peril which impended over them; but every man believed that this accident had happened beside the intention of the doer. Fools! to think by shutting their eyes to evade destiny, or that any other cup remained for them but that which their great Antinous had tasted!

Then Ulysses revealed himself to all in that presence, and that he was the man whom they held to be dead at Troy, whose palace they had usurped, whose wife in his lifetime they had sought in impious marriage, and that for this reason destruction was come upon them. And he dealt his deadly arrows among them, and there was no avoiding him, nor escaping from his horrid person; and Telemachus by his side plied them thick with those murderous lances from which there was no retreat, till fear itself made them valiant, and danger gave them eyes to understand the peril. Then they which had swords drew them, and some with shields that could find them, and some with tables and benches snatched up in haste, rose in a mass to overwhelm and crush those two: yet they singly bestirred themselves like men, and defended themselves against that great host; and through tables, shields, and all, right through, the arrows of Ulysses clove, and the irresistible lances of Telemachus; and many lay dead, and all had wounds. And Minerva, in the likeness of a bird, sate upon the beam which went across the hall, clapping her wings with a fearful noise: and sometimes the great bird would fly among them, cuffing at the swords and at the lances, and up and down the hall would go, beating her wings, and troubling every thing, that it was frightful to behold; and it frayed the blood from the cheeks of those heaven-hated suitors. But to Ulysses and his son she appeared in her own divine similitude, with her snake-fringed shield, a goddess armed, fighting their battles. Nor did that dreadful pair desist till they had laid all their foes at their feet. At their feet they lay in shoals: like fishes when the fishermen break up their nets, so they lay gasping and sprawling at the feet of Ulysses and his son. And Ulysses remembered the prediction of Tiresias, which said that he was to perish by his own guests, unless he slew those who knew him not.

Then certain of the queen's household went up, and told Penelope what had happened; and how her lord Ulysses was come home, and had slain the suitors. But she gave no heed to their words, but thought that some frenzy possessed them, or that they mocked her; for it is the property of such extremes of sorrow as she had felt not to believe when any great joy cometh. And she rated and chid them exceedingly for troubling her. But they the more persisted in their asseverations of the truth of what they had affirmed; and some of them had seen the slaughtered bodies of the suitors dragged forth of the hall. And they said, "That poor guest, whom you talked with last night, was Ulysses." Then she was yet more fully persuaded that they mocked her; and she wept. But they said, "This thing is true which we have told. We sat within, in an inner room in the palace, and the doors of the hall were shut on us: but we heard the cries and the groans of the men that were killed, but saw nothing, till at length your son called to us to come in; and, entering, we saw Ulysses standing in the midst of the slaughtered." But she, persisting in her unbelief, said that it was some god which had deceived them to think it was the person of Ulysses.

By this time, Telemachus and his father had cleansed their hands from the slaughter, and were come to where the queen was talking with those of her household; and, when she saw Ulysses, she stood motionless, and had no power to speak, — sudden surprise and joy and fear and many passions so strove within her. Sometimes she was clear that it was her husband that she saw, and sometimes the alteration which twenty years had made in his person (yet that was not much) perplexed her, that she knew not what to think, and for joy she could not believe, and yet for joy she would not but believe; and, above all, that sudden change from a beggar to a king troubled her, and wrought uneasy scruples in her mind. But Telemachus, seeing her strangeness, blamed her, and called her an ungentle and tyrannous mother; and said that she showed a too great curiousness of modesty to abstain from embracing his father, and to have doubts of his person, when, to all present, it was evident that he was the very real and true Ulysses.

Then she mistrusted no longer; but ran and fell upon Ulysses' neck, and said, "Let not my husband be angry that I held off so long with strange delays: it is the gods, who, severing us for so long time, have caused this unseemly distance in me. If Menelaus' wife had used half my caution, she would never have taken so freely to a stranger's bed; and she might have spared us all these plagues which have come upon us through her shameless deed."

These words, with which Penelope excused herself, wrought more affection in Ulysses than if, upon a first sight, she had given up herself implicitly to his embraces; and he wept for joy to possess a wife so discreet, so answering to his own staid mind, that had a depth of wit proportioned to his own, and one that held chaste virtue at so high a price. And he thought the possession of such a one cheaply purchased with the loss of all Circe's delights, and Calypso's immortality of joys; and his long labors and his severe sufferings past seemed as nothing, now they were crowned with the enjoyment of his virtuous and true wife, Penelope. And as sad men at sea, whose ship has gone to pieces nigh shore, swimming for their lives, all drenched in foam and brine, crawl up to some poor patch of land, which they take possession of with as great a joy as if they had the world given them in fee, — with such delight did this chaste wife cling to her lord restored, till the dark night fast coming on reminded her of that more intimate and happy union, when, in her long-widowed bed, she should once again clasp a living Ulysses.

So, from that time, the land had rest from the suitors. And the happy Ithacans, with songs and solemn sacrifices of praise to the gods, celebrated the return of Ulysses; for he that had been so long absent was returned to wreak the evil upon the heads of the doers: in the place where they had done the evil, there wreaked he his vengeance upon them.

TALES.

TALES.

REMINISCENCES OF JUKE JUDKINS, ESQ.,

OF BIRMINGHAM.*

I AM the only son of a considerable brazier in Birmingham, who, dying in 1803, left me successor to the business, with no other encumbrance than a sort of rent-charge, which I am enjoined to pay out of it, of ninety-three pounds sterling *per annum*, to his widow, my mother; and which the improving state of the concern, I bless God, has hitherto enabled me to discharge with punctuality. (I say, I am enjoined to pay the said sum, but not strictly obligated: that is to say, as the will is worded, I believe the law would relieve me from the payment of it; but the wishes of a dying parent should in some sort have the effect of law.) So that, though the annual profits of my business, on an average of the last three or four years, would appear to an indifferent observer, who should inspect my shop-books, to amount to the sum of one thousand three hundred and three pounds, odd shillings, the real proceeds in that time have fallen short of that sum to the amount of the aforesaid payment of ninety-three pounds sterling annually.

* From "The New Monthly Magazine," 1826.

I was always my father's favorite. He took a delight, to the very last, in recounting the little sagacious tricks and innocent artifices of my childhood. One manifestation thereof I never heard him repeat without tears of joy trickling down his cheeks. It seems, that when I quitted the parental roof (Aug. 27, 1788), being then six years and not quite a month old, to proceed to the Free School at Warwick, where my father was a sort of trustee, my mother — as mothers are usually provident on these occasions — had stuffed the pockets of the coach, which was to convey me and six more children of my own growth that were going to be entered along with me at the same seminary, with a prodigious quantity of gingerbread, which I remember my father said was more than was needed : and so indeed it was ; for, if I had been to eat it all myself, it would have got stale and mouldy before it had been half spent. The consideration whereof set me upon my contrivances how I might secure to myself as much of the gingerbread as would keep good for the next two or three days, and yet none of the rest in manner be wasted. I had a little pair of pocket-compasses, which I usually carried about me for the purpose of making draughts and measurements, at which I was always very ingenious, of the various engines and mechanical inventions in which such a town as Birmingham abounded. By the means of these, and a small penknife which my father had given me, I cut out the one-half of the cake, calculating that the remainder would reasonably serve my turn ; and subdividing it into many little slices, which were curious to see for the neatness and niceness of their proportion, I sold it out in so many pennyworths to my young companions as served us all the way to Warwick, which is a distance of some twenty miles from this town: and very merry, I assure you, we made ourselves with it, feasting all the way. By this honest stratagem, I put double the prime cost of the gingerbread into my purse, and secured as much as I thought would keep good and moist for my next two or three days' eating. When I told this to my parents on their first visit to me at Warwick, my father (good man) patted me on the cheek, and stroked my head, and seemed as if he could never make enough of me; but my mother unaccountably burst into tears, and said "it was a very niggardly action," or some such expression, and that "she would rather it would please God to take me" — meaning, God help me, that I should die — "than that she should live to see me grow up a *mean man:*" which shows the difference of parent from parent, and how some mothers are more harsh and intolerant to their children than some fathers; when we might expect quite the contrary. My father, however, loaded me with presents from that time, which made me the envy of my school-fellows. As I felt this growing disposition in them, I naturally sought to avert it by all the means in my power; and from that time I used to eat my little packages of fruit, and other nice things, in a corner, so privately that I was never found out. Once, I remember, I had a huge apple sent me, of that sort which they call *cats'-heads.* I concealed this all day under my pillow; and at night, but not before I had ascertained that my bed-fellow was sound asleep, — which I did by pinching him rather smartly two or three times, which he seemed to perceive no more than a dead person, though once or twice he made a motion as he would turn, which frightened me, — I say, when I had made all sure, I fell to work upon my apple; and, though it was as big as an ordinary man's two fists, I made shift to get through before it was time to get up. And a more delicious feast I never made; thinking all night what a good parent I had (I mean my father) to send me so many nice things, when the poor lad that lay by me had no parent or friend in the world to send him any thing nice: and, thinking of his desolate condition, I munched and munched as silently as I could, that I might not set him a-longing if he overheard me. And yet, for all this considerateness and attention to other people's feelings, I was never much a favorite with my school-fellows; which I have often wondered at, seeing that I never defrauded any one of them of the value of a halfpenny, or told stories of them to their master, as some little lying boys would do, but was ready to do any of them all the services in my power that were consistent with my own well-doing. I think nobody can be expected to go further than that. But I am detaining my reader too long in recording of my juvenile days. It is time I should go forward to a season when it became natural that I should have some thoughts of marrying, and, as they say, settling in the world. Nevertheless, my reflections on what I may call the boyish period of my life may have their use to some readers. It is pleasant to trace the man in the boy; to observe shoots of generosity in those young years; and to watch the progress of liberal sentiments, and what I may call a genteel way of thinking, which is discernible in some children at a very early age, and usually lays the foundation of all that is praiseworthy in the manly character afterwards.

With the warmest inclinations towards that way of life, and a serious conviction of its superior advantages over a single one, it has been the strange infelicity of my lot never to have entered into the respectable estate of matrimony. Yet I was once very near it. I courted a young woman in my twenty-seventh year; for so early I began to feel symptoms of the tender passion! She was well to do in the world, as they call it; but yet not such a fortune, as, all things considered, perhaps I might have pretended to. It was not my own choice altogether; but my mother very strongly pressed me to it. She was always putting it to me, that "I had comings-in sufficient, — that I need not stand upon a portion;" though the young woman, to do her justice, had considerable expectations, which yet did not quite come up to my mark, as I told you before. She had this saying always in her mouth, that "I had money enough; that it was time I enlarged my housekeeping, and to show a spirit befitting my circumstances." In short, what with her importunities, and my own desires *in part* co-operating, — for, as I said, I was not yet quite twenty-seven, — a time when the youthful feelings may be pardoned, if they show a little impetuosity, — I resolved, I say, upon all these considerations, to set about the business of courting in right earnest. I was a young man then; and having a spice of romance in my character (as the reader has doubtless observed long ago), such as that sex is apt to be taken with, I had reason in no long time to think my addresses were any thing but disagreeable. Certainly the happiest part of a young man's life is the time when he is going a-courting. All the generous impulses are then awake, and he feels a double existence in participating his hopes and wishes with another being. Return yet again for a brief moment, ye visionary views, — transient enchantments! ye moonlight rambles with Cleora in the Silent Walk at Vauxhall, (N.B. — About a mile from Birmingham, and resembling the gardens of that name near London, only that the price of admission is lower,) when the nightingale has suspended her notes in June to listen to our loving discourses, while the moon was overhead! (for we generally used to take our tea at Cleora's mother's before we set out, not so much to save expenses as to avoid the publicity of a repast in the gardens, — coming in much about the time of half-price, as they call it,) — ye soft intercommunions of soul, when, exchanging mutual vows, we prattled of coming felicities! The loving disputes we have had under those trees, when this house (planning our future settlement) was rejected, because, though cheap, it was dull; and the other house was given up, because, though agreeably situated, it was too high-rented! — one was too much in the heart of the town, another was too far from business. These minutiæ will seem impertinent to the aged and the prudent. I write them only to the young. Young lovers, and passionate as being young (such were Cleora and I then), alone can understand me. After some weeks wasted, as I may now call it, in this sort of amorous colloquy, we at length fixed upon the house in the High Street, No. 203, just vacated by the death of Mr. Hutton of this town, for our future residence. I had all the time lived in lodgings (only renting a shop for business), to be near my mother, — near, I say: not in the same house; for that would have been to introduce confusion into our housekeeping, which it was desirable to keep separate. Oh the loving wrangles, the endearing differences, I had with Cleora, before we could quite make up our minds to the house that was to receive us! — I pretending, for argument's sake, the rent was too high, and she insisting that the taxes were moderate in proportion; and love at last reconciling us in the same choice. I think at that time, moderately speaking, she might have had any thing out of me for asking. I do not, nor shall ever, regret that my character at that time was marked with a tinge of prodigality. Age comes fast enough upon us, and, in its good time, will prune away all that is inconvenient in these excesses. Perhaps it is right that it should do so. Matters, as I said, were ripening to a conclusion between us, only the house was yet not absolutely taken, — some necessary arrangements, which the ardor of my youthful impetuosity could hardly brook at that time (love and youth will be precipitate), — some preliminary arrangements, I say, with the landlord, respecting fixtures, — very necessary things to be considered in a young man about to settle in the world, though not very accordant with the impatient state of my then passions, — some obstacles about the valuation of the fixtures, — had hitherto precluded (and I shall always think providentially) my final closes with his offer; when one of those accidents, which, unimportant in themselves, often arise to give a turn to the most serious intentions of our life, intervened, and put an end at once to my projects of wiving and of housekeeping.

I was never much given to theatrical entertainments; that is, at no time of my life was I ever what they call a regular play-goer: but on some occasion of a benefit-night, which was expected to be very productive, and indeed turned out so, Cleora expressing a desire to be present, I could do no less than offer, as I did very willingly, to squire her and her mother to the pit. At that time, it was not customary in our town for tradesfolk, except some of the very topping ones, to sit, as they now do, in the boxes. At the time appointed, I waited upon the ladies, who had brought with them a young man, a distant relation, whom it seems they had invited to be of the party. This a little disconcerted me, as I had about me barely silver enough to pay for our three selves at the door, and did not at first know that their relation had proposed paying for himself. However, to do the young man justice, he not only paid for himself, but for the old lady besides; leaving me only to pay for two, as it were. In our passage to the theatre, the nótice of Cleora was attracted to some orange wenches that stood about the doors vending their commodities. She was leaning on my arm; and I could feel her every now and then giving me a nudge, as it is called, which I afterwards discovered were hints that I should buy some oranges. It seems, it is a custom at Birmingham, and perhaps in other places, when a gentleman treats ladies to the play, — especially when a full night is expected, and that the house will be inconveniently warm, — to provide them with this kind of fruit, oranges being esteemed for their cooling property. But how could I guess at that, never having treated ladies to a play before, and being, as I said, quite a novice at these kind of entertainments? At last, she spoke plain out, and begged that I would buy some of "those oranges," pointing to a particular barrow. But, when I came to examine the fruit, I did not think the quality of it was answerable to the price. In this way, I handled several baskets of them; but something in them all displeased me. Some had thin rinds, and some were plainly over-ripe, which is as great a fault as not being ripe enough; and I could not (what they call) make a bargain. While I stood haggling with the women, secretly determining to put off my purchase till I should get within the theatre, where I expected we should have better choice, the young man, the cousin (who, it seems, had left us without my missing him), came running to us with his pockets stuffed out with oranges, inside and out, as they say. It seems, not liking the look of the barrow-fruit any more than myself, he had slipped away to an eminent fruiterer's, about three doors distant, which I never had the sense to think of, and had lain out a matter of two shillings in some of the best St. Michael's, I think, I ever tasted. What a little hinge, as I said before, the most important affairs in life may turn upon! The mere inadvertence to the fact that there was an eminent fruiterer's within three doors of us, though we had just passed it without the thought once occurring to me, which he had taken advantage of, lost me the affection of my Cleora. From that time, she visibly cooled towards me; and her partiality was as visibly transferred to this cousin. I was long unable to account for this change in her behavior; when one day, accidentally discoursing of oranges to my mother, alone, she let drop a sort of reproach to me, as if I had offended Cleora by my *nearness*, as she called it, that evening. Even now, when Cleora has been wedded some years to that same officious relation, as I may call him, I can hardly be persuaded that such a trifle could have been the motive to her inconstancy; for could she suppose that I would sacrifice my dearest hopes in her to the paltry sum of two shillings, when I was going to treat her to the play, and her mother too (an expense of more than four times that amount), if the young man had not interfered to pay for the latter, as I mentioned? But the caprices of the sex are past finding out: and I begin to think my mother was in the right; for doubtless women know women better than we can pretend to know them.*

CUPID'S REVENGE.†

LEONTIUS, Duke of Lycia, who in times past had borne the character of a wise and just governor, and was endeared to all ranks of his subjects, in his latter days fell into a sort of dotage, which manifested itself in an extravagant fondness for his daughter Hidaspes. This young maiden, with the Prince Leucippus, her brother, were the only remembrances left to him of a

* These "Reminiscences" were advertised to be continued; but this chapter of them is all that ever appeared.—EDITOR.

† This story was originally published in "Harper's Magazine." It was printed from the author's manuscript, which the publishers purchased of Lamb's friend, Thomas Allsop. By the kind permission of the Messrs. Harper, "Cupid's Revenge" appears in this volume.—EDITOR.

deceased and beloved consort. For *her*, nothing was thought too precious. Existence was of no value to him but as it afforded opportunities of gratifying her wishes. To be instrumental in relieving her from the least little pain or grief, he would have lavished his treasures to the giving-away of the one-half of his dukedom.

All this deference on the part of the parent had yet no power upon the mind of the daughter to move her at any time to solicit any unbecoming suit, or to disturb the even tenor of her thoughts. The humility and dutifulness of her carriage seemed to keep pace with his apparent willingness to release her from the obligations of either. She might have satisfied her wildest humors and caprices; but, in truth, no such troublesome guests found harbor in the bosom of the quiet and unaspiring maiden.

Thus far the prudence of the princess served to counteract any ill effects which this ungovernable partiality in a parent was calculated to produce in a less virtuous nature than Hidaspes'; and this foible of the duke's, so long as no evil resulted from it, was passed over by the courtiers as a piece of harmless frenzy.

But upon a solemn day, — a sad one, as it proved for Lycia, — when the returning anniversary of the princess's birth was kept with extraordinary rejoicings, the infatuated father set no bounds to his folly, but would have his subjects to do homage to her for that day, as to their natural sovereign; as if he, indeed, had been dead, and she, to the exclusion of the male succession, was become the rightful ruler of Lycia. He saluted her by the style of Duchess; and with a terrible oath, in the presence of his nobles, he confirmed to her the grant of all things whatsoever that she should demand on that day, and for the six next following; and if she should ask any thing, the execution of which must be deferred until after his death, he pronounced a dreadful curse upon his son and successor if he failed to see to the performance of it.

Thus encouraged, the princess stepped forth with a modest boldness; and, as if assured of no denial, spake as follows.

But, before we acquaint you with the purport of her speech, we must premise, that in the land of Lycia, which was at that time pagan, above all their other gods the inhabitants did in an especial manner adore the deity who was supposed to have influence in the disposing of people's affections in *love*. Him, by the name of God Cupid, they feigned to be a *beautiful boy*, and *winged;* as indeed, between young persons, these frantic passions are usually least under constraint; while the wings might signify the haste with which these ill-judged attachments are commonly dissolved, and do indeed go away as lightly as they come, flying away in an instant to light upon some newer fancy. They painted him *blindfolded*, because these silly affections of lovers make them blind to the defects of the beloved object, which every one is quick-sighted enough to discover but themselves; or because love is for the most part led blindly, rather than directed by the open eye of the judgment, in the hasty choice of a mate. Yet, with that inconsistency of attributes with which the heathen people commonly over-complimented their deities, this blind love, this Cupid, they figured with a bow and arrows;

and, being sightless, they yet feigned him to be a notable archer and an unerring marksman. No heart was supposed to be proof against the point of his inevitable dart. By such incredible fictions did these poor pagans make a shift to excuse their vanities, and to give a sanction to their irregular affections, under the notion that love was irresistible; whereas, in a well-regulated mind, these amorous conceits either find no place at all, or, having gained a footing, are easily stifled in the beginning by a wise and manly resolution.

This frenzy in the people had long been a source of disquiet to the discreet princess; and many were the conferences she had held with the virtuous prince, her brother, as to the best mode of taking off the minds of the Lycians from this vain superstition. An occasion, furnished by the blind grant of the old duke, their father, seemed now to present itself.

The courtiers then, being assembled to hear the demand which the princess should make, began to conjecture, each one according to the bent of his own disposition, what the thing would be that she should ask for. One said, "Now surely she will ask to have the disposal of the revenues of some wealthy province, to lay them out — as was the manner of Eastern princesses — in costly dresses and jewels becoming a lady of so great expectancies." Another thought that she would seek an extension of power, as women naturally love rule and dominion. But the most part were in hope that she was about to beg the hand of some neighbor prince in marriage, who, by the wealth and contiguity of his dominions, might add strength and safety to the realm of Lycia. But in none of these things was the expectation of these crafty and worldly-minded courtiers gratified; for Hidaspes, first making lowly obeisance to her father, and thanking him on bended knees for so great grace conferred upon her, — according to a plan preconcerted with Leucippus, — made suit as follows: —

"Your loving care of me, O princely father! by which in my tenderest age you made up to me for the loss of a mother at those years when I was scarcely able to comprehend the misfortune, and your bounties to me ever since, have left me nothing to ask for myself, as wanting and desiring nothing. But, for the people whom you govern, I beg and desire a boon. It is known to all nations, that the men of Lycia are noted for a vain and fruitless superstition, — the more hateful as it bears a show of true religion, but is indeed nothing more than a self-pleasing and bold wantonness. Many ages before this, when every man had taken to himself a trade, as hating idleness far worse than death, some one that gave himself to sloth and wine, finding himself by his neighbors rebuked for his unprofitable life, framed to himself a god, whom he pretended to obey in his dishonesty; and, for a name, he called him Cupid. This god of merely man's creating — as the nature of man is ever credulous of any vice which takes part with his dissolute conditions — quickly found followers enough. They multiplied in every age, especially among your Lycians, who to this day remain adorers of this drowsy deity, who certainly was first invented in drink, as sloth and luxury are commonly the first movers in these idle love-passions. This *winged boy* — for so they fancy him — has his sacri fices, his loose images set up in the land, through all the villages; nay, your own sacred palace is not exempt from them, to the scandal of sound devotion, and dishonor of the true deities, which are only they who give good gifts to man, — as Ceres, who gives us corn; the planter of the olive, Pallas; Neptune, who directs the track of ships over the great ocean, and binds distant lands together in friendly commerce; the inventor of medicine and music, Apollo; and the cloud-compelling Thunderer of Olympus: whereas the gifts of this idle deity — if indeed he have a being at all out of the brain of his frantic worshippers — usually prove destructive and pernicious. My suit, then, is, that this unseemly idol throughout the land be plucked down, and cast into the fire; and that the adoring of the same may be prohibited on pain of death to any of your subjects henceforth found so offending."

Leontius, startled at this unexpected demand from the princess, with tears besought her to ask some wiser thing, and not to bring down upon herself and him the indignation of so great a god.

"There is no such god as you dream of," said then Leucippus boldly, who had hitherto forborne to second the petition of the princess; "but a vain opinion of him has filled the land with love and wantonness. Every young man and maiden, that feel the least desire to one another, dare in no case to suppress it; for they think it to be Cupid's motion, and that he is a god!"

Thus pressed by the solicitations of both his children, and fearing the oath which he had taken, in an evil hour the misgiving father consented; and a proclamation was sent throughout all the provinces for the putting-down of the idol, and suppression of the established Cupid-worship.

Notable, you may be sure, was the stir made in all places among the priests, and among the artificers in gold, in silver, or in marble, who made a gainful trade, either in serving at the altar, or in the manufacture of the images no longer to be tolerated. The cry was clamorous as that at Ephesus when a kindred idol was in danger; for "great had been Cupid of the Lycians." Nevertheless, the power of the duke, backed by the power of his more popular children, prevailed; and the destruction of every vestage of the old religion was but as the work of one day throughout the country.

And now, as the pagan chronicles of Lycia inform us, the displeasure of Cupid went out, — the displeasure of a great god, — flying through all the dukedom, and sowing evils. But, upon the first movers of the profanation, his angry hand lay heaviest; and there was imposed upon them a strange misery, that all might know that Cupid's revenge was mighty. With his arrows hotter than plagues, or than his own anger, did he fiercely right himself; nor could the prayers of a few concealed worshippers, nor the smoke arising from an altar here and there which had escaped the general overthrow, avert his wrath, or make him to cease from vengeance, until he had made of the once-flourishing country of Lycia a most wretched land. He sent no famines, he let loose no cruel wild beasts among them, — inflictions with one or other of which the rest of the Olympian deities are fabled to have visited the nations under their displeasure, — but took a nearer course of his own; and his invisible arrows went to the *moral heart* of Lycia, infecting and filling court and country with desires of unlawful marriages, unheard-of and monstrous affections, prodigious and misbecoming unions.

The symptoms were first visible in the changed bosom of Hidaspes. This exemplary maiden, — whose cold modesty, almost to a failing, had discouraged the addresses of so many princely suitors that had sought her hand in marriage, — by the venom of this inward pestilence, came on a sudden to cast eyes of affection upon a mean and deformed creature, Zoilus by name, who was a dwarf, and lived about the palace, the common jest of the courtiers. In her besotted eyes he was grown a goodly gentleman: and to her maidens, when any of them reproached him with the defect of his shape in her hearing, she would reply, that " to them, indeed, he might appear defective, and unlike a man, as, indeed, no man was like unto him; for in form and complexion he was beyond painting. He is like," she said, " to nothing that we have seen; yet he doth resemble Apollo, as I have fancied him, when, rising in the east, he bestirs himself, and shakes daylight from his hair." And, overcome with a passion which was heavier than she could bear, she confessed herself a wretched creature, and implored forgiveness of God Cupid, whom she had provoked; and, if possible, that he would grant it to her that she might enjoy her love. Nay, she would court this piece of deformity to his face; and when the wretch, supposing it to be done in mockery, has said that he could wish himself more ill-shaped than he was, so it would contribute to make her grace merry, she would reply, " Oh! think not that I jest; unless it be a jest not to esteem my life in comparison with thine; to hang a thousand kisses in an hour upon those lips; unless it be a jest to vow that I am willing to become your wife, and to take obedience upon me." And by his "own white hand," taking it in hers, — so strong was the delusion, — she besought him to swear to marry her.

The term had not yet expired of the seven days within which the doting duke had sworn to fulfil her will, when, in pursuance of this frenzy, she presented herself before her father, leading in the dwarf by the hand, and, in the face of all the courtiers, solemnly demanding his hand in marriage. And, when the apish creature made show of blushing at the unmerited honor, she, to comfort him, bade him not to be ashamed; for, "in her eyes, he was worth a kingdom."

And now, too late, did the fond father repent him of his dotage. But when by no importunity he could prevail upon her to desist from her suit, for his oath's sake he must needs consent to the marriage. But the ceremony was no sooner, to the derision of all present, performed, than, with the just feelings of an outraged parent, he commanded the head of the presumptuous bridegroom to be stricken off, and committed the distracted princess close prisoner to her chamber, where, after many deadly swoonings, with intermingled outcries upon the cruelty of her father, she, in no long time after, died; making ineffectual appeals, to the last, to the mercy of the offended Power, — the Power that had laid its heavy hand upon her, to the bereavement of her good judgment first, and finally to the extinction of a life that might have proved a blessing to Lycia.

Leontius had scarcely time to be sensible of her danger before a fresh cause for mourning overtook him. His son Leucippus, who had hitherto been a pattern of strict life and modesty, was stricken with a second arrow from the deity, offended for his overturned altars, in which the prince had been a chief instrument. The god caused his heart to fall away, and his crazed fancy to be smitten with the excelling beauty of a wicked widow, by name Bacha. This woman, in the first days of her mourning for her husband, by her dissembling tears and affected coyness had drawn Leucippus so cunningly into her snares, that, before she would grant him a return of love, she extorted from the easy-hearted prince a contract of marriage, to be fulfilled in the event of his father's death. This guilty intercourse, which they covered with the name of marriage, was not carried with such secrecy but that a rumor of it ran about the palace, and by some officious courtier was brought to the ears of the old duke, who, to satisfy himself of the truth, came hastily to the house of Bacha, where he found his son courting. Taking the prince to task roundly, he sternly asked who that creature was that had bewitched him out of his honor thus. Then Bacha, pretending ignorance of the duke's person, haughtily demanded of Leucippus what saucy old man that was, that without leave had burst into the house of an afflicted widow to hinder her paying her tears (as she pretended) to the dead. Then the duke declaring himself, and threatening her for having corrupted his son, giving her the reproachful terms of witch and sorceress, Leucippus mildly answered, that he "did her wrong." The bad woman, imagining that the prince for very fear would not betray their secret, now conceived a project of monstrous wickedness; which was no less than to insnare the father with the same arts which had subdued the son, that she might no longer be a concealed wife, nor a princess only under cover, but, by a union with the old man, become at once the true and acknowledged Duchess of Lycia. In a posture of humility, she confessed her ignorance of the duke's quality; but, now she knew it, she besought his pardon for her wild speeches, which proceeded, she said, from a distempered head, which the loss of a dear husband had affected. He might command her life, she told him, which was now of small value to her. The tears which accompanied her words, and her mourning weeds (which, for a blind to the world, she had not yet cast off), heightening her beauty, gave a credence to her protestations of her innocence. But the duke continuing to assail her with reproaches, with a matchless confidence, assuming the air of injured virtue, in a somewhat lofty tone she replied, that though he were her sovereign, to whom in any lawful cause she was bound to submit, yet, if he sought to take away her honor, she stood up to defy him. *That*, she said, was a jewel dearer than any he could give her, which, so long as she should keep, she should esteem herself richer than all the princes of the earth that were without it. If the prince, his son, knew any thing to her dishonor, let him tell it. And here she challenged Leucippus before his father to speak the worst of her. If he would, however, sacrifice a woman's character to please an unjust humor of the duke's, she saw no remedy, she said, now *he* was dead (meaning her late husband) that with his life would have defended her reputation.

Thus appeared to, Leucippus, who had stood a while astonished at her confident falsehoods, though ignorant of the full drift of them, considering that not the reputation only, but probably the life, of a woman whom he had so loved, and who had made such sacrifices to him of love and beauty, depended upon his absolute concealment of their contract, framed his mouth to a compassionate untruth, and with solemn asseverations confirmed to his father her assurances of her innocence. He denied not that with rich gifts he had assailed her virtue, but had found her relentless to his solicitations; that gold nor greatness had any power over her. Nay, so far he went on to give force to the protestations of this artful woman, that he confessed to having offered marriage to her, which she, who scorned to listen to any second wedlock, had rejected.

All this while, Leucippus secretly prayed to Heaven to forgive him while he uttered these bold untruths; since it was for the prevention of a greater mischief only, and had no malice in it.

But, warned by the sad sequel which ensued, be thou careful, young reader, how in any case you tell a lie. Lie not, if any man but ask you "how you do," or "what o'clock it is." Be sure you make no false excuse to screen a friend that is most dear to you. Never let the most well-intended falsehood escape your lips; for Heaven, which is entirely Truth, will make the seed which you have sown of untruth to yield miseries a thousand-fold upon yours, as it did upon the head of the ill-fated and mistaken Leucippus.

Leontius, finding the assurances of Bacha so confidently seconded by his son, could no longer withhold his belief; and, only forbidding their meeting for the future, took a courteous leave of the lady, presenting her at the same time with a valuable ring, in recompense, as he said, of the injustice which he had done her in his false surmises of her guiltiness. In truth, the surpassing beauty of the lady, with her appearing modesty, had made no less impression upon the heart of the fond old duke than they had awakened in the bosom of his more pardonable son. His first design was to make her his mistress; to the better accomplishing of which, Leucippus was dismissed from the court, under the pretext of some honorable employment abroad. In his absence, Leontius spared no offers to induce her to comply with his purpose. Continually he solicited her with rich offers, with messages, and by personal visits. It was a ridiculous sight, if it were not rather a sad one, to behold this second and worse dotage, which by Cupid's wrath had fallen upon this fantastical *old new lover*. All his occupation now was in dressing and pranking himself up in youthful attire to please the eyes of his new mistress. His mornings were employed in the devising of trim fashions, in the company of tailors, embroiderers, and feather-dressers. So infatuated was he with these vanities, that, when a servant came and told him that his daughter was dead, — even she whom he had but lately so highly prized, — the words seemed spoken to a deaf person. He either could not or would not understand them; but, like one senseless, fell to babbling about the shape of a new hose and doublet. His crutch, the faithful prop of long aged years, was discarded; and he resumed the youthful fashion of a sword by his side, when his years wanted strength to have drawn it. In this condition of folly, it was no difficult task for the widow, by affected pretences of honor, and arts of amorous denial, to draw in this doting duke to that which she had all along aimed at, — the offer of his crown in marriage. She was now Duchess of Lycia! In her new elevation, the mask was quickly thrown aside, and the impious Bacha appeared in her true qualities. She had never loved the duke, her husband; but had used him as the instrument of her greatness. Taking advantage of his amorous folly, which seemed to gain growth the nearer he approached to his grave, she took upon her the whole rule of Lycia; placing and displacing, at her will, all the great officers of state; and filling the court with creatures of her own, the agents of her guilty pleasures, she removed from the duke's person the oldest and trustiest of his dependants.

Leucippus, who at this juncture was returned from his foreign mission, was met at once with the news of his sister's death and the strange wedlock of the old duke. To the memory of Hidaspes he gave some tears; but these were swiftly swallowed up in his horror and detestation of the conduct of Bacha. In his first fury, he resolved upon a full disclosure of all that had passed between him and his wicked step-mother. Again, he thought, by killing Bacha, to rid the world of a monster. But tenderness for his father recalled him to milder counsels. The fatal secret, nevertheless, sat upon him like lead, while he was determined to confide it to no other. It took his sleep away, and his desire of food; and, if a thought of mirth at any time crossed him, the dreadful truth would recur to check it, as if a messenger should have come to whisper to him of some friend's death. With difficulty he was brought to wish their highnesses faint joy of their marriage; and, at the first sight of Bacha, a friend was fain to hold his wrist hard to prevent him from fainting. In an interview, which after, at her request, he had with her alone, the bad woman shamed not to take up the subject lightly; to treat as a trifle the marriage vow that had passed between them; and, seeing him sad and silent, to threaten him with the displeasure of the duke, his father, if by words or looks he gave any suspicion to the world of their dangerous secret. "What had happened," she said, "was by no fault of hers. People would have thought her mad if she had refused the duke's offer. She had used no arts to entrap his father. It was Leucippus' own resolute denial of any such thing as a contract having passed between them which had led to the proposal."

The prince, unable to extenuate his share of blame in the calamity, humbly besought her, that "since, by his own great fault, things had been brought to their present pass, she would only live honest for the future, and not abuse the credulous age of the old duke, as he well knew she had the power to do. For himself, seeing that life was no longer desirable to him, if his death was judged by her to be indispensable to her security, she was welcome to lay what trains she pleased to compass it, so long as she would only suffer his father to go to his grave in peace, since *he* had never wronged her."

This temperate appeal was lost upon the heart of Bacha, who from that moment was secretly bent upon effecting the destruction of Leucippus. Her project was, by feeding the ears of the duke with exaggerated praises of his son, to awaken a jealousy in the old man, that she secretly preferred Leucippus. Next, by wilfully insinuating the great popularity of the prince (which was no more indeed than the truth) among the Lycians, to instil subtle fears into the duke that his son had laid plots for circumventing his life and throne. By these arts she was working upon the weak mind of the duke almost to distraction, when, at a meeting concocted by herself between the prince and his father, the latter taking Leucippus soundly to task for these alleged treasons, the prince replied only by humbly drawing his sword, with the intention of laying it at his father's feet; and begging him, since he suspected him, to sheathe it in his own bosom, for of his life he had been long weary. Bacha entered at the crisis, and, ere Leucippus could finish his submission, with loud outcries alarmed the courtiers, who, rushing into the presence, found the prince with sword in hand indeed, but with far other intentions than this bad woman imputed to him, plainly accusing him of having drawn it upon his father! Leucippus was quickly disarmed; and the old duke, trembling between fear and age, committed him to close prison, from which, by Bacha's aims, he never should have come out alive but for the interference of the common people, who, loving their prince, and equally detesting Bacha, in a simultaneous mutiny arose, and rescued him from the hands of the officers.

The court was now no longer a place of living for Leucippus; and hastily thanking his countrymen for his deliverance, which in his heart he rather deprecated than welcomed, as one that wished for death, he took leave of all court hopes, and, abandoning the palace, betook himself to a life of penitence in solitudes.

Not so secretly did he select his place of penance, in a cave among lonely woods and fastnesses, but that his retreat was traced by Bacha; who, baffled in her purpose, raging like some she-wolf, despatched an emissary of her own to destroy him privately.

There was residing at the court of Lycia, at this time, a young maiden, the daughter of Bacha by her first husband, who had hitherto been brought up in the obscurity of a poor country abode with an uncle; but whom Bacha now publicly owned, and had prevailed upon the easy duke to adopt as successor to the throne in wrong of the true heir, his suspected son Leucippus.

This young creature, Urania by name, was as artless and harmless as her mother was crafty and wicked. To the unnatural Bacha she had been an object of neglect and aversion; and for the project of supplanting Leucippus only had she fetched her out of retirement. The bringing-up of Urania had been among country hinds and lasses: to tend her flocks or superintend her neat dairy had been the extent of her breeding. From her calling, she had contracted a pretty rusticity of dialect, which, among the fine folks of the court, passed for simplicity and folly. She was the unfittest instrument for an ambitious design that could be chosen; for her manners in a palace had a tinge still of her old occupation; and, to her mind, the lowly shepherdess's life was best.

Simplicity is oft a match for prudence: and Urania was not so simple but she understood that she had been sent for to court only in the prince's wrong; and in her heart she was determined to defeat any designs that might be contriving against her brother-in-law. The melancholy bearing of Leucippus had touched her with pity. This wrought in her a kind of love, which, for its object, had no further end than the well-being of the beloved. She looked for no return of it, nor did the possibility of such a blessing in the remotest way occur to her, — so vast a distance she had imaged between her lowly bringing-up and the courtly breeding and graces of Leucippus. Hers was no raging flame, such as had burned destructive in the bosom of poor Hidaspes. Either the vindictive god in mercy had spared this young maiden, or the wrath of the confounding *Cupid* was restrained by a higher Power from discharging the most malignant of his arrows against the peace of so much innocence. Of the extent of her mother's malice she was too guileless to have entertained conjecture; but from hints and whispers, and, above all, from that tender watchfulness with which a true affection like Urania's tends the safety of its object, — fearing even where no cause for fear subsists, — she gathered that some danger was impending over the prince, and with simple heroism resolved to countermine the treason.

It chanced upon a day that Leucippus had been indulging his sad meditations in forests far from human converse, when he was struck with the appearance of a human being, so unusual in that solitude. There stood before him a seeming *youth*, of delicate appearance, clad in coarse and peasantly attire. "He was come," he said, "to seek out the prince, and to be his poor boy and servant, if he would let him."—"Alas! poor youth," replied Leucippus: "why do you follow me, who am as poor as you are?"—"In good faith," was his pretty answer, "I shall be well and rich enough if you will but love me." And, saying so, he wept. The prince, admiring this strange attachment in a boy, was moved with compassion; and seeing him exhausted, as if with long travel and hunger, invited him in to his poor habitation, setting such refreshments before him as that barren spot afforded. But by no entreaties could he be prevailed upon to take any sustenance; and all that day, and for the two following, he seemed supported only by some gentle flame of love that was within him. He fed only upon the sweet looks and courteous entertainment which he received from Leucippus. Seemingly, he wished to die under the loving eyes of his master. "I cannot eat," he prettily said; "but I shall eat to-morrow."—"You will be dead by that time," replied Leucippus. "I shall be well then," said he; "since you will not love me." Then the prince asking him why he sighed so, "To think," was his innocent reply, "that such a fine man as you should die, and no gay lady love him."—"But you will love me," said Leucippus. "Yes, sure," said he, "till I die; and, when I am in heaven, I shall wish for you." "This is a love," thought the other, "that I never yet heard tell of. But come, thou art sleepy, child: go in, and I will sit with thee." Then, from some words which the poor youth dropped, Leucippus, suspecting that his wits were beginning to ramble, said, "What portends this?"—"I am not sleepy," said the youth; "but you are sad. I would that I could do any thing to make you merry!

Shall I sing?" But soon, as if recovering strength, "There is one approaching!" he wildly cried out. "Master, look to yourself!"

His words were true: for now entered, with provided weapon, the wicked emissary of Bacha, that we told of; and, directing a mortal thrust at the prince, the supposed boy, with a last effort, interposing his weak body, received it in his bosom, thanking the heavens in death that he he had saved "so good a master."

Leucippus, having slain the villain, was at leisure to discover, in the features of his poor servant, the countenance of his devoted sister-in-law! Through solitary and dangerous ways she had sought him in that disguise; and, finding him, seems to have resolved upon a voluntary death by fasting, — partly that she might die in the presence of her beloved, and partly that she might make known to him in death the love which she wanted boldness to disclose to him while living, but chiefly because she knew, that, by her demise, all obstacles would be removed that stood between her prince and his succession to the throne of Lycia.

Leucippus had hardly time to comprehend the strength of love in his Urania, when a trampling of horses resounded through his solitude. It was a party of Lycian horsemen, that had come to seek him, dragging the detested Bacha in their train, who was now to receive the full penalty of her misdeeds. Amidst her frantic fury upon the missing of her daughter, the old duke had suddenly died, not without suspicion of her having administered poison to him. Her punishment was submitted to Leucippus, who was now, with joyful acclaims, saluted as the rightful Duke of Lycia. He, as no way moved with his great wrongs, but considering her simply as the parent of Urania, saluting her only by the title of "Wicked Mother," bade her to live. "That reverend title," he said, and pointed to the bleeding remains of her child, "must be her pardon. He would use no extremity against her, but leave her to Heaven." The hardened mother, not at all relenting at the sad spectacle that lay before her, but making show of dutiful submission to the young duke, and with bended knees approaching him, suddenly with a dagger inflicted a mortal stab upon him; and, with a second stroke stabbing herself, ended both their wretched lives.

Now was the tragedy of Cupid's wrath awfully completed; and, the race of Leontius failing in the deaths of both his children, the chronicle relates, that under their new duke, Ismenus, the offence to the angry Power was expiated; his statues and altars were, with more magnificence than ever, re-edified; and he ceased thenceforth from plaguing the land.

Thus far the pagan historians relate erring. But from this vain idol story a not unprofitable moral may be gathered against the abuse of the natural but dangerous *passion of love*. In the story of Hidaspes, we see the preposterous linking of beauty with deformity; of princely expectancies with mean and low conditions, in the case of the prince, her brother; and of decrepit age with youth, in the ill end of their doting father, Leontius. By their examples we are warned to decline all *unequal and ill-assorted unions*.

THE DEFEAT OF TIME;

OR, A TALE OF THE FAIRIES.*

TITANIA and her moonlight elves were assembled under the canopy of a huge oak, that served to shelter them from the moon's radiance, which, being now at her full noon, shot forth intolerable rays, — intolerable, I mean, to the subtile texture of their little shadowy bodies, — but dispensing an agreeable coolness to us grosser mortals. An air of discomfort sate upon the queen and upon her courtiers. Their tiny friskings and gambols were forgot; and even Robin Goodfellow, for the first time in his little airy life, looked grave. For the queen had had melancholy forebodings of late, founded upon an ancient prophecy laid up in the records of Fairyland, that the date of fairy existence should be *then* extinct when men should cease to believe in them. And she knew how that the race of the Nymphs, which were her predecessors, and had been the guardians of the sacred floods, and of the silver fountains, and of the consecrated hills and woods, had utterly disappeared before the chilling touch of man's incredulity; and she sighed bitterly at the approaching fate of herself and of her subjects, which was dependent upon so fickle a lease as the capricious and ever mutable faith of man. When, as if to realize her fears, a melancholy shape came gliding in, and *that* was—Time, who with his intolerable scythe

* From Hone's "Table-book."

mows down kings and kingdoms; at whose dread approach the fays huddled together as a flock of timorous sheep; and the most courageous among them crept into acorn-cups, not enduring the sight of that ancientest of monarchs. Titania's first impulse was to wish the presence of her false lord, King Oberon, — who was far away, in the pursuit of a strange beauty, a fay of Indian Land, — that with his good lance and sword, like a faithful knight and husband, he might defend her against Time. But she soon checked that thought as vain; for what could the prowess of the mighty Oberon himself, albeit the stoutest champion in Fairyland, have availed against so huge a giant, whose bald top touched the skies? So, in the mildest tone, she besought the spectre, that in his mercy he would overlook and pass by her small subjects, as too diminutive and powerless to add any worthy trophy to his renown. And she besought him to employ his resistless strength against the ambitious children of men, and to lay waste their aspiring works; to tumble down their towers and turrets, and the Babels of their pride, — fit objects of his devouring scythe, — but to spare her and her harmless race, who had no existence beyond a dream; frail objects of a creed that lived but in the faith of the believer. And with her little arms, as well as she could, she grasped the stern knees of Time; and, waxing speechless with fear, she beckoned to her chief attendants, and maids of honor, to come forth from their hiding-places, and to plead the plea of the fairies. And one of those small, delicate creatures came forth at her bidding, clad all in white like a chorister; and in a low, melodious tone, not louder than the hum of a pretty bee, — when it seems to be demurring whether it shall settle upon this sweet flower or that before it settles, — set forth her humble petition. "We fairies," she said, "are the most inoffensive race that live, and least deserving to perish. It is we that have the care of all sweet melodies, that no discords may offend the sun, who is the great soul of music. We rouse the lark at morn; and the pretty Echoes, which respond to all the twittering choir, are of our making. Wherefore, great King of Years, as ever you have loved the music which is raining from a morning cloud sent from the messenger of day, the lark, as he mounts to heaven's gate, beyond the ken of mortals; or if ever you have listened with a charmed ear to the night-bird, that —

'In the flowery spring,
Amidst the leaves set, makes the thickets ring
Of her sour sorrows, sweetened with her song,' —

spare our tender tribes, and we will muffle up the sheep-bell for thee, that thy pleasure take no interruption whenever thou shalt listen unto Philomel."

And Time answered, that "he had heard that song too long; and he was even wearied with that ancient strain that recorded the wrong of Tereus. But, if she would know in what music Time delighted, it was, when sleep and darkness lay upon crowded cities, to hark to the midnight chime which is tolling from a hundred clocks, like the last knell over the soul of a dead world; or to the crush of the fall of some age-worn edifice, which is as the voice of himself when he disparteth kingdoms."

A second female fay took up the plea, and said, "We be the handmaids of the Spring, and tend upon the birth of all sweet buds: and the pastoral cowslips are our friends; and the pansies; and the violets, like nuns; and the quaking harebell is in our wardship; and the hyacinth, once a fair youth, and dear to Phœbus."

Then Time made answer, in his wrath striking the harmless ground with his hurtful scythe, that "they must not think that he was one that cared for flowers, except to see them wither, and to take her beauty from the rose."

And a third fairy took up the plea, and said, "We are kindly things; and it is we that sit at evening, and shake rich odors from sweet bowers upon discoursing lovers, that seem to each other to be their own sighs; and we keep off the bat and the owl from their privacy, and the ill-boding whistler; and we flit in sweet dreams across the brains of infancy, and conjure up a smile upon its soft lips to beguile the careful mother, while its little soul is fled for a brief minute or two to sport with our youngest fairies."

Then Saturn (which is Time) made answer, that "they should not think that he delighted in tender babes, that had devoured his own, till foolish Rhea cheated him with a stone, which he swallowed, thinking it to be the infant Jupiter." And thereat, in token, he disclosed to view his enormous tooth, in which appeared monstrous dints left by that unnatural meal; and his great throat, that seemed capable of devouring up the earth and all its inhabitants at one meal. "And for lovers," he continued, "my delight is, with a hurrying hand to snatch them away from their love-meetings by stealth at nights; and, in absence, to stand like a motionless statue, or their leaden planet of mishap (whence I had my name), till I make their minutes seem ages."

Next stood up a male fairy, clad all in green, like a forester or one of Robin Hood's mates, and, doffing his tiny cap, said, "We are small foresters, that live in woods, training the young boughs in graceful intricacies, with blue snatches of the sky between: we frame all shady roofs and arches rude; and sometimes, when we are plying our tender hatchets, men say that the tapping woodpecker is nigh. And it is we that scoop the hollow cell of the squirrel, and carve quaint letters upon the rinds of trees, which, in sylvan solitudes, sweetly recall to the mind of the heat-oppressed swain, ere he lies down to slumber, the name of his fair one, dainty Aminta, gentle Rosalind, or chastest Laura, as it may happen."

Saturn, nothing moved with this courteous address, bade him be gone, or, "if he would be a woodman, to go forth and fell oak for the fairies' coffins which would forthwith be wanting. For himself, he took no delight in haunting the woods, till their golden plumage (the yellow leaves) were beginning to fall, and leave the brown-black limbs bare, like Nature in her skeleton dress."

Then stood up one of those gentle fairies that are good to man, and blushed red as any rose while he told a modest story of one of his own good deeds. "It chanced upon a time," he said, "that while we were looking cowslips in the meads, while yet the dew was hanging on the buds like beads, we found a babe left in its swathing-clothes, — a little sorrowful, deserted thing, begot of love, but begetting no love in others; guiltless of shame, but doomed to shame for its parents' offence in bringing it by indirect courses into the world. It was pity to see the abandoned little orphan left to the world's care by an unnatural mother. How the cold dew kept wetting its childish coats! and its little hair, how it was bedabbled, that was like gossamer! Its pouting mouth, unknowing how to speak, lay half opened like a rose-lipped shell; and its cheek was softer than any peach, upon which the tears, for very roundness, could not long dwell, but fell off, in clearness like pearls,— some on the grass, and some on his little hand; and some haply wandered to the little dimpled well under his mouth, which Love himself seemed to have planned out, but less for tears than for smilings. Pity it was, too, to see how the burning sun had scorched its helpless limbs; for it lay without shade or shelter, or mother's breast, for foul weather or fair. So, having compassion on its sad plight, my fellows and I turned ourselves into grasshoppers, and swarmed about the babe, making such shrill cries as that pretty little chirping creature makes in its mirth, till with our noise we attracted the attention of a passing rustic, a tender-hearted hind, who, wondering at our small but loud concert, strayed aside curiously, and found the babe, where it lay in the remote grass, and, taking it up, lapped it in his russet coat, and bore it to his cottage, where his wife kindly nurtured it till it grew up a goodly personage. How this babe prospered afterwards, let proud London tell. This was that famous Sir Thomas Gresham, who was the chiefest of her merchants, the richest, the wisest. Witness his many goodly vessels on the Thames, freighted with costly merchandise, jewels from Ind, and pearls for courtly dames, and silks of Samarcand. And witness, more than all, that stately Bourse (or Exchange) which he caused to be built, a mart for merchants from east and west, whose graceful summit still bears, in token of the fairies' favors, his chosen crest, the grasshopper. And, like the grasshopper, may it please you, great king, to suffer us also to live, partakers of the green earth!"

The fairy had scarce ended his plea, when a shrill cry, not unlike the grasshopper's, was heard. Poor Puck — or Robin Goodfellow, as he is sometimes called — had recovered a little from his first fright, and, in one of his mad freaks, had perched upon the beard of old Time, which was flowing, ample, and majestic; and was amusing himself with plucking at a hair which was indeed so massy, that it seemed to him that he was removing some huge beam of timber, rather than a hair; which Time by some ill chance perceiving, snatched up the impish mischief with his great hand, and asked what it was.

"Alas!" quoth Puck, "a little random elf am I, born in one of Nature's sports; a very weed, created for the simple, sweet enjoyment of myself, but for no other purpose, worth, or need, that ever I could learn. 'Tis I that bob the angler's idle cork, till the patient man is ready to breathe a curse. I steal the morsel from the gossip's fork, or stop the sneezing chanter in mid psalm; and, when an infant has been born with hard or homely features, mothers say I changed the child at nurse: but to fulfil any graver purpose I have not wit enough, and hardly the will. I am a pinch of lively dust to frisk upon the wind: a tear would make a puddle of me; and so I tickle myself with the lightest straw, and shun all griefs that might make me stagnant. This is my small philosophy."

Then Time, dropping him on the ground, as a thing too inconsiderable for his vengeance, grasped fast his mighty scythe: and now, not Puck alone, but the whole state of fairies, had gone to inevitable wreck and destruction, had not a timely apparition interposed, at whose boldness Time was astounded; for he came not with the habit or the forces of a deity, who alone might cope with Time, but as a simple mortal, clad as you might see a forester that hunts after wild conies by the cold moonshine; or a stalker of stray deer, stealthy and bold. But by the golden lustre in his eye, and the passionate wanness in his cheek, and by the fair and ample space of his forehead, which seemed a palace framed for the habitation of all glorious thoughts, he knew that this was his great rival, who had power given him to rescue whatsoever victims Time should clutch, and to cause them to live for ever in his immortal verse. And, muttering the name of Shakspeare, Time spread his roc-like wings, and fled the controlling presence; and the liberated court of the fairies, with Titania at their head, flocked around the gentle ghost, giving him thanks, nodding to him, and doing him courtesies, who had crowned them henceforth with a permanent existence, to live in the minds of men, while verse shall have power to charm, or midsummer moons shall brighten.

. . . .

What particular endearments passed between the fairies and their poet, passes my pencil to delineate; but, if you are curious to be informed, I must refer you, gentle reader, to the "Plea of the Midsummer Fairies," a most agreeable poem lately put forth by my friend Thomas Hood; of the first half of which the above is nothing but a meagre and a harsh prose abstract. Farewell!

The words of Mercury are harsh after the songs of Apollo.

MARIA HOWE;

OR, THE EFFECT OF WITCH-STORIES.*

I WAS brought up in the country. From my infancy I was always a weak and tender-spirited girl, subject to fears and depressions. My parents, and particularly my mother, were of a very different disposition. They were what is usually called gay. They loved pleasure and parties and visiting; but, as they found the turn of my mind to be quite opposite, they gave themselves little trouble about me, but upon such occasions generally left me to my choice, which was much oftener to stay at home, and indulge myself in my solitude, than to join in their rambling visits. I was always fond of being alone, yet always in a manner afraid. There was a book-closet which led into my mother's dressing-room. Here I was extremely fond of being shut up by myself, to take down whatever volumes I pleased, and pore upon them, — no matter whether they were fit for my years or no, or whether I understood them.

* This and the two following juvenile stories are from "Mrs. Leicester's School." — EDITOR.

Here, when the weather would not permit my going into the dark walk (*my walk*, as it was called) in the garden, — here, when my parents have been from home, I have staid for hours together, till the loneliness, which pleased me so at first, has at length become quite frightful, and I have rushed out of the closet into the inhabited parts of the house, and sought refuge in the lap of some one of the female servants, or of my aunt, who would say, seeing me look pale, that Maria had been frightening herself with some of those *nasty books:* so she used to call my favorite volumes, which I would not have parted with, no, not with one of the least of them, if I had had the choice to be made a fine princess, and to govern the world. But my aunt was no reader. She used to excuse herself, and say that reading hurt her eyes. I have been naughty enough to think that this was only an excuse; for I found that my aunt's weak eyes did not prevent her from poring ten hours a day upon her Prayer-book, or her favorite Thomas à Kempis. But this was always her excuse for not reading any of the books I recommended. My aunt was my father's sister. She had never been married. My father was a good deal older than my mother, and my aunt was ten years older than my father. As I was often left at home with her, and as my serious disposition so well agreed with hers, an intimacy grew up between the old lady and me; and she would often say that she loved only one person in the world, and that was me. Not that she and my parents were on very bad terms; but the old lady did not feel herself respected enough. The attention and fondness which she showed to me, conscious as I was that I was almost the only being she felt any thing like fondness to, made me love her, as it was natural: indeed, I am ashamed to say, that I fear I almost loved her better than both my parents put together. But there was an oddness, a silence, about my aunt, which was never interrupted but by her occasional expressions of love to me, that made me stand in fear of her. An odd look from under her spectacles would sometimes scare me away, when I had been peering up in her face to make her kiss me. Then she had a way of muttering to herself, which, though it was good words and religious words that she was mumbling, somehow I did not like. My weak spirits, and the fears I was subject to, always made me afraid of any personal singularity or oddness in any one. I am ashamed, ladies, to lay open so many particulars of our family; but indeed it is necessary to the understanding of what I am going to tell you of a very great weakness, if not wickedness, which I was guilty of towards my aunt. But I must return to my studies, and tell you what books I found in the closet, and what reading I chiefly admired. There was a great "Book of Martyrs," in which I used to read, or rather I used to spell out meanings; for I was too ignorant to make out many words: but there it was written all about those good men who chose to be burned alive, rather than forsake their religion, and become naughty Papists. Some words I could make out, some I could not: but I made out enough to fill my little head with vanity; and I used to think I was so courageous I could be burned too; and I would put my hands upon the flames which were pictured in the pretty pictures which the book had, and feel them. But you know, ladies, there is a great difference between the flames in a picture, and real fire; and I am now ashamed of the conceit which I had of my own courage, and think how poor a martyr I should have made in those days. Then there was a book not so big, but it had pictures in. It was called Culpepper's "Herbal." It was full of pictures of plants and herbs; but I did not much care for that. Then there was Salmon's "Modern History," out of which I picked a good deal. It had pictures of Chinese gods, and the great hooded serpent, which ran strangely in my fancy. There were some law-books too; but the old English frightened me from reading them. But, above all, what I relished was Stackhouse's "History of the Bible," where there was the picture of the ark, and all the beasts getting into it. This delighted me, because it puzzled me: and many an aching head have I got with poring into it, and contriving how it might be built, with such and such rooms, to hold all the world, if there should be another flood; and sometimes settling what pretty beasts should be saved, and what should not; for I would have no ugly or deformed beast in my pretty ark. But this was only a piece of folly and vanity, that a little reflection might cure me of. Foolish girl that I was, to suppose that any creature is really ugly, that has all its limbs contrived with heavenly wisdom, and was doubtless formed to some beautiful end! — though a child cannot comprehend it. Doubtless a frog or a toad is not uglier in itself than a squirrel or a pretty green lizard; but we want understanding to see it.

These fancies, ladies, were not so very foolish or naughty, perhaps, but they may be forgiven in a child of six years old; but what I am going to tell, I shall be ashamed of, and repent, I hope, as long as I live. It will teach me not to form rash judgments. Besides the picture of the ark, and many others which I have forgot, Stackhouse contained one picture which made more impression upon my childish understanding than all the rest: it was the picture of the raising-up of Samuel, which I used to call the Witch-of-Endor picture. I was always very fond of picking up stories about witches. There was a book called "Glanvil on Witches," which used to lie about in this closet: it was thumbed about, and showed it had been much read in former times. This was my treasure. Here I used to pick out the strangest stories. My not being able to read them very well, probably made them appear more strange and out of the way to me. But I could collect enough to understand that witches were old women, who gave themselves up to do mischief; how, by the help of spirits as bad as themselves, they lamed cattle, and made the corn not grow; and how they made images of wax to stand for people that had done them any injury, or they thought had done them injury; and how they burned the images before a slow fire, and stuck pins in them; and the persons which these waxen images represented, however far distant, felt all the pains and torments in good earnest which were inflicted in show upon these images: and such a horror I had of these wicked witches, that though I am now better instructed, and look upon all these stories as mere idle tales, and invented to fill people's heads with nonsense, yet I cannot recall to mind the horrors which I then felt, without shuddering, and feeling something of the old fit return.

This foolish book of witch-stories had no pictures in it; but I made up for them out of my own fancy, and out of the great picture of the raising-up of Samuel, in Stackhouse. I was not old enough to understand the difference there was between these silly, improbable tales, which imputed such powers to poor old women, who are the most helpless things in the creation, and the narrative in the Bible, which does not say that the witch, or pretended witch, raised up the dead body of Samuel by her own power, but, as it clearly appears, he was permitted by the divine will to appear, to confound the presumption of Saul; and that the witch herself was really as much frightened and confounded at the miracle as Saul himself, not expecting a real appearance, but probably having prepared some juggling, sleight-of-hand tricks, and sham appearance, to deceive the eyes of Saul; whereas neither she, nor any one living, had ever the power to raise the dead to life, but only He who made them from the first. These reasons I might have read in Stackhouse itself, if I had been old enough, and have read them in that very book since I was older; but, at that time, I looked at little beyond the picture.

These stories of witches so terrified me, that my sleeps were broken; and, in my dreams, I always had a fancy of a witch being in the room with me. I know now that it was only nervousness; but though I can laugh at it now as well as you, ladies, if you knew what I suffered, you would be thankful that you have had sensible people about you to instruct you, and teach you better. I was let grow up wild, like an ill weed; and thrived accordingly. One night, that I had been terrified in my sleep with my imaginations, I got out of bed, and crept softly to the adjoining room. My room was next to where my aunt usually sat when she was alone. Into her room I crept for relief from my fears. The old lady was not yet retired to rest, but was sitting with her eyes half open, half closed; her spectacles tottering upon her nose; her head nodding over her Prayer-book; her lips mumbling the words as she read them, or half read them, in her dozing posture; her grotesque appearance, her old-fashioned dress, resembling what I had seen in that fatal picture in Stackhouse. All this, with the dead time of night, as it seemed to me (for I had gone through my first sleep), joined to produce a wicked fancy in me, that the form which I had beheld was not my aunt, but some witch. Her mumbling of her prayers confirmed me in this shocking idea. I had read in Glanvil of those wicked creatures reading their prayers *backwards;* and I thought that this was the operation which her lips were at this time employed about. Instead of flying to her friendly lap for that protection which I had so often experienced when I have been weak and timid, I shrunk back, terrified and bewildered, to my bed, where I lay, in broken sleeps and miserable fancies, till the morning, which I had so much reason to wish for, came. My fancies a little wore away with the light; but an impression was fixed, which could not for a long time be done away. In the day-time, when my father and mother were about the house, when I saw them familiarly speak to my aunt, my fears all vanished; and when the good creature has taken me upon her knees, and shown me any kindness more than ordinary, at such times I have melted into tears, and longed to tell her what naughty, foolish fancies I had had of her. But, when night returned, that figure which I had seen recurred,—the posture, the half-closed eyes, the mumbling and muttering which I had heard. A confusion was in my head, *who* it was I had seen that night: it was my aunt, and it was not my aunt; it was that good creature, who loved me above all the world, engaged at her good task of devotions,—perhaps praying for some good to me. Again, it was a witch, a creature hateful to God and man, reading backwards the good prayers; who would perhaps destroy me. In these conflicts of mind I passed several weeks, till, by a revolution in my fate, I was removed to the house of a female relation of my mother's in a distant part of the country, who had come on a visit to our house, and observing my lonely ways, and apprehensive of the ill effect of my mode of living upon my health, begged leave to take me home to her house to reside for a short time. I went, with some reluctance at leaving my closet, my dark walk, and even my aunt, who had been such a source of both love and terror to me. But I went, and soon found the grand effects of a change of scene. Instead of melancholy closets and lonely avenues of trees, I saw lightsome rooms and cheerful faces. I had companions of my own age. No books were allowed me but what were rational and sprightly,—that gave me mirth, or gave me instruction. I soon learned to laugh at witch-stories; and when I returned, after three or four months' absence, to our own house, my good aunt appeared to me in the same light in which I had viewed her from my infancy, before that foolish fancy possessed me; or rather, I should say, more kind, more fond, more loving than before. It is impossible to say how much good that lady (the kind relation of my mother's that I spoke of) did to me by changing the scene. Quite a new turn of ideas was given to me. I became sociable and companionable. My parents soon discovered a change in me; and I have found a similar alteration in them. They have been plainly more fond of me since that change, as from that time I learned to conform myself more to their way of living. I have never since had that aversion to company, and going out with them, which used to make them regard me with less fondness than they would have wished to show. I impute all that I had to complain of in their neglect to my having been a little unsociable, uncompanionable mortal. I lived in this manner for a year or two, passing my time between our house and the lady's who so kindly took me in hand, till, by her advice, I was sent to this school; where I have told you, ladies, what, for fear of ridicule, I never ventured to tell any person besides, — the story of my foolish and naughty fancy.

SUSAN YATES;

OR, FIRST GOING TO CHURCH.

I WAS born and brought up in a house in which my parents had all their lives resided, which stood in the midst of that lonely tract of land called the Lincolnshire Fens. Few families besides our own lived near the spot; both because it was reckoned an unwholesome air, and because its distance from any town or market made it an inconvènient situation. My father was in no very affluent circumstances; and it was a sad necessity which he was put to, of having to go many miles to fetch any thing from the nearest village, which was full seven miles distant, through a sad, miry way, that at all times made it heavy walking, and, after rain, was almost impassable. But he had no horse or carriage of his own.

The church, which belonged to the parish in which our house was situated, stood in this village; and its distance being, as I said before, seven miles from our house, made it quite an impossible thing for my mother or me to think of going to it. Sometimes, indeed, on a fine dry Sunday, my father would rise early, and take a walk to the village, just to see how *goodness thrived*, as he used to say; but he would generally return tired, and the worse for his walk. It is scarcely possible to explain to any one who has not lived in the fens what difficult and dangerous walking it is. A mile is as good as four,

I have heard my father say, in those parts. My mother, who, in the early part of her life, had lived in a more civilized spot, and had been used to constant church-going, would often lament her situation. It was from her I early imbibed a great curiosity and anxiety to see that thing which I had heard her call a church, and so often lament that she could never go to. I had seen houses of various structures, and had seen in pictures the shapes of ships and boats, and palaces and temples, but never rightly any thing that could be called a church, or that could satisfy me about its form. Sometimes I thought it must be like our house; and sometimes I fancied it must be more like the house of our neighbor, Mr. Sutton, which was bigger and handsomer than ours. Sometimes I thought it was a great hollow cave, such as I have heard my father say the first inhabitants of the earth dwelt in. Then I thought it was like a wagon or a cart, and that it must be something movable. The shape of it ran in my mind strangely; and one day I ventured to ask my mother, what was that foolish thing she was always longing to go to, and which she called a church. Was it any thing to eat or drink? or was it only like a great huge plaything, to be seen and stared at? I was not quite five years of age when I made this inquiry.

This question, so oddly put, made my mother smile: but, in a little time, she put on a more grave look, and informed me that a church was nothing that I had supposed it; but it was a great building, far greater than any house which I had seen, where men and women and children came together twice a day, on Sundays, to hear the Bible read, and make good resolutions for the week to come. She told me that the fine music which we sometimes heard in the air came from the bells of St. Mary's Church, and that we never heard it but when the wind was in a particular point. This raised my wonder more than all the rest; for I had somehow conceived that the noise which I heard was occasioned by birds up in the air, or that it was made by the angels, whom (so ignorant I was till that time) I had always considered to be a sort of birds: for, before this time, I was totally ignorant of any thing like religion; it being a principle of my father, that young heads should not be told too many things at once, for fear they should get confused ideas, and no clear notions of any thing. We had always, indeed, so far observed Sundays, that no work was done upon that day; and upon that day I wore my best muslin frock, and was not allowed to sing or to be noisy: but I never understood why that day should differ from any other. We had no public meetings: indeed, the few straggling houses which were near us would have furnished but a slender congregation; and the loneliness of the place we lived in, instead of making us more sociable, and drawing us closer together, as my mother used to say it ought to have done, seemed to have the effect of making us more distant, and averse to society, than other people. One or two good neighbors, indeed, we had, but not in numbers to give me an idea of church attendance.

But now my mother thought it high time to give me some clearer instruction in the main points of religion; and my father came readily into her plan. I was now permitted to sit up half an hour later on Sunday evening, that I might hear a portion of Scripture read, which had always been their custom; though, by reason of my tender age, and my father's opinion on the impropriety of children being taught too young, I had never till now been an auditor. I was taught my prayers, and those things which you, ladies, I doubt not, had the benefit of being instructed in at a much earlier age.

The clearer my notions on these points became, they only made me more passionately long for the privilege of joining in that social service from which it seemed that we alone, of all the inhabitants of the land, were debarred; and, when the wind was in that point which enabled the sound of the distant bells of St. Mary's to be heard over the great moor which skirted our house, I have stood out in the air to catch the sounds, which I almost devoured: and the tears have come into my eyes, when sometimes they seemed to speak to me, almost in articulate sounds, to *come to church*, and because of the great moor which was between me and them I could not come; and the too tender apprehensions of these things have filled me with a religious melancholy. With thoughts like these, I entered into my seventh year.

And now the time was come, when the great moor was no longer to separate me from the object of my wishes and of my curiosity. My father having some money left him by the will of a deceased relation, we ventured to set up a sort of a carriage: no very superb one, I assure you, ladies; but, in that part of the world, it was looked upon with some envy by our poorer neighbors. The first party of pleasure which my father proposed to take in it was to the village where I had so often wished to go; and my mother and I were to accompany him: for it was very fit, my father observed, that little Susan should go to church, and learn how to behave herself; for we might sometime or other have occasion to live in London, and not always be confined to that out-of-the-way spot.

It was on a Sunday morning that we set out, my little heart beating with almost breathless expectation. The day was fine, and the roads as good as they ever are in those parts. I was so happy and so proud! I was lost in dreams of what I was going to see. At length, the tall steeple of St. Mary's Church came in view. It was pointed out to me by my father as the place from which that music had come which I had heard over the moor, and fancied to be angels singing. I was wound up to the highest pitch of delight at having visibly presented to me the spot from which had proceeded that unknown friendly music; and when it began to peal, just as we approached the village, it seemed to speak, "*Susan is come!*" as plainly as it used to invite me *to come* when I heard it over the moor. I pass over our alighting at the house of a relation, and all that passed till I went with my father and mother to church.

St. Mary's Church is a great church for such a small village as it stands in. My father said it had been a cathedral, and that it had once belonged to a monastery; but the monks were all gone. Over the door, there was stone-work representing the saints and bishops; and here and there, along the sides of the church, there were figures of men's heads, made in a strange, grotesque way. I have since seen the same sort of figures in the round tower of the Temple Church in London. My father said they were very improper ornaments for such a place; and so I now think them: but it seems the people who built these great churches, in old times, gave themselves more liberties than they do now; and I remember, that when I first saw them, and before my father had made this observation, though they were so ugly and out of shape, and some of them seemed to be grinning, and distorting their features with pain or with laughter, yet, being placed upon a church to which I had come with such serious thoughts, I could not help thinking they had some serious meaning; and I looked at them with wonder, but without any temptation to laugh. I somehow fancied they were the representation of wicked people, set up as a warning.

When we got into the church, the service was not begun; and my father kindly took me round to show me the monuments, and every thing else remarkable. I remember seeing one of a venerable figure, which my father said had been a judge. The figure was kneeling, as if it were alive, before a sort of desk, with a book, I suppose the Bible, lying on it. I somehow fancied the figure had a sort of life in it, it seemed so natural; or that the dead judge, that it was done for, said his prayers at it still. This was a silly notion: but I was very young, and had passed my little life in a remote place, where I had never seen any thing, nor knew any thing; and the awe which I felt at first being in a church took from me all power but that of wondering. I did not reason about any thing: I was too young. Now I understand why monuments are put up for the dead, and why the figures which are put upon them are described as doing the actions which they did in their lifetimes, and that they are a sort of pictures set up for our instruction. But all was new and surprising to me on that day,—the long windows with little panes, the pillars, the pews made of oak, the little hassocks for the people to kneel on, the form of the pulpit, with the sounding-board over it, gracefully carved in flower-work. To you, who have lived all your lives in populous places, and have been taken to church from the earliest time you can remember, my admiration of these things must appear strangely ignorant; but I was a lonely young creature, that had been brought up in remote places, where there was neither church, nor church-going inhabitants. I have since lived in great towns, and seen the ways of churches and of worship; and I am old enough now to distinguish between what is essential in religion, and what is merely formal or ornamental.

When my father had done pointing out to me the things most worthy of notice about the church, the service was almost ready to begin: the parishioners had most of them entered, and taken their seats; and we were shown into a pew, where my mother was already seated. Soon after, the clergyman entered, and the organ began to play what is called the Voluntary. I had never seen so many people assembled before. At first, I thought that all eyes were upon me, and that because I was a stranger. I was terribly ashamed and confused at first: but my mother helped me to find out the places in the Prayer-book; and being busy about that took off some of my painful apprehensions. I was no stranger to the order of the service, having often read in the Prayer-book at home: but, my thoughts being confused, it puzzled me a little to find out the responses and other things which I thought I knew so well; but I went through it tolerably well. One thing which has often troubled me since is, that I am afraid I was too full of myself, and of thinking how happy I was, and what a privilege it was for one that was so young to join in the service with so many grown people; so that I did not attend enough to the instruction which I might have received. I remember, I foolishly applied every thing that was said, to myself, so as it could mean nobody but myself, I was so full of my own thoughts. All that assembly of people seemed to me as if they were come together only to show me the way of a church. Not but I received some very affecting impressions from some things which I heard that day: but the standing-up and the sitting-down of the people, the organ, the singing, — the way of all these things took up more of my attention than was proper; or I thought it did. I believe I behaved better, and was more serious, when I went a second time and a third time: for now we went, as a regular thing, every Sunday; and continued to do so, till, by a still further change for the better in my father's circumstances, we removed to London. Oh! it was a happy day for me, my first going to St. Mary's Church: before that day, I used to feel like a little outcast in the wilderness; like one that did not belong to the world of Christian people. I have never felt like a little outcast since. But I never can hear the sweet noise of bells, that I don't think of the angels singing, and what poor but pretty thoughts I had of angels in my uninstructed solitude.

ARABELLA HARDY;

OR, THE SEA VOYAGE.

I WAS born in the East Indies. I lost my father and mother young. At the age of five, my relations thought it proper that I should be sent to England for my education. I was to be intrusted to the care of a young woman who had a character for great humanity and discretion; but just as I had taken leave of my friends, and we were about to take our passage, the young woman suddenly fell sick, and could not go on board. In this unpleasant emergency, no one knew how to act. The ship was at the very point of sailing, and it was the last which was to sail for the season. At length, the captain, who was known to my friends, prevailed upon my relation, who had come with us to see us embark, to leave the young woman on shore, and to let me embark separately. There was no possibility of getting any other female attendant for me, in the short time allotted for our preparation; and the opportunity of going by that ship was thought too valuable to be lost. No other ladies happened to be going; and so I was consigned to the care of the captain and his crew, — rough and unaccustomed attendants for a young creature, delicately brought up as I had been: but, indeed, they did their best to make me not feel the difference. The unpolished sailors were my nursery-maids and my waiting-women. Every thing was done by the captain and the men to accommodate me, and make me easy. I had a little room made out of the cabin, which was to be considered as my room, and nobody might enter into it. The first mate had a great character for bravery, and all sailor-like accomplishments; but with all this he had a gentleness of manners, and a pale, feminine cast of face, from ill health and a weakly constitution, which subjected him to some ridicule from the officers, and caused him to be named Betsy. He did not much like the appellation; but he submitted to it the better, saying that those who gave him a woman's name well knew that he had a man's heart, and that, in the face of danger, he would go as far as any man. To this young man, whose real name was Charles Atkinson, by a lucky thought of the captain, the care of me was especially intrusted. Betsy was proud of his charge; and, to do him justice, acquitted himself with great diligence and adroitness through the whole of the voyage. From the beginning, I had somehow looked upon Betsy as a woman, hearing him so spoken of; and this reconciled me in some measure to the want of a maid, which I had been used to. But I was a managcablc girl at all times, and gave nobody much trouble.

I have not knowledge enough to give an account of my voyage, or to remember the names of the seas we passed through, or the lands which we touched upon, in our course. The chief thing I can remember (for I do not recollect the events of the voyage in any order) was Atkinson taking me upon deck to see the great whales playing about in the sea. There was one great whale came bounding up out of the sea, and then he would dive into it again, and then he would come up at a distance where nobody expected him; and another whale was following after him. Atkinson said they were at play, and that the lesser whale loved that bigger whale, and kept it company all through the wide seas: but I thought it strange play, and a frightful kind of love; for I every minute expected they would come up to our ship, and toss it. But Atkinson said a whale was a gentle creature, and it was a sort of sea-elephant; and that the most powerful creatures in nature are always the least hurtful. And he told me how men went out to take these whales, and stuck long pointed darts into them; and how the sea was discolored with the blood of these poor whales for many miles' distance: and I admired the courage of the men; but I was sorry for the inoffensive whale. Many other pretty sights he used to show me, when he was not on watch, or doing some duty for the ship. No one was more attentive to his duty than he: but, at such times as he had leisure, he would show me all pretty sea-sights, — the dolphins and porpoises that came before a storm; and all the colors which the sea changed to,—how sometimes it was a deep blue, and then a deep green, and sometimes it would seem all on fire. All these various appearances he would show me, and attempt to explain the reason of them to me as well as my young capacity would admit of. There was a lion and a tiger on board, going to England as a present to the king; and it was a great diversion to Atkinson and me, after I had got rid of my first terrors, to see the ways of these beasts in their dens, and how venturous the sailors were in putting their hands through the grates, and patting their rough coats. Some of the men had monkeys, which ran loose about; and the sport was for the men to lose them, and find them again. The monkeys would run up the shrouds, and pass from rope to rope, with ten times greater alacrity than the most experienced sailor could follow them: and sometimes they would hide themselves in the most unthought-of places; and, when they were found, they would grin, and make mouths, as if they had sense. Atkinson described to me the ways of these little animals in their native woods; for he had seen them. Oh, how many ways he thought of to amuse me in that long voyage!

Sometimes he would describe to me the odd shapes and varieties of fishes that were in the sea; and tell me tales of the sea-monsters that lay hid at the bottom, and were seldom seen by men; and what a glorious sight it would be if our eyes could be sharpened to behold all the inhabitants of the sea at once, swimming in the great deeps, as plain as we see the gold and silver fish in a bowl of glass. With such notions he enlarged my infant capacity to take in many things.

When in foul weather I have been terrified at the motion of the vessel as it rocked backwards and forwards, he would still my fears, and tell me that I used to be rocked so once in a cradle; and that the sea was God's bed, and the ship our cradle, and we were as safe in that greater motion as when we felt that lesser one in our little wooden sleeping-places. When the wind was up, and sang through the sails, and disturbed me with its violent clamors, he would call it music, and bid me hark to the sea-organ; and with that name he quieted my tender apprehensions. When I have looked around with a mournful face at seeing all *men* about me, he would enter into my thoughts, and tell me pretty stories of his mother and his sisters, and a female cousin that he loved better than his sisters, whom he called Jenny; and say, that, when we got to England, I should go and see them; and how fond Jenny would be of his little daughter, as he called me. And, with these images of women and females which he raised in my fancy, he quieted me for a while. One time, and never but once, he told me that Jenny had promised to be his wife, if ever he came to England; but that he had his doubts whether he should live to get home, for he was very sickly. This made me cry bitterly.

That I dwell so long upon the attention of this Atkinson, is only because his death, which happened just before we got to England, affected me so much, that he alone of all the ship's crew has engrossed my mind ever since; though, indeed, the captain and all were singularly kind to me, and strove to make up for my uneasy and unnatural situation. The boatswain would pipe for my diversion, and the sailor-boy would climb the dangerous mast for my sport. The rough foremast-man would never willingly appear before me till he had combed his long black hair smooth and sleek, not to terrify me. The officers got up a sort of play for my amusement; and Atkinson, or, as they called him, Betsy, acted the heroine of the piece. All ways that could be contrived were thought upon to reconcile me to my lot. I was the universal favorite: I do not know how deservedly; but I suppose it was because I was alone, and there was no female in the ship besides me. Had I come over with female relations or attendants, I should have excited no particular curiosity: I should have required no uncommon attentions. I was one little woman among a crew of men; and I believe the homage which I have read that men universally pay to women was in this case directed to me, in the absence of all other womankind. I do not know how that might be; but I was a little princess among them, and I was not six years old.

I remember, the first drawback which happened to my comfort was Atkinson's not appearing the whole of one day. The captain tried to reconcile me to it by saying that Mr. Atkinson was confined to his cabin; that he was not quite well, but a day or two would restore him. I begged to be taken in to see him; but this was not granted. A day, and then another, came, and another, and no Atkinson was visible; and I saw apparent solicitude in the faces of all the officers, who nevertheless strove to put on their best countenances before me, and to be more than usually kind to me. At length, by the desire of Atkinson himself, as I have since learned, I was permitted to go into his cabin, and see him. He was sitting up, apparently in a state of great exhaustion: but his face lighted up when he saw me; and he kissed me, and told me that he was going a great voyage, far longer than that which we had passed together, and he should never come back. And, though I was so young, I understood well enough that he meant this of his death; and I cried sadly: but he comforted me, and told me that I must be his little executrix, and perform his last will, and bear his last words to his mother and his sisters, and to his cousin Jenny, whom I should see in a short time; and he gave me his blessing, as a father would bless his child; and he sent a last kiss by me to all his female relations; and he made me promise that I would go and see them, when I got to England. And soon after this he died: but I was in another part of the ship when he died; and I was not told it till we got to shore, which was a few days after; but they kept telling me that he was better and better, and that I should soon see him, but that it disturbed him to talk with any one. Oh, what a grief it was, when I learned that I had lost an old shipmate, that had made an irksome situation so bearable by his kind assiduities! and to think that he was gone, and I could never repay him for his kindness!

When I had been a year and a half in England, the captain, who had made another voyage to India and back, thinking that time had alleviated a little the sorrow of Atkinson's relations, prevailed upon my friends, who had the care of me in England, to let him introduce me to Atkinson's mother and sisters. Jenny was no more. She had died in the interval; and I never saw her. Grief for his death had brought on a consumption, of which she lingered about a twelvemonth, and then expired. But in the mother and the sisters of this excellent young man I have found the most valuable friends I possess on this side the great ocean. They received me from the captain as the little *protégée* of Atkinson: and from them I have learned passages of his former life; and this in particular,—that the illness of which he died was brought on by a wound, of which he never quite recovered, which he got in a desperate attempt, when he was quite a boy, to defend his captain against a superior force of the enemy which had boarded him, and which, by his premature valor inspiriting the men, they finally succeeded in repulsing. This was that Atkinson, who, from his pale and feminine appearance, was called Betsy: this was he whose womanly care of me got him the name of a woman; who, with more than female attention, condescended to play the handmaid to a little unaccompanied orphan, that fortune had cast upon the care of a rough sea-captain and his rougher crew.

POEMS.

POEMS.

EXISTENCE, CONSIDERED IN ITSELF, NO BLESSING.*

FROM THE LATIN OF PALINGENIUS.

The poet, after a seeming approval of suicide from a consideration of the cares and crimes of life, finally rejecting it, discusses the negative importance of existence, contemplated in itself, without reference to good or evil.

OF these sad truths consideration had,
Thou shalt not fear to quit this world so mad,
So wicked: but the tenet rather hold
Of wise Calanus and his followers old,
Who with their own wills their own freedom wrought,
And by self-slaughter their dismissal sought
From this dark den of crime, this horrid lair
Of men, that savager than monsters are;
And, scorning longer in this tangled mesh
Of ills, to wait on perishable flesh,
Did with their desperate hands anticipate
The too, too slow relief of lingering fate.
And if religion did not stay thine hand,
And God, and Plato's wise behests, withstand,
I would in like case counsel thee to throw
This senseless burden off, of cares below.

* From the "London Athenæum," 1832.

Not wine, as wine, men choose, but as it came
From such or such a vintage: 'tis the same
With life, which simply must be understood
A blank negation, if it be not good.
But if 'tis wretched all, — as men decline
And loathe the sour lees of corrupted wine, —
'Tis so to be contemned. Merely TO BE
Is not a boon to seek, or ill to flee;
Seeing that every vilest little THING
Has it in common, — from a gnat's small wing,
A creeping worm, down to the moveless stone,
And crumbling bark from trees. Unless TO BE,
And TO BE BLEST, be one, I do not see
In bare existence, *as* existence, aught
That's worthy to be loved or to be sought.

THE PARTING SPEECH OF THE CELESTIAL MESSENGER TO THE POET.*

FROM THE LATIN OF PALINGENIUS, IN THE ZODIACUS VITÆ.

BUT now time warns (my mission at an end)
That to Jove's starry court I re-ascend;
From whose high battlements I take delight
To scan your earth, diminished to the sight,
Pendant and round, and, as an apple, small,
Self-propt, self-balanced, and secure from fall
By her own weight; and how with liquid robe
Blue Ocean girdles round her tiny globe,

* From the "London Athenæum," 1832.

While lesser Nereus, gliding like a snake,
Betwixt her lands his flexile course doth take,
Shrunk to a rivulet; and how the Po,
The mighty Ganges, Tanais, Ister, show
No bigger than a ditch which rains have swelled.
Old Nilus' seven proud mouths I late beheld,
And mocked the watery puddles. Hosts steel-clad
Ofttimes I thence beheld; and how the sad
Peoples are punished by the fault of kings,
Which from the purple fiend Ambition springs.
Forgetful of mortality, they live
In hot strife for possessions fugitive,
At which the angels grieve. Sometimes I trace
Of fountains, rivers, seas, the change of place;
By ever-shifting course, and Time's unrest,
The vale exalted, and the mount deprest
To an inglorious valley; ploughshares going
Where tall trees reared their tops, and fresh trees growing
In antique postures; cities lose their site;
Old things wax new. Oh! what a rare delight
To him, who, from this vantage, can survey
At once stern Afric and soft Asia,
With Europe's cultured plains, and, in their turns,
Their scattered tribes! — those whom the hot Crab burns,
The tawny Ethiops; Orient Indians;
Getulians; ever-wandering Scythians;
Swift Tartan hordes; Cilicians rapacious,
And Parthians with black-bended bow pugnacious;
Sabeans incense bring; men of Thrace;
Italian, Spaniard, Gaul; and that rough race

Of Britons, rigid as their native colds;
With all the rest the circling sun beholds.
But clouds and elemental mists deny
These visions blest to any fleshly eye.

HERCULES PACIFICATUS.*

A TALE FROM SUIDAS.

In days of yore, ere early Greece
Had dreamed of patrols or police,
A crew of rake-hells *in terrorem*
Spread wide, and carried all before 'em;
Rifled the poultry and the women,
And held that all things were in common;
Till Jove's great son the nuisance saw,
And did abate it by club law.
Yet not so clean he made his work,
But here and there a rogue would lurk
In caves and rocky fastnesses,
And shunned the strength of Hercules.

Of these, more desperate than others,
A pair of ragamuffin brothers
In secret ambuscade joined forces,
To carry on unlawful courses.
These robbers' names — enough to shake us —
Were Strymon one, the other Cacus;
And, more the neighborhood to bother,
A wicked dam they had for mother,

* From the "Englishman's Magazine," 1831.

Who knew their craft, but not forbid it:
And whatsoe'er they nymmed she hid it;
Received them with delight and wonder
When they brought home some special plunder;
Called them her darlings, and her white boys,
Her ducks, her dildings; all was right, boys.
"Only," she said, "my lads, have care
Ye fall not into Black Back's snare;
For, if he catch, he'll maul your *corpus*,
And clapper-claw you to some purpose."
She was, in truth, a kind of witch;
Had grown by fortune-telling rich;
To spells and conjurings did tackle her,
And read folks' dooms by light oracular,
In which she saw as clear as daylight
What mischief on her bairns would a-light.
Therefore she had a special loathing
For all that owned that sable clothing.

Who can 'scape fate, when we're decreed to't?
The graceless brethren paid small heed to't.
A brace they were of sturdy fellows,
As we may say, that feared no colors;
And sneered with modern infidelity
At the old gypsy's fond credulity.
It proved all true, though, as she'd mumbled;
For on a day the varlets stumbled
On a green spot, — *sit linguæ fides*, —
('Tis Suidas tells it,) where Alcides,
Secure, as fearing no ill neighbor,
Lay fast asleep after a "Labor."
His trusty oaken plant was near:

The prowling rogues look round, and leer,
And each his wicked wits 'gan rub,
How to bear off the famous club;
Thinking that they, *sans* price or hire, would
Carry't straight home, and chop for fire-wood:
'Twould serve their old dame half a winter.
You stare; but, faith, it was no splinter:
I would not, for much money, spy
Such beam in any neighbor's eye.
The villains, these exploits not dull in,
Incontinently fell a-pulling.
They found it heavy, no slight matter,
But tugged and tugged it, till the clatter
Woke Hercules, who in a trice
Whipt up the knaves, and, with a splice
He kept on purpose, — which before
Had served for giants many a score, —
To end of club tied each rogue's head fast;
Strapping feet too, to keep them steadfast;
And pickaback them carries townwards,
Behind his brawny back, head-downwards;
(So foolish calf — for rhyme, I bless X. —
Comes *nolens volens* out of Essex;)
Thinking to brain them with his *dextra*,
Or string them up upon the next tree.
That club — so equal fates condemn —
They thought to catch has now catched them.

Now, Hercules, we may suppose,
Was no great dandy in his clothes;
Was seldom, save on Sundays, seen
In calimanco or nankeen;

On anniversaries, would try on
A jerkin, spick-span new, from lion;
Went bare for the most part, to be cool,
And save the time of his groom of the stole.
Besides, the smoke he had been in,
In Stygian Gulf, had dyed his skin
To a natural sable, — a right hell-fit,
That seemed to careless eyes black velvet.

The brethren from their station scurvy,
Where they hung dangling topsy-turvy,
With horror view the black costume;
And each presumes his hour is come:
Then softly to themselves 'gan mutter
The warning words their dame did utter,
Yet not so softly, but with ease
Were overheard by Hercules.
Quoth Cacus, "This is he she spoke of,
Which we so often made a joke of."
"I see," said the other; "thank our sin for't,
'Tis Black Back, sure enough: we're in for't."

His godship, who, for all his brag
Of roughness, was at heart a wag,
At his new name was tickled finely,
And fell a-laughing most divinely.
Quoth he, "I'll tell this jest in heaven;
The musty rogues shall be forgiven;"
So, in a twinkling, did uncase them,
On mother-earth once more to place them.
The varlets, glad to be unhampered,
Made each a leg, then fairly scampered.

A FRAGMENT.

[His Satanic Majesty seems to have been exceedingly popular with the English bards and bardlings of thirty and odd years ago. The London booksellers' counters were covered with "Devil's Walks," "True Devil's Walks," "Devil's Drives," "Devil's Progresses," "Devil's Bargains," and I know not how many more poems on the same renowned personage. Not only Southey and Coleridge chose Beelzebub for the subject of a poem, but even Elia sung of Satan, and told in immortal verse the true and wonderful history of the Devil's courtship and marriage; which Moxon published in a dainty little tome, with six humorous designs, price one shilling. The exact title of the work, the bibliographical reader will be pleased to learn, is "Satan in Search of a Wife; with the whole Progress of his Courtship and Marriage, and who danced at the Wedding. By an Eye-witness."

And, although the market was rather overstocked with poems concerning the Evil One, Lamb's little effusion had a pretty fair sale. The copyright on a shilling volume must have been small; yet Elia, in a letter to Moxon, says, "You hinted that there might be something under ten pounds by and by accruing to me, — *devil's money* (you are sanguine; say seven pounds ten shillings)."

The merits of this *jeu d'esprit* may be very small; indeed, I have no doubt that it is about the poorest thing its author ever printed: yet should I like to see it — because Charles Lamb wrote it. But I have not been able to find a copy of "Satan in Search of a Wife."

The following extract from the work, which I found in an old number of the "London Athenæum," will, I hope, be acceptable to some of Lamb's readers. If we cannot get the whole cake, let us be thankful for the smallest bit thereof. — EDITOR.]

THE Devil was sick and queasy of late,
And his sleep and his appetite failed him :
His ears they hung down ; and his tail it was clapped
Between his poor hoofs, like a dog that's been rapped.
None knew what the devil ailed him.

He tumbled and tossed on his mattress o' nights,
That was fit for a fiend's disportal ;
For 'twas made of the finest of thistle and thorn,

Which Alecto herself had gathered, in scorn
Of the best down-beds that are mortal.

His giantly chest in earthquakes heaved,
With groanings corresponding;
And mincing and few were the words he spoke,
While a sigh, like some delicate whirlwind, broke
From a heart that seemed desponding.

Now, the Devil an old wife had for his dam;
I think none e'er was older:
Her years — old Parr's were nothing to them;
And a chicken to her was Methusalem,
You'd say, could you behold her.

She remembered Chaos a little child,
Strumming upon hand-organs:
At the birth of old Night a gossip she sat,
The ancientest there; and was godmother at
The christening of the Gorgons.

Her bones peeped through a rhinoceros' skin,
Like a mummy through its cerement;
But she had a mother's heart, and guessed
What pinched her son, whom she thus addressed
In terms that bespoke endearment: —

"What ails my Nicky, my darling imp,
My Lucifer bright, my Beelze?
My pig, my pug-with-a-curly-tail,
You are not well: can a mother fail
To see *that* which all hell see?"

"O mother dear! I am dying, I fear:
Prepare the yew and the willow,
And the cypress black; for I get no ease,
By day or by night, for the cursed fleas
That skip about my pillow."

"Your pillow is clean, and your pillow-beer,
For I wash'd 'em in Styx last night, son,
And your blankets both, and dried them upon
The brimstony banks of Acheron:
It is not the *fleas* that bite, son.
. . . . .
I wish my Nicky is not in love."
"O mother, you have nicked it!"
And he turned his head aside with a *blush:*
Not red-hot pokers, or crimson plush,
Could half so deep have pricked it.

FOR THE ALBUM OF MISS ——, FRENCH TEACHER AT MRS. GISBORN'S SCHOOL, ENFIELD.*

IMPLORED for verse, I send you what I can;
But you are so exact a French-woman,
As I am told, Jemima, that I fear
To wound with English your Parisian ear,
And think I do your curious volume wrong,
With lines not written in the Frenchman's tongue.
Had I a knowledge equal to my will,
With airy *chansons* I your leaves would fill;

* From "Blackwood's Magazine," 1829.

With *fables* that should emulate the vein
Of sprightly Gresset or of La Fontaine;
Or *scenès comiques* that should approach the air
Of your favorite, renownèd Molière.
But at my suit the Muse of France looks sour,
And strikes me dumb! Yet what is in my power
To testify respect for you, I pray
Take in plain English, — our rough Enfield way.

TO C. ADERS, ESQ.,*

ON HIS COLLECTION OF PAINTINGS BY THE OLD GERMAN MASTERS.

FRIENDLIEST of men, Aders, I never come
Within the precincts of this sacred room,
But I am struck with a religious fear,
Which says, "Let no profane eye enter here."
With imagery from heaven the walls are clothed,
Making the things of time seem vile and loathed.
Spare saints, whose bodies seem sustained by love,
With martyrs old in meek procession move.
Here kneels a weeping Magdalen, less bright
To human sense for her blurred cheeks; in sight
Of eyes new-touched by Heaven, more winning fair
Than when her beauty was her only care.
A hermit here strange mysteries doth unlock
In desert sole, his knees worn by the rock.
There angel harps are sounding, while below
Palm-bearing virgins in white order go.

* From Hone's "Year-book."

Madonnas, varied with so chaste design
While all are different, each seems genuine,
And hers the only Jesus: hard outline
And rigid form, by Durer's hand subdued
To matchless grace and sacro-sanctitude, —
Durer, who makes thy slighted Germany
Vie with the praise of paint-proud Italy.

Whoever enterest here, no more presume
To name a parlor or a drawing-room;
But, bending lowly to each holy story,
Make this thy chapel and thine oratory.

LETTERS.

LETTERS.

TO A BOOKSELLER.

THANK you for the books.* I am ashamed to take tithe thus of your press. I am worse to a publisher than the two Universities and the British Museum. A. C. I will forthwith read. B. C. (I can't get out of the A, B, C) I have more than read. Taken altogether, 'tis too lovely; but what delicacies! I like most "King Death;" glorious 'bove all, "The Lady with the Hundred Rings;" "The Owl;" "Epistle to What's his Name"† (here may be I'm partial); "Sit down, Sad Soul;" "The Pauper's Jubilee" (but that's old, and yet 'tis never old); "The Falcon;" "Felon's Wife;" damn "Madame Pasty" (but that is borrowed);

Apple-pie is very good,
And so is apple-pasty;
But ——
O Lord! 'tis very nasty:

but chiefly the dramatic fragments, — scarce three of which should have escaped my specimens, had an antique name been prefixed. They exceed his first. So much for the nonsense of poetry: now to the se-

* "The Maid of Eloan," by Allan Cunningham; and Barry Cornwall's "Songs and Dramatic Fragments."

† Charles Lamb.

rious business of life. Up a court (Blandford Court) in Pall Mall (exactly at the back of Marlborough House), with iron gate in front, and containing two houses, at No. 2, did lately live Leishman, my tailor. He is moved somewhere in the neighborhood, devil knows where. Pray find him out, and give him the opposite. I am so much better, though my head shakes in writing it, that, after next Sunday, I can well see F. and you. Can you throw B. C. in? Why tarry the wheels of my "Hogarth"?

CHARLES LAMB.

TO J. PAYNE COLLIER.

THE GARDEN OF ENGLAND, Dec. 10.

DEAR J. P. C.,—I know how zealously you feel for our friend S. T. Coleridge; and I know that you and your family attended his lectures four or five years ago. He is in bad health, and worse mind: and, unless something is done to lighten his mind, he will soon be reduced to his extremities; and even these are not in the best condition. I am sure that you will do for him what you can; but at present he seems in a mood to do for himself. He projects a new course, not of physic, nor of metaphysic, nor a new course of life, but a new course of lectures on Shakspeare and poetry. There is no man better qualified (always excepting number one); but I am pre-engaged for a series of dissertations on Indian and India-pendence, to be completed, at the expense of the company, in I know not (yet) how many volumes foolscap folio. I am busy getting up my Hindoo mythology; and, for the purpose, I am once more enduring Southey's curse (of "Kehama"). To be serious, Coleridge's state and affairs make me so; and there are particular reasons just now, and have been any time for the last twenty years, why he should succeed. He will do so with a little encouragement. I have not seen him lately; and he does not know that I am writing.

Yours (for Coleridge's sake) in haste,

C. Lamb.

TO JOSEPH COTTLE.

Dear Sir, — It is so long since I have seen or heard from you, that I fear that you will consider a request I have to make as impertinent. About three years since, when I was in Bristol, I made an effort to see you by calling at Brunswick Square; but you were from home. The request I have to make is, that you would very much oblige me, if you have any small portrait of yourself, by allowing me to have it copied, to accompany a selection of the likenesses of "Living Bards" which a most particular friend of mine is making. If you have no objection, and would oblige me by transmitting such portrait, I will answer for taking the greatest care of it, and for its safe return. I hope you will pardon the liberty.

From an old friend and well-wisher,

Charles Lamb.

TO THE SAME.

Dear Sir,—My friend, whom you have obliged by the loan of your picture, has had it very nicely copied (and a very spirited drawing it is; so every one thinks who has seen it). The copy is not much inferior to yours, done by a daughter of Joseph's, R. A.

I accompany the picture with my warm thanks, both for that, and your better favor, the "Messiah," which I assure you I have read through with great pleasure. The verses have great sweetness, and a New-Testament plainness about them which affected me very much. I could just wish, that, in page 63, you had omitted the lines 71 and 72, and had ended the period with—

> "The willowy brook was there, but that sweet sound—
> When to be heard again on earthly ground?"

Two very sweet lines, and the sense perfect.

And in page 154, line 68,—

> "He spake, 'I come, ordained a world to save,
> To be baptized by thee in Jordan's wave.'"

These words are hardly borne out by the story, and seem scarce accordant with the modesty with which our Lord came to take his common portion among the baptismal candidates. They also anticipate the beauty of John's recognition of the Messiah, and the subsequent confirmation by the Voice and Dove.

You will excuse the remarks of an old brother bard, whose career, though long since pretty well stopped, was co-eval in its beginning with your own, and who is sorry his lot has been always to be so distant from you.

It is not likely that C. L. will see Bristol again; but, if J. C. should ever visit London, he will be a most welcome visitor to C. L. My sister joins in cordial remembrances.

Dear sir, yours truly, CHARLES LAMB.

TO THE SAME.

LONDON, INDIA HOUSE, May 26, 1829.

MY DEAR SIR, — I am quite ashamed of not having acknowledged your kind present earlier; but that unknown something, which was never yet discovered, though so often speculated upon, which stands in the way of lazy folks answering letters, has presented its usual obstacle. It is not forgetfulness nor disrespect nor incivility, but terribly like all these bad things.

I have been in my time a great epistolary scribbler: but the passion, and with it the facility, at length wears out; and it must be pumped up again by the heavy machinery of duty or gratitude, when it should run free. I have read your "Fall of Cambria" with as much pleasure as I did your "Messiah." Your Cambrian poem I shall be tempted to repeat oftenest, as human poems take me in a mood more frequently congenial than divine. The character of Llewellyn pleases me more than any thing else, perhaps; and then some of the lyrical pieces are fine varieties.

It was quite a mistake that I could dislike any thing you should write against Lord Byron; for I have a thorough aversion to his character, and a very moderate admiration of his genius: he is great in so little a way.

To be a poet is to be the man, not a petty portion of occasional low passion worked up in a permanent form of humanity. Shakspeare has thrust such rubbishly feelings into a corner, — the dark dusky heart of Don John, in the "Much Ado about Nothing." The fact is, I have not seen your "Expostulatory Epistle" to him. I was not aware, till your question, that it was out. I shall inquire, and get it forthwith.

Southey is in town, whom I have seen slightly; Wordsworth expected, whom I hope to see much of. I write with accelerated motion; for I have two or three bothering clerks and brokers about me, who always press in proportion as you seem to be doing something that is not business. I could exclaim a little profanely; but I think you do not like swearing.

I conclude, begging you to consider that I feel myself much obliged by your kindness; and shall be most happy at any and at all times to hear from you.

Dear sir, yours truly, CHARLES LAMB.

TO A FARMER AND HIS WIFE.

TWELFTH DAY, '23.

THE pig was above my feeble praise. It was a dear pigmy. There was some contention as to who should have the ears; but, in spite of his obstinacy (deaf as these little creatures are to advice), I contrived to get at one of them.

It came in boots too, which I took as a favor. Generally these pretty toes, pretty toes! are missing; but I suppose he wore them to look taller.

He must have been the least of his race. His little foots would have gone into the silver slipper. I take him to have been a Chinese and a female.

If Evelyn could have seen him, he would never have farrowed two such prodigious volumes; seeing how much good can be contained in — how small a compass!

He crackled delicately.

I left a blank at the top of my letter, not being determined which to address it to: so farmer and farmer's wife will please to divide our thanks. May your granaries be full, and your rats empty, and your chickens plump, and your envious neighbors lean, and your laborers busy, and you as idle and as happy as the day is long!

VIVE L'AGRICULTURE!

How do you make your pigs so little?
They are vastly engaging at the age:
    I was so myself.
Now I am a disagreeable old hog,
A middle-aged gentleman-and-a-half.
My faculties, thank God, are not much impaired!

I have my sight, hearing, taste, pretty perfect; and can read the Lord's Prayer in common type, by the help of a candle, without making many mistakes.

Believe me, that, while my faculties last, I shall ever cherish a proper appreciation of your many kindnesses in this way, and that the last lingering relish of past favors upon my dying memory will be the smack of that little ear. It was the left ear, which is lucky. Many happy returns, not of the pig, but of the New Year, to both! Mary, for her share of the pig and the memoirs, desires to send the same.

Yours truly, C. LAMB.

TO S. T. COLERIDGE.

THESES QUÆDAM THEOLOGICÆ.

[The careful reader will observe that these famous theological propositions as here given, just as they were sent to Coleridge, differ somewhat from the transcript of them given in the letter to Southey, published in Talfourd's "Life and Letters of Charles Lamb." Here you have the original theses themselves: there you have a revised and amended copy of them. The letter to Coleridge accompanying these learned and knotty questions is not included in any edition of Lamb's Works. "Mr. Coleridge," says Cottle, in his "Reminiscences of Coleridge and Southey," "at first appeared greatly hurt at this letter." — EDITOR.]

First, Whether God loves a lying angel better than a true man?

Second, Whether the Archangel Uriel could affirm an untruth? and, if he could, whether he would?

Third, Whether honesty be an angelic virtue, or not rather to be reckoned among those qualities which the schoolmen term *virtutes minus splendidæ?*

Fourth, Whether the higher order of Seraphim illuminati ever sneer?

Fifth, Whether pure intelligences can love?

Sixth, Whether the Seraphim ardentes do not manifest their virtues by the way of vision and theory? and whether practice be not a sub-celestial and merely human virtue?

Seventh, Whether the vision beatific be any thing more or less than a perpetual representment to each individual angel of his own present attainments and future capabilities, somehow in the manner of mortal looking-glasses, reflecting a perpetual complacency and self-satisfaction?

Eighth, and last, Whether an immortal and amenable soul may not come to be condemned at last, and the man never suspect it beforehand?

LEARNED SIR, MY FRIEND, — Presuming on our long habits of friendship, and emboldened further by your late liberal permission to avail myself of your correspondence in case I want any knowledge (which I intend to do when I have no Encyclopædia or Ladies' Magazine at hand to refer to in any matter of science), I now submit to your inquiries the above theological propositions, to be by you defended or oppugned, or both, in the schools of Germany; whither, I am told, you are departing, to the utter dissatisfaction of your native Devonshire, and regret of universal England, but to my own individual consolation, if, through the channel of your wished return, learned sir, my friend, may be transmitted to this our island, from those famous theological wits of Leipsic and Göttingen, any rays of illumination, in vain to be derived from the home growth of our English halls and colleges. Finally wishing, learned sir, that you may see Schiller, and swing in a wood (*vide* poems), and sit upon a tun, and eat fat hams of Westphalia,

I remain
Your friend and docile pupil to instruct,
CHARLES LAMB.

TO THOMAS HOOD.*

AND what dost thou at the Priory? *Cucullus non facit Monachum.* English me that, and challenge old Lignum Janua to make a better.

My old New River has presented no extraordinary novelties lately; but there Hope sits every day, speculating upon traditionary gudgeons. I think she has taken the fisheries. I now know the reason why our forefathers were denominated East and West Angles. Yet is there no lack of spawn; for I wash my hands in fishets that come through the pump every morning thick

* Then "unrheumatizing himself" at Hastings.

as motelings, — little things that perish untimely, and never taste the brook. You do not tell me of those romantic land bays that be as thou goest to Lover's Seat: neither of that little churchling in the midst of a wood (in the opposite direction, nine furlongs from the town), that seems dropped by the Angel that was tired of carrying two packages; marry, with the other he made shift to pick his flight to Loretto. Inquire out, and see my little Protestant Loretto. It stands apart from trace of human habitation; yet hath it pulpit, reading-desk, and trim front of massiest marble, as if Robinson Crusoe had reared it to soothe himself with old church-going images. I forget its Xtian name, and what she-saint was its gossip.

You should also go to No. 13, Standgate Street; a Baker, who has the finest collection of marine monsters in ten sea-counties, — sea-dragons, polypi, mer-people, most fantastic. You have only to name the old gentleman in black (not the Devil) that lodged with him a week (he'll remember) last July, and he will show courtesy. He is by far the foremost of the savans. His wife is the funniest thwarting little animal! They are decidedly the Lions of green Hastings. Well, I have made an end of my say. My epistolary time is gone by when I could have scribbled as long (I will not say as agreeable) as thine was to both of us. I am dwindled to notes and letterets. But, in good earnest, I shall be most happy to hail thy return to the waters of old Sir Hugh. There is nothing like inland murmurs, fresh ripples, and our native minnows.

"He sang in meads, how sweet the brooklets ran,
To the rough ocean and red restless sands."

I design to give up smoking; but I have not yet fixed upon the equivalent vice. I must have *quid pro quo;* or *quo pro quid*, as Tom Woodgate would correct me. My service to him. C. L.*

TO THE SAME.

DEAR LAMB, — You are an impudent varlet; but I will keep your secret. We dine at Ayrton's on Thursday, and shall try to find Sarah and her two spare beds for that night only. Miss M. and her tragedy may be dished: so may *not* you and your rib. Health attend you.

Yours, T. HOOD, ESQ.

ENFIELD.

Miss Bridget Hood sends love.†

* "The letter came to hand too late for me to hunt the 'Lions;' but on a subsequent visit to the same Cinque Port with my wife, though we verified the little Loretto, we could not find the Baker, or even his man, howbeit we tried at every shop that had the least sign of bakery or cakery in its window. The whole was a batch of *fancy* bread, — one of those fictions which the writer was apt to pass off upon his friends." — HOOD.

† The secret alluded to in this "notelet" was, that the article in the "Gem," entitled "The Widow," and published under Lamb's well-known signature, was written by Hood.

Of course, the reader will see by the subscription, T. Hood, *Esq.*, that the letter was not written by the author of the "Song of the Shirt." Miss Bridget Hood is Mary Lamb; and the writer of the epistle is Charles Lamb himself. — EDITOR.

TO LEIGH HUNT.

ILLUSTREZZIMO SIGNOR, — I have obeyed your mandate to a tittle. I accompany this with a volume; but what have you done with the first I sent you? Have you swapped it with some lazzaroni for macaroni, or pledged it with a gondolierer for a passage? Peradventuri the Cardinal Gonsalvi took a fancy to it: his Eminence has done my Nearness an honor. 'Tis but a step to the Vatican. As you judge, my works do not enrich the workman; but I get vat I can fòr 'em. They keep dragging me on, a poor, worn mill-horse, in the eternal round of the damned magazine; but 'tis they are blind, not I. Colburn (where I recognize with delight the gay W. Honeycomb renovated) hath the ascendency.* I was with the Novellos last week. They have a large, cheap house and garden, with a dainty library (magnificent) without books; but, what will make you bless yourself (I am too old for wonder), something has touched the right organ in Vincentio at last. He attends a Wesleyan chapel on Kingsland Green. He at first tried to laugh it off, — he only went for the singing; but the cloven foot — I retract — the lamb's trotters are at length apparent. Mary Isabella attributes it to a lightness induced by his headaches; but I think I see in it a less accidental influence.

* A series of pleasant, gossiping articles by Leigh Hunt, called "The Family Journal," and pretended to be written by a descendant of Mr. Spectator's friend, Will Honeycomb. — EDITOR.

Mr. Clark is at perfect staggers! the whole fabric of his infidelity is shaken. He has no one to join him in his horse-insults and indecent obstreperousnesses against Christianity; for Holmes (the bonny Holmes) is gone to Salisbury to be organist, and Isabella and the Clark make but a feeble quorum. The children have all neat little clasped pray-books; and I have laid out seven shillings eight pence in Watts's Hymns for Christmas presents for them. The eldest girl alone holds out. She has been at Boulogne, skirting upon the vast focus of Atheism, and imported bad principles in patois French. But the strongholds are crumbling. N. appears as yet to have but a confused notion of the Atonement. It makes him giddy, he says, to think much about it; but such giddiness is spiritual sobriety. Well, Byron is gone; and —— is now the best poet in England. Fill up the gap to your fancy. Barry Cornwall has at last carried the pretty A. S. They are just in the treacle-moon. Hope it won't clog his wings (gaum, we used to say at school). Mary, my sister, has worn me out with eight weeks' cold and toothache, her average complement in the winter; and it will not go away. She is otherwise well, and reads novels all day long. She has had an exempt year, a good year; for which, forgetting the minor calamity, she and I are most thankful. Alsager is in a flourishing house, with wife and children about him, in Mecklenburg Square,—almost too fine to visit. Baron Field is come home from Sydney; but as yet I can hear no tidings of a pension. He is plump and friendly; his wife, really a very superior woman. He resumes the bar. I have got acquainted with Mr. Irving, the Scotch preacher, whose fame must have reached you. He is a humble disciple at the foot of Gamaliel S. T. C. Judge how his own sectarists must stare, when I tell you he has dedicated a book to S. T. C., acknowledging to have learnt more of the nature of faith, Christianity, and Christian Church, from him than from all the men he ever conversed with! He is a most amiable, sincere, modest man in a room, this Boanerges in the temple. Mrs. Montague told him the dedication would do him no good. 'That shall be a reason for doing it,' was his answer. Judge, now, whether this man be a quack. Dear H., take this imperfect notelet for a letter: it looks so much the more like conversing on nearer terms. Love to all the Hunts, old friend Thornton, and all. Yours ever,

C. Lamb.

TO MRS. SHELLEY.

Enfield, July 26, 1827.

Dear Mrs. Shelley, — At the risk of throwing away some fine thoughts, I must write to say how pleased we were with your very kind remembering of us (who have unkindly run away from all our friends) before you go. Perhaps you are gone, and then my tropes are wasted. If any piece of better fortune has lighted upon you than you expected, but less than we wish you, we are rejoiced. We are here trying to like solitude, but have scarce enough to justify the experiment. We get some, however. The six days are our sabbath; the seventh — why, Cockneys will come for a little fresh air, and so —

But by *your month*, or October at furthest, we hope to see Islington: I, like a giant refreshed with the leaving-off of wine; and Mary, pining for Mr. Moxon's books and Mr. Moxon's society. Then we shall meet.

I am busy with a farce in two acts;* the incidents tragi-comic. I can do the dialogue *commey for;* but the damned plot — I believe I must omit it altogether. The scenes come after one another like geese, not marshalling like cranes or a Hyde-Park review. The story is as simple as G. D., and the language plain as his spouse. The characters are three women to one man; which is one more than laid hold on him in the "Evangely." I think that prophecy squinted towards my drama.

I want some Howard Paine to sketch a skeleton of artfully succeeding scenes through a whole play, as the courses are arranged in a cookery-book: I to find wit, passion, sentiment, character, and the like trifles: to lay in the dead colors, — I'd Titianesque 'em up: to mark the channel in a cheek (smooth or furrowed, yours or mine); and, where tears should course, I'd draw the waters down: to say where a joke should come in or a pun be left out: to bring my *personæ* on and off like a Beau Nash; and I'd Frankenstein them there: to bring three together on the stage at once; they are so shy with me, that I can get no more than two; and there they stand till it is the time, without being the season, to withdraw them.

I am teaching Emma Latin, to qualify her for a superior governess-ship; which we see no prospect of

* "The Pawnbroker's Daughter."

her getting. 'Tis like feeding a child with chopped hay from a spoon. Sisyphus — his labors were as nothing to it.

Actives and passives jostle in her nonsense, till a deponent enters, like Chaos, more to embroil the fray. Her prepositions are suppositions; her conjunctions copulative have no connection in them; her concords disagree; her interjections are purely English "Ah!" and "Oh!" with a yawn and a gape in the same tongue; and she herself is a lazy, blockheadly supine. As I say to her, ass *in præsenti* rarely makes a wise man *in futuro*.

But I dare say it was so with you when you began Latin, and a good while after.

Good-by! Mary's love.

Yours truly, C. LAMB.

TO THE EDITOR OF THE "TABLE-BOOK."

DEAR SIR, — Somebody has fairly played a *hoax* on you (I suspect that pleasant rogue M–x–n *) in sending the sonnet in my name, inserted in your last number. True it is that I must own to the verses being mine, but not written on the occasion there pretended; for I have not yet had the pleasure of seeing the lady † in the part of Emmeline, and I have understood that the force of her acting in it is rather in the expression of new-born sight than of the previous want of it. The lines were really written upon her performance in the

* Edward Moxon. † Miss Kelley.

"Blind Boy," and appeared in the "Morning Chronicle" some years back. I suppose our facetious friend thought that they would serve again, like an old coat new turned.

Yours (and his nevertheless),

C. LAMB.

TO THE SAME.

SIR, — A correspondent in your last number rather hastily asserts that there is no other authority than Davenport's tragedy * for the poisoning of Matilda by King John. It oddly enough happens, that in the same number appears an extract from a play of Heywood's, of an older date, in two parts; in which play the fact of such poisoning, as well as her identity with Maid Marian, are equally established. Michael Drayton also hath a legend, confirmatory (as far as poetical authority can go) of the violent manner of her death. But neither he nor Davenport confounds her with Robin's mistress. Besides the named authorities, old Fuller (I think) somewhere relates, as matter of chronicle history, that, old Fitzwalter (he is called Fitzwater both in Heywood and in Davenport) being banished after his daughter's murder (some years subsequently), King John, at a tournament in France, being delighted with the valiant bearing of a combatant in the lists, and inquiring his name, was told that it was his old faithful servant, Fitzwalter, who desired nothing more heartily than to be reconciled to his liege; and an

* "King John and Matilda," a tragedy by Robert Davenport.

affecting reconciliation followed. In the common collection, called "Robin Hood's Garland" (I have not seen Ritson's), no mention is made, if I remember, of the nobility of Marian. Is she not the daughter of plain Squire Gamwell of old Gamwell Hall? Sorry that I cannot gratify the curiosity of your "disembodied spirit"* (who as such is, methinks, sufficiently "veiled" from our notice) with more authentic testimonies, I rest

Your humble abstracter, C. L.

TO P. G. PATMORE.

DEAR P., — I am poorly. I have been to a funeral, where I made a pun, to the consternation of the rest of the mourners; and we had wine. I can't describe to you the howl which the widow set up at proper intervals. Dash could; for it was not unlike what he makes.†

The letter I sent you was directed to the care of E. White, India House, for Mrs. Hazlitt; *which* Mrs. Hazlitt, I don't yet know: but A. has taken it to France on speculation. Really it is embarrassing. There is Mrs.

* The signature of the correspondent referred to in the first sentence of the letter.

† Hood, in his charming "Literary Reminiscences," relates the following story concerning this dog and his sometime master: "I remember, in one of our strolls, being called to account very pompously by the proprietor of an Enfield villa, who asserted that my dog Dash, who never hunted any thing in his dog-days, had chased the sheep: whereupon Elia, taking the dog's part, said, very emphatically, 'Hunt *lambs*, sir? why, he has never hunted me!'" — EDITOR.

present H., Mrs. late H., and Mrs. John H.; and to which of the three Mrs. Wigginses it appertains, I don't know. I wanted to open it; but it's transportation. I am sorry you are plagued about your book. I would strongly recommend you to take for one story Massinger's "Old Law." It is exquisite. I can think of no other.

Dash is frightful this morning. He whines, and stands up on his hind-legs. He misses Beckey, who is gone to town. I took him to Barnet the other day; and he couldn't eat his victuals after it. Pray God his intellects be not slipping.

Mary is gone out for some soles. I suppose it's no use to ask you to come and partake of 'em, else there's a steam-vessel.*

I am doing a tragi-comedy in two acts, and have got on tolerably; but it will be refused, or worse. I never had luck with any thing my name was put to.

Oh, I am so poorly! I *waked* it at my cousin's the bookbinder's, who is now with God; or, if he is not, it's no fault of mine.

We hope the frank wines do not disagree with Mrs. Patmore. By the way, I like her.

Did you ever taste frogs? Get them, if you can. They are little Lilliput rabbits, only a thought nicer.

Christ, how sick I am! — not of the world, but of the widow's shrub. She's sworn under six thousand pounds; but I think she perjured herself. She howls in E *la;* and I comfort her in B flat. You understand music?

If you haven't got "Massinger," you have nothing to

* Mr. Patmore was then at Paris.

do but go to the first bibliotheque you can light upon at Boulogne, and ask for it (Gifford's edition) ; and, if they haven't got it, you can have "Athalie," par Monsieur Racine, and make the best of it! But that "Old Law" 's delicious!

"No shrimps!" (That's in answer to Mary's question about how the soles are to be done.)

I am uncertain where this *wandering* letter may reach you. What you mean by "Poste Restante," God knows. Do you mean I must pay the postage? So I do to Dover.

We had a merry passage with the widow at the Commons. She was howling, — part howling, and part giving directions to the proctor, — when, crash! down went my sister through a crazy chair, and made the clerks grin; and I grinned, and the widow tittered; *and then I knew that she was not inconsolable.* Mary was more frightened than hurt.

She'd make a good match for anybody (by "she," I mean the widow).

> "If he bring but a *relict* away,
> He is happy, nor heard to complain." — *Shenstone.*

Procter has got a wen growing out at the nape of his neck, which his wife wants him to have cut off: but I think it rather an agreeable excrescence; like his poetry, redundant. Hone has hanged himself for debt. Godwin was taken up for picking pockets. Beckey takes to bad courses. Her father was blown up in a steam-machine. The coroner found it insanity. I should not like him to sit on my letter.*

* The reader, says Mr. Patmore, need not be told that all the above items of home-news are pure fiction.

Do you observe my direction? Is it Gaelic? — classical?

Do try and get some frogs. You must ask for "grenouilles" (green eels). They don't understand "frogs;" though it's a common phrase with us.

If you go through Bulloign (Boulogne), inquire if old Godfrey is living, and how he got home from the crusades. He must be a very old man now.

If there is any thing new in politics or literature in France, keep it till I see you again; for I'm in no hurry. Chatty-Briant (Chateaubriand) is well, I hope.

I think I have no more news; only give both our loves ("all three," says Dash) to Mrs. Patmore, and bid her get quite well, as I am at present, bating qualms, and the grief incident to losing a valuable relation.*

C. L.

LONDRES, July 19, 1827.

* In this and some of his other letters, Lamb writes very much in the manner in which Shakspeare's fools and jesters — in some respects the wisest and thoughtfulest characters in his works — talk. If his words be "light as air," they vent "truths deep as the centre." If the "Fool" in "Lear" had written letters to his friends and acquaintances, I think they would have marvellously resembled this epistle to Patmore; and if, in saying this, I compliment the "Fool," I hope I do not derogate from the genius of Elia. Jaques, you remember, after hearing the "motley fool" moral on the time, declares that "motley's the only wear;" and I opine that Lamb would consider it no small praise to be likened, in wit, wisdom, and eloquence, to Touchstone, or to the clown in "Twelfth Night." — EDITOR.

THE END.

Boston: Printed by John Wilson and Son.

www.ingramcontent.com/pod-product-compliance
Lightning Source LLC
La Vergne TN
LVHW011148110826
845150LV00006B/1186

* 9 7 8 1 4 2 5 5 4 8 6 8 1 *